Acclaim for Tim Marks's

Confidence of a

CHAMPION

**BECOMING WHO YOU WERE CREATED TO BE
BY LETTING GO OF LIES FROM THE PAST**

"Tim Marks's first book *Voyage of Viking* was the kind of book that you never wanted to end, and his latest, *Confidence of a Champion*, makes you want to strive to be a champion in all that you do. Having the pleasure of knowing Tim as a friend and business partner, I appreciate the authenticity of his words. I have personally witnessed Tim not only teach these principles but also do his best to *live* them. *Confidence of a Champion* goes deeper into the emotional and spiritual mechanics of success than any other book I have read. I count it a favorite of mine, and I know it will have a lasting impact on the lives of many as they pursue their dreams."

—Claude Hamilton, leadership and personal-development
expert and co-founder of LIFE

"As someone who has struggled in this area, I can assure you Confidence of a Champion is spot on. I wish I had had this book years ago to help develop myself. Many times while reading Tim's explanations of the causes of and solutions for low confidence, I thought: 'This is exactly how I used to feel and think!' Grab this book today and start becoming who you were meant to be."

—Dan Hawkins, leadership and personal-development
expert a ¹ co-founder of LIFE

CONFIDENCE OF A
CHAMPION

BECOMING WHO YOU WERE CREATED TO BE
BY LETTING GO OF LIES FROM THE PAST

TIM MARKS

Foreword by
CHRIS BRADY

CONFIDENCE OF A
CHAMPION

TIM MARKS

Second Edition, June 2013
10 9 8 7 6 5 4

Published by:

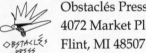

Obstaclés Press
4072 Market Place Dr.
Flint, MI 48507

Printed in the United States of America

ISBN 978-0-9858020-9-7

Cover design and layout by Norm Williams - nwa-inc.com

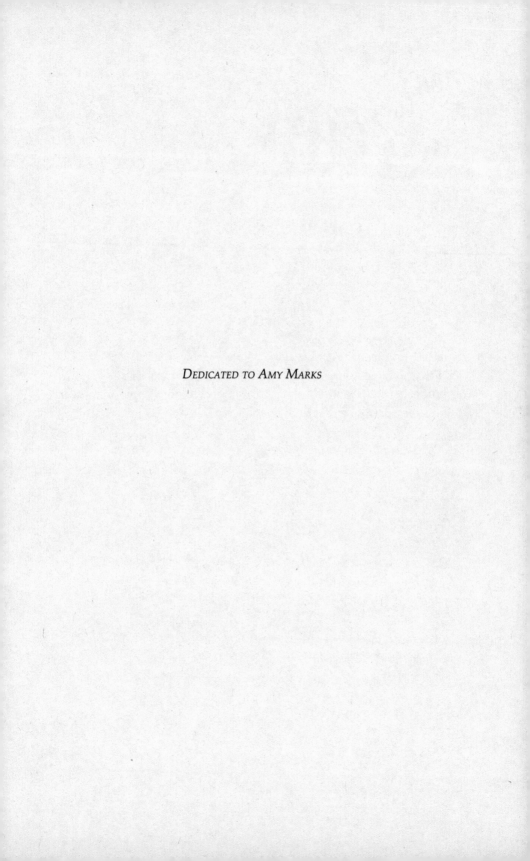

DEDICATED TO AMY MARKS

CONTENTS

ACKNOWLEDGMENTS

No one writes a book without assistance from others. To quote the late Zig Ziglar, "You can have everything in life you want if you will just help enough other people get what they want."[1] Many people have helped me learn success principles over time, and that cumulative knowledge has aided in the creation of this book. Interestingly, my whole self-development journey began with listening to a Zig Ziglar audio years ago, and I am forever grateful for that. I would like to thank Zig for all the things he has taught me through his books and CDs. I believe this book, or any other book I have written or may write in the future, would not have happened were it not for Zig Ziglar touching my life with his teachings.

I want to thank my writer CJ Calvert, who has just been a blessing to work with. He excels at asking questions, reframing ideas, and "wordsmithing" the thoughts I want to convey. He is willing to do whatever it takes to get any project done, but particularly on this one, he has jumped through hoops to create and deliver the book I desired.

Due to the great talent and skill of my graphic designer Norm Williams, the layout and cover design embody and arouse confidence and provide the perfect complement to the message of the book. Thank you, Norm.

I also want to thank my good friend Chris Brady for being an inspiration to me. His writing ability is nothing short of world-class. I have been in awe of the books he has written. His capacity to produce ideas and bring them to life on the printed page is inspiring. I am grateful to Chris for reviewing this book and providing valuable input to make it better.

CONFIDENCE OF A CHAMPION

In addition, I offer sincere appreciation to my mentor Orrin Woodward. I learned many of the lessons in this book from him, either directly or through books and audios that he recommended.

My pastor Dr. Tom Ascol provided a great blessing by offering his wisdom to help improve this book, in particular chapter 6, which contains crucial information that was difficult to communicate effectively. I thank him for challenging me and encouraging me to get it right.

And, of course, I would like to thank my family for showing me grace while I took time away from them to write this book. Cameron, Mya, Nash, and Max, I love you dearly. Most especially, I want to thank my loving wife Amy. You are the most important person on earth to me. You continue to teach me through your grace and gentle spirit. Whenever I am struck by a Goliath, you are by my side to dust me off. I love you.

Finally, I want to thank my Lord and Savior Jesus Christ and praise Him for all the grace and blessings in my life.

FOREWORD

There are many books that are entertaining, while others are informative. Still others are profound, and some stir the reader to action. Once in a while, a book comes along that accomplishes all of these in one whack. The book you are holding in your hands does just that.

Tim Marks is a most delightful author, mostly because his writing, like his life, is a straightforward adventure. In our many years of friendship, I have been privileged to see Tim from a vantage point that allowed insight into his real character. I've seen him under attack, in pain, hurt, and exhausted. I have also seen him win huge victories, achieve stellar recognitions, and hit difficult goals. Through either extreme, Tim has remained the same admirable person. His consistency is certainly one of his most dominant traits, along with the penchant for action that throbbed throughout his first bestselling book *Voyage of a Viking*. In addition to being consistent and action-oriented, Tim is also very honest about personal limitations and weaknesses that many people would more naturally mask or cover up. Because of this, Tim's writings come directly from the heart with no trimmings or dressing. What results is a "what you see is what you get" style that resonates with readers of all backgrounds. Candor, it seems, is a most attractive quality in a writer.

There are lots of books on self-improvement, personal development, and success and achievement. After one has read through much of the genre, some of the material can begin to seem repetitive and at times even a little shallow. *Confidence of a Champion* is radically different. This is true partly because books on the internal mental game of confidence are rare, if not downright nonexistent. But it is also true because such a book could not be written by anyone except someone like Tim Marks, who not only strongly experienced

13

except someone like Tim Marks, who not only strongly experienced each of the pangs of low self-esteem confessed in these pages but also grew confident to the point where he later felt secure enough to share them openly and honestly. Further, and more notably, Tim Marks teaches from a position of significant success, a position that required him to overcome a lack of confidence so severe that most people never even approach it. The extreme between the "before and after" Tim Marks is one of his most instructive attributes.

One additional unique quality of this book that bears mentioning is its disarming humor. Often surprising and abrupt but always on point, Tim's self-deprecation is as attractive as it is witty. Again, this comes from Tim's total refusal to pose as anything except himself. This, too, is an object lesson that supports the overall aim of the book. If Tim can grow comfortable enough to poke such fun at himself and the silly situations that surround us in life, perhaps others can grow to that level as well.

If you are a person who has ever suffered from a lack of self-confidence (and really, who among us hasn't?) or would simply like to grow more confident, then this book is for you. It delves into the very core of confidence itself and explicates some of the most credible theories to explain it. But far from being a theoretical book full of musings, *Confidence of a Champion* is nothing if not practical. Applications, tips, and recommendations for growing one's confidence are scattered throughout. So turn the page and begin a learning adventure that just may turn out to be the most important step you'll take all year. No matter who you are, you will get something special out of this book. Of that, I am confident!

Sincerely,
Chris Brady
New York Times bestselling author and co-founder of LIFE

INTRODUCTION

"I'm not old enough to play baseball or football. I'm not eight yet. My mom told me when you start baseball, you aren't going to be able to run that fast because you had an operation. I told Mom I wouldn't need to run that fast. When I play baseball, I'll just hit them out of the park. Then I'll be able to walk."

– Edward J. McGrath, Jr.

Have you ever met people who have a certain power or charismatic aura when they walk into a room? Everyone turns their attention to them. They seem to be the "Top dog" or "Queen Bee" at the head of the table. They walk effortlessly among the people at a party, introducing themselves to strangers and making small talk. They stride onto stage in front of a thousand people and launch into a speech or sermon as if they are chatting with best friends over coffee. They seem completely comfortable in their own skin and at peace with themselves. They have the guts to stand up for what they believe and go after what they want in life. Have you ever wondered how they do that? They've got CONFIDENCE. And through this book, I'm going to help you build your confidence so you can live the life you've always wanted.

Author Norman Vincent Peale once said, "Believe in yourself! Have faith in your abilities. Without a humble but reasonable confidence in your own powers you cannot be successful or happy."[2] He went on

> *People have genius inside them, but may lack the confidence to bring their dreams to life.*

to share a remarkable story of an American sailor during the Korean conflict who spoke up and took action in the most desperate of circumstances. In Peale's words:

An American destroyer lay at harbor one clear, moonlit night. The quartermaster, making a routine check of the ship, suddenly stopped short. He saw a big, black object floating not far off. Aghast, he realized at once that it was a floating contact mine, which had broken loose from a minefield and was slowly drifting with the ebbing tide right toward the ship.

Grabbing the intercom, he quickly summoned the captain and the duty officer to the scene. A general alarm was sounded. The entire ship went into action. Officers and men stared fearfully at the slowly approaching mine. Feverishly, the situation was appraised as disaster hung in the balance. Various suggestions were rapidly put forward by the officers. Should they up anchor? No, there wasn't time. Start the engines and shift the position of the ship? No, that wasn't feasible, for the propeller wash would only suck the mine inward more rapidly. Could the mine be exploded with gunfire? No, it was too close to the ship's magazine. What then should be done? Launch a boat and push it away with poles? This wouldn't work, for it was a contact mine and there was no time to disarm it. Tragedy seemed imminent.

Suddenly, an ordinary seaman out-thought all of his superior officers. "Get the fire hoses!" he shouted. Everyone instinctively realized that his suggestion made sense. A stream of water was played into the sea between the ship and the floating mine, creating a current that carried the mine into waters where it could be safely exploded by gunfire. Quite a man, that ordinary seaman. He had within himself the ability to think cool and straight in a crisis situation. Such abilities are definitely built into each of us, perhaps to a greater extent in some more than in others, but no normal human being is lacking in creative potential.[3]

Why Is Confidence So Important?

"If you have no confidence in self, you are twice defeated in the race of life. With confidence, you have won even before you have started." – *Marcus Tullius Cicero*

Our level of confidence affects every area of our lives. It affects our success in business and personal relationships; even our health and fitness can be affected by our level of confidence. As Helen Keller said, "Nothing can be done without hope and confidence."[4] I remember hearing about the concept of building confidence years ago and how it would help in my work and

> *People have genius inside them, but may lack the confidence to bring their dreams to life.*

personal relationships. I was given a book back in 2000 called *How to Have Confidence and Power When Dealing with People* by Les Giblin. Since I was an engineer, my first reaction was "This is for salespeople or teachers—you know, people who work with *people*." After I finally read the book, it dawned on me that we all work with people, but some of us don't do it very well. And a large part of that has to do with our confidence.

Because of a lack of confidence, far too many people have dreams that die with them. Sydney Smith said, "A great deal of talent is lost to the world for want of a little courage. Every day sends to their graves obscure men whose timidity prevented them from making a first effort."[5] It is tragic to imagine the incalculable number of inventions not built, songs not composed, books not written, buildings not constructed, businesses not launched, relationships not started (and children not born) because someone didn't have confidence. People have genius inside them but may lack the confidence to bring their dreams to life.

How would your life improve if you had more confidence? How would your success at work or in your personal life improve? In this book, I intend to help you find out. This book is for you if you have:

17

- ever walked into a room and felt uncertain or uneasy meeting new people.
- ever stopped yourself from striking up a conversation with a stranger for fear of rejection.
- ever sat at a boardroom table brimming with suggestions but were afraid to raise your hand.
- ever been asked to speak in front of an audience, either at work, church, or school or in your community, and were terrified.
- ever hesitated to make that important phone call.
- ever felt unworthy while at a job interview.
- ever been sure everyone was talking about you and what a lousy job you were doing.
- ever doubted yourself and your ability to succeed.
- regularly put yourself down.

This book is a "prescription pill" for anyone who struggles to feel more confident. If you have friends, colleagues, or loved ones who face such a burden, this book is designed for them. If *you* struggle with a lack of confidence, we are going to tackle the reasons why and give you the tools to develop it.

Life doesn't give us what we wish for; it often gives us what we have the confidence to pursue. Throughout hundreds of hours of mentoring sessions with people who had many talents but were held back by a lack of confidence, I felt there was never one good book that I could hand them to help them. I hope this is that "one good book" for you.

Does the World Need Another Self-Help Book on Confidence?

"It's what you learn after you know it all that counts."

– Harry S. Truman

Many of the books today that I've read on confidence are just people-skills books. That's fine to a point, but if your self-image is in the dumps because of something deeper, all the people-skills training in the world isn't going to have the impact you want until you address the real root cause.

Some popular books will teach you how to get "fired up" or "motivated." That's good to a point as well, but I believe there is a world of difference between a short-term psychological effect and a life-changing shift in the way we view ourselves. Because of that, we need to approach with caution a lot of the self-help, "name-it, claim-it" content available today. I have heard of people trying everything to improve their confidence: hypnosis, acupuncture, pills, or even attempting to acquire a different personality temperament.

This book aims to be different from any other book that's on the market (at least that I have ever been able to find). My goal is not to offer just another self-help book (although there are certainly great ones out there). This won't be a theology book (although there are great ones of those out there as well). The goal is to help you apply God's principles to the way you feel about yourself and develop the gifts that the Creator has given you. I want to help you identify what creates confidence and get you on the path to creating a healthy self-image so you can achieve the victories you want in life.

Whether You Are Christian or Not, This Book Is for You

In writing this book, I recognize that many people with different worldviews and religious beliefs will be reading these words. Let me say upfront that I am a Christian, and I am going to mention God and the Bible in this book. If you are not Christian, some of my spiritual anecdotes may not relate to you. I want to

> *Your level of confidence is based on your personal mixture of three ingredients: self-esteem, self-image, and self-worth.*

apologize in advance if you feel offended by any part of this book, for it is not my intention to offend. However, I *don't* apologize for my mention of God, for as a Christian, I wouldn't have integrity if I didn't write the book honoring my beliefs.

To my friends and readers who are atheist or agnostic, Jewish, Muslim, Buddhist, or anything in between, I would say this book will still have tremendous value for you. May I gently suggest that you "eat the meat and spit out the bones"? What I mean is this: please look past the references that don't connect with you and focus on the content that does. These principles work. While it is my hope that in time you will be inspired to dig more deeply into some of the ideas with which you disagree, the goal of this book is not to try to force people to change their worldviews (though we may discuss them together). The goal of this book is to help you learn to build your confidence.

To my theological friends: I know you will probably read this book and pick it apart. You will quote scripture, chapter and verse, and critique some of the things I say. An atheist might quote Anna Freud in saying, "I was always looking outside myself for strength and confidence but it comes from within. It is there all the time."[6] What I would say in response is that we don't need confidence in ourselves; rather, we need confidence in God. I know the only way to truly find self-worth as a Christian is to find it in our Lord and Savior Jesus Christ and in Him alone—not in any of our works or deeds. I know all of my blessings come from Him. But if I don't try to do my best, be all that God intends me to be, and do all that I can for His glory every day, then maybe I'm not seeking to do *His will*, but rather *my own*.

As a Christian, I know there is only one way to find one's true self-image, and that is in the image of God Himself. He has created us, and until we can see our relationship with Him and make sure that relationship is right, I don't think we'll ever be truly doing something long-term that is worthy of our whole life's effort. What I'm sharing in this book are God's principles as I have learned them through years of studying, being mentored, and mentoring others. May you, my theological friends, be inspired as well!

WHAT IS CONFIDENCE?

Confidence is a high level of belief or certainty in someone or something. For example, I am confident the sun will rise tomorrow. I am also confident the staircase will support my weight. When thinking of my doctor, I am confident in his ability to prescribe appropriate treatments.

Self-confidence is simply *belief in yourself*. It is the belief that you can handle a certain situation or task. For example, I am a confident driver because I have certainty and belief in my ability to handle myself behind the wheel. Possessing social confidence means you are unafraid to walk into a room and shake hands with strangers. Having professional confidence means you feel capable of doing your job well. Confidence affects the way you carry yourself in the world, in your interactions with people, and in the actions that you do or don't take. Your level of confidence is based on your personal mixture of three ingredients: self-esteem, self-image, and self-worth. While these terms tend to be used interchangeably, there are subtle yet important differences between them:

- **Self-esteem** is how much you like yourself.
- **Self-image** is how you view yourself.
- **Self-worth** is how much value you see in yourself.

Let's discuss each of those ingredients in detail.

Self-Esteem. Positive self-esteem is a feeling that you like and accept yourself. The opposite of self-esteem is self-loathing. Glenn R. Schiraldi, author of *10 Simple Solutions for Building Self-Esteem*, writes that self-esteem "is a realistic, appreciative opinion of oneself. *Realistic* means we are dealing in the truth, being accurately and honestly aware of our strengths, weaknesses, and everything in between.

Appreciative, however, means we have overall good feelings about the person we see."[7]

In his book *Honoring the Self*, Nathaniel Branden describes how different levels of self-esteem can affect people. He writes, "A person who does not feel competent in the performance of some particular task, such as flying an airplane, designing a computer program, or operating a business, does not necessarily suffer from poor self-esteem. But a physically healthy person who feels fundamentally inadequate to the normal challenges of life, such as earning a living, certainly does. A person who feels undeserving of some particular award or honor, such as the Nobel Prize or universal adulation for having dashed off a fairly simple love song, again does not necessarily lack good self-esteem. But a person who feels undeserving of happiness, who feels unworthy of any joy or reward in life, surely has a self-esteem deficiency."[8] In order to have confidence, you must like yourself.

Self-Image. This is the way you view yourself. Brian Tracy says, "The person we believe ourselves to be will always act in a manner consistent with our self-image."[9] Self-image is connected to our self-esteem, but they are a little different. For example, let's suppose you are very tall. If you have a positive self-image, you might say to yourself, "Because I am tall, I command attention and have an advantage playing basketball." Your self-esteem then says, "I like myself for being tall." Or the opposite might occur. If you have a negative self-image, you might say to yourself, "Because I am tall, I'm gangly, my head scrapes the roof, and I stick out in a crowd." Your self-esteem then says, "I *don't* like myself for being tall."

Maxwell Maltz, author of *Psycho-Cybernetics*, says, "The 'self-image' sets the boundaries of individual accomplishment. It defines what you can and cannot do. Expand the self-image and you expand the 'area of the possible.' The development of an adequate, realistic self-image will seem to imbue the individual with new capabilities [and] new

> *To have a healthy self-image, you need to view yourself in a positive way.*

talents and literally turn failure into success."[10] To have a healthy self-image, you need to view yourself in a positive way.

Self-Worth. This is the recognition of your fundamental value and worth. I read once, "If you really put a small value upon yourself, rest assured that the world will not raise your price."[11] Low self-worth says, "I don't matter. If I were to vanish, no one would notice or care. I'm worthless." Obviously, these are the tragic words we would hear from someone very depressed or, in the worst cases, even suicidal. If you have these thoughts, I would strongly recommend that you reach out to your pastor, a counselor, your spouse, or a trusted friend. You are being lied to by the evil one. A high level of self-worth says, "I *do* matter. The world is a better place because I was born. My life is making an important difference to those around me. I am doing, and will continue to do, great things with my life. I am a valuable person."

Often, people with low feelings of self-worth will think they are flawed or deficient in some way. They might have made a mistake which they think is unforgivable. They might have gone through terrible circumstances and view themselves as "damaged goods." I want you to know that everyone has value, no matter what flaws they

> *Everyone has value,*
> *no matter what flaws*
> *they think they have.*

think they have. Consider the following story from Orrin Woodward's book *RESOLVED*:

A water bearer in China had two large pots, each hung on each end of a pole, which he carried across his neck. One of the pots had a crack in it, while the other pot was perfect and always delivered a full portion of water. At the end of the long walk from the stream to the house, the cracked pot was only half-full. For a full two years, this went on daily, with the bearer delivering only one and a half pots of water to his house.

Of course, the perfect pot was proud of its accomplishments, perfect for what it was made to do. The poor cracked pot, on the other hand, was ashamed of its imperfection. It was miserable that it was able to accomplish only half of what it was made to do.

After two years of feeling a bitter failure, the poor cracked pot spoke to the water bearer one day by the stream. "I am ashamed of myself, and I want to apologize to you. I have been able to deliver only half my load because this crack on my side causes water to leak as you walk all the way back to your house. Because of my flaw, you have to do all of this work, and you don't get the full value of your efforts," the pot said.

The bearer said to the pot, "Did you notice that there are flowers only on your side of the path, but not on the other pot's side? That's because I have always known your flaw. So I planted flower seeds on your side of the path, and every day, while we walk back, you water them. For two years, I have been able to pick these beautiful flowers to decorate the table. Without you being just the way you are, there would not be this beauty to grace the house.[12]

What Confidence Is NOT

"Always hold your head up, but be careful to keep your nose at a friendly level."

– Max L. Forman

Confidence is not arrogance or having a big ego. Ego (or self-importance) is a person's perceived value in comparison to others. Some say EGO stands for "Edging God Out." If people are arrogant and have a big ego, they think the world revolves around them and that others are less important than they are. Arrogance is like a twenty-six-year-old minimum-wage earner with a rented Ferrari pretending to be successful while living in his mom's basement. That isn't confidence; that's a facade.

Damon Throop says, "It is easy to tell confidence from pride. Confidence lifts, encourages, helps, and is full of gratitude. Pride demeans, mocks, destroys, and is bitter and resentful."[13] Confidence is not about intimidating others or being a bully. Nor is beating your chest or raising your voice or pounding your fist on the table. Confidence is also not the impression you give other people because you probably look more confident to them than you feel. If any of this describes you, this book will help you find answers that will be valuable as well.

What's Your "Confidence Quotient"?

Ever since Daniel Goleman's excellent book *Emotional Intelligence* popularized the IQ variation of "EQ" or "emotional intelligence," there have been a lot of other Qs making the rounds. In his book *RESOLVED*, Orrin Woodward discusses Dr. Paul Stoltz's concept of AQ, which stands for "adversity quotient." PQ, as proposed by Dr. Robert Rohm, an expert on DISC personality strategies, is "personality quotient." I'd like to share another Q for you to consider: your CQ or "confidence quotient."[14]

How confident are you? Here is a series of statements, both positive and negative, to help you dig into your belief about yourself.

Under the positive statements, give yourself a point for every one you put a check mark beside. Tally up your check marks to arrive at a total "positive" score. Then give yourself a point for each negative statement you do *not* place a check mark beside. For example, if you have twelve check marks out of twenty total negative statements, give yourself eight points. If you have five check marks beside negative statements, give yourself fifteen points. Finally, add your positive and negative scores together for a combined total score out of forty possible points. This is your confidence quotient.

Obviously, this test isn't scientific; it is simply a way of highlighting some of the limiting or empowering beliefs you may currently have about yourself. When you are clear about what you are thinking, you can get to work on changing your viewpoint to a more empowering one.

Positive Statements

- ❑ Generally I love and accept myself for who I am.
- ❑ One of the things I am most proud of is that I always live out my values, beliefs, and convictions.
- ❑ I openly admit my mistakes and am willing to seek correction.
- ❑ I feel very valuable and unstoppable most of the time in my job or profession.
- ❑ Overall, I am pleased with what I have accomplished in life.
- ❑ I don't need to knock other people down to feel good about myself.
- ❑ I have no problem meeting new people. I enjoy being around others, particularly at social gatherings.
- ❑ No matter what, I know I am loved (by God, my dog, or someone else).
- ❑ I deserve everything I have, both good and bad.
- ❑ I am a happy, carefree person.
- ❑ I am pretty happy with who I have turned out to be as a person.
- ❑ Unless I respect them, I really don't care what other people think about me.
- ❑ I am a self-starter and love to be involved in new projects.
- ❑ I see a challenge as a new opportunity and not an obstacle.
- ❑ I can make decisions fairly quickly, and many times they are right.
- ❑ I feel as if I am at least as smart as most of the people with whom I work.
- ❑ If other people succeed, it doesn't take away from me; I am genuinely happy for them.

❑ I have the guts to go after what I want in life.

❑ I know that no matter what problem I face, I will find a way to handle it.

❑ I am loved and am deserving of love.

_____ **TOTAL OUT OF 20**

Negative Statements

❑ I am very fearful of criticism, disapproval, or any type of rejection.

❑ I need constant affirmation from someone I respect to feel confident in the work I do.

❑ I often feel depressed or beat up on myself over things I've said and done.

❑ All in all, I feel like a failure.

❑ I wish I had more respect for myself.

❑ I am afraid to attend a movie alone or go to a restaurant alone for fear of what others might think.

❑ I tend to have higher standards for myself than others.

❑ I often change the way that I act so people will accept me.

❑ I avoid disagreements with people because I know my point of view is often wrong.

❑ I love to argue with people and put them in their place.

❑ If people question my ideas, I get angry.

❑ The only reason my wife respects me is because God told her she has to.

❑ I am afraid of being made to look like a fool.

❑ I am afraid to ask that special someone out for a date.

❑ I feel as if I need anxiety medicine in order to be around crowds.

❑ I feel like a failure as a parent.

❑ My parents are or were perfectionists, and they made me live up to their standards.

❑ Meeting new people makes me nervous.

❑ I procrastinate on major decisions for fear of making the wrong one.

❑ I don't feel worthy of love.

____ **TOTAL OUT OF 20** (Remember to count only the boxes you *don't* place a check mark beside.)

_____ **COMBINED TOTAL OUT OF 40**

Now that you have scored your confidence in the previous pages, you have an idea of where you stand. You may even wish to keep a daily journal about what is happening in your life, what might have happened each day to throw you off your game, and what you can do next time to bounce back with greater confidence. If a journal was good enough to help Ben Franklin live his thirteen virtues, it's good enough to help us track and live the one quality of confidence.

The Story of a Candy Salesman Named John

I think we all enjoy stories of people who once didn't have confidence and then, through a series of events, gained confidence and had massive success. One of my favorite stories is of a little boy named John who grew up in Ohio. He was a shy little boy because his father William, the very man he needed to be able to look up to and respect the most, treated him poorly. William was actually a shyster who sold snake-oil potions and lotions to people, telling them the lotions would actually cure cancer and other ailments. Often he would be run out of town for months at a time, leaving his young family without any money to make ends meet.

Because of this, young John was forced to learn at a young age how to be an entrepreneur. He developed businesses; his favorite was selling candy. One time, the young boy had just made some money selling candy so that his mom could buy groceries when his dad returned home after having been out of town for several months. In the middle of the night, his father woke up and stole John's money from him. William actually said, "I cheat my boys every chance I get. I want to make them sharp." When the young boy woke up to discover his money stolen, his father's words of warning rang in his ears: "Son, never trust anyone, including me, your own father."[15]

As John grew and became a young man, he started a family of his own. He found his way, going from career to career and business to business. Finally he got involved in a new industry in which most people were failing. John knew he had to do something different to be successful, but he lacked the necessary confidence. What he needed to do was meet a railroad tycoon who would be able to ship his product throughout the country and put him ahead of all his competitors. The railroad tycoon whom John was to meet was in New York City and was well known as a shrewd businessman. The day John was scheduled to get on the train to New York to meet this man, he providentially missed the train by about six minutes. That train crashed, and all the passengers aboard died. John knew this moment was ordained by God and that missing the train was part of His plan.[16]

John felt very confident that God had called him to bring this product to people's lives and, in the process, become very wealthy. Therefore, as he traveled on a later train to New York, his second attempt, he rethought his business plan. He knew the railroad tycoon he was going to meet was someone who chewed up and spat out people and was quite accustomed to getting his way in any business deal. But John had a different plan. He walked into the meeting, named the price he would pay to ship his product, and stated the volume of business he would give the railroad tycoon. To everybody's surprise, the deal went through.[17]

The New York City railroad tycoon was Cornelius Vanderbilt. The young man who had once lacked confidence was John D. Rockefeller, who would go on to launch Standard Oil. And the rest, as they say, is history.[18]

Let's Begin This Journey

Many of you may be thinking, "Tim, you have no idea who I am or what I've gone through. You don't know what's happened to me to shake my confidence." It's true that I may not know your name; but I've worked with thousands of people and personally counseled hundreds, from ditch-diggers to doctors, from people who are simply a little nervous speaking in front of a crowd to those who have suffered terrible childhood abuse. I am confident that the ideas in this book, ideas which have changed lives, will have a similar and positive effect in yours as well.

Here is a breakdown of what we will be covering:

Chapter 1: Know Your Worth.

The foundation of confidence is recognizing your inherent value. We are going to talk about how and why you are a worthwhile person and how you can specifically identify your strengths and talents and recognize that every person, including you, is a unique and irreplaceable being.

Chapter 2: Stop Comparing.

Without an objective standard to determine worth, people tend to look for the next most obvious yardstick: the guy standing next to them. Whether a person thinks he is inferior to others or has his nose in the air, comparison is a deadly game that has no place in a self-assured person. We're going to dig into some of the wrong thinking that leads to comparison, recognize that the grass isn't greener on the other side, and learn that lifting people up as idols is a quick way to be let down.

Chapter 3: Manage Your Self-Talk.

Confident people speak to themselves differently. They look on the bright side of things, catch the negative thoughts that slip into their minds, and rewrite the language they use to describe their world. We are going to unearth the old scripts running in your brain and discuss how to reframe negative situations. And we will discuss the power of words on your attitude and learn how to silence the critic within.

Chapter 4: Take Action!

Confident people say yes to life more often. They take action rather than talking themselves out of being involved. We are going to discuss how to have confidence when making phone calls, introducing yourself to new people, and speaking in front of an audience. We will cover how to take action in spite of fear and doubt and how confident actions create a confident person.

Chapter 5: Cut Your Anchors.

We all carry around baggage from our past, most especially our childhood. Whether we struck out at home plate, were bullied at school, or even got hurt by our parents, those events can leave a lasting imprint on our level of confidence. We are going to wade into some dark waters and look at what might be holding you back. With work, you can learn to cut the anchors that have kept you from becoming the best you can be.

Chapter 6: Fight Fear with Faith.
Romans 8:31 says, "If God is for us, who can be against us?" Sometimes when we feel we have no strength, courage, or capability left, the ultimate source of confidence is the one we can look toward. Fear shrinks when faith is strong.

You have taken a brave step in even picking up a book on confidence. It tells me that you are humble enough to be open to new ideas and hungry enough to learn. My hope is that the words and ideas on the following pages will serve to inspire, uplift, and transform you in a positive way, allowing you to reach all your personal and professional goals. May this book help you achieve the confidence you seek.

Let's get cranking!

1

KNOW YOUR WORTH

"The most delightful surprise in life is to suddenly recognize your own worth."

– Maxwell Maltz

In her fantastic book *A Place of Healing*, author Joni Eareckson Tada tells a story about visiting the Notre Dame cathedral in Paris. She was stunned at how dirty and black it appeared. After years of neglect, the soot and smoke and grime had covered up a masterpiece. She could barely make out the ornate designs, carvings of gargoyles, and other striking features. Years later when she saw a picture of that same cathedral, she couldn't believe how beautiful it was. Scaffolds had been erected, construction crews were sandblasting and cleaning it, and now the beautiful stone work and colors were popping out and coming to life.

Mrs. Tada draws a parallel to how we can accumulate grime over our inner worth. She calls it getting a *film over our soul*. If we don't deal with certain aspects of our past, including our mistaken negative beliefs about ourselves, we will always struggle with self-confidence. This negative film that forms over our soul affects the way we feel about ourselves and even the way we see others. For decades, people living in Paris, France, didn't realize the cathedral was slowly getting as nasty and dirty as it was because the accumulation of filth and grime was so gradual. When the cathedral was sandblasted clean, it seemed as if a whole new building had emerged. The ornate carvings and beauty were always there, but they needed to be scrubbed clean in order to be enjoyed.

I believe the same thing is true for each of us: just as a great cathedral in Paris was put together by master craftsmen over decades, moving and carving great slabs of stone, a master craftsman has put His creativity and focus into us, crafting each of us into a unique and irreplaceable being. No matter how much dirt and grime and soot may be covering our souls, it can be washed away daily to reveal the beauty beneath. Our inherent value isn't determined by the soot and grime that covers our soul.

Consider this: if you crumple up a dollar bill, what is it worth? A dollar! You see, although something may look crumpled on the outside, that doesn't automatically lower its value. If we look like a crumpled dollar bill in the world's eyes, it doesn't matter. We are still valuable. In the inspring book *Encouragement: The Key to Caring*, Dr. Larry Crabb says, "We somehow fail to grasp that God's acceptance makes anyone else's rejection no more devastating than a misplaced dollar would be to a millionaire. We foolishly believe that other people's acceptance represents a legitimate measure of our value."[20] However, the world tends to assign to us the value that we see in ourselves. If we think we are worth being treated well, it's amazing to see that reaction reflected back to us. But if we think we are worthless, it makes it hard for others to treat us any differently. As Denis Waitley said, "It's not who you are that holds you back; it's who you think you are not."[21]

> *A master craftsman has put His creativity and focus into us, crafting each of us into a unique and irreplaceable being.*

EVERYONE HAS VALUE

"A bar of iron costs $5, made into horseshoes its worth is $12, made into needles its worth is $3,500, made into balance springs for watches its worth is $300, 000. Your own value is determined also by what you are able to make of yourself."

– Author Unknown

"To have that sense of one's intrinsic worth which constitutes self-respect is potentially to have everything."

– Joan Didion

Y ou are priceless. If you have ever doubted it, consider this miraculous example of courage and the value attached to it. On May 8, 2012, a thirty-two-year-old former chiropractor named Claire Lomas finished the 26.2-mile London Marathon. The marathon was sponsored by billionaire business mogul Richard Branson's company Virgin, and Ms. Lomas was greeted at the finish line by Branson's daughter, Holly, who presented her with a medal for endurance. It was unusual to give a medal to anyone running the marathon at that point, as all the other participants had long since finished the race *sixteen days earlier.* The original crowds had packed up and gone home. But two weeks later, new crowds were eagerly forming at the finish line, cheering Claire on, despite her snail-like pace. You see, the reason for her slow pace, and the reason for awarding her a medal for endurance, was that Claire Lomas is paralyzed from the chest down.

After a 2007 horse riding accident shattered her back, Claire thought that she would never walk again. But because of incredible advances in technology, Claire was able to stroll painstakingly toward the finish line using an amazing device called the ReWalk suit. It looks like something out of a science-fiction movie: a robotic contraption you stand in, with robotic legs that do the walking for you. Thanks to plummeting costs, the price tag for the ReWalk suit is a "reasonable" £43,000 or about US$52,000, which for most still is not chump change.

The sum of $52,000 to allow you to walk a distance in an entire day that would take everyone else an hour—that's the price you would have to pay to barely regain your ability to move again after such a crushing accident. And most of us saunter through our day giving no thought to the blessed miracle of walking. We think nothing of our mobility, let alone the gift of our other senses: the ability to hold our spouse and kids in a big bear hug, to watch a sunset, to hear wonderful music, or to taste chocolate. What would those things be worth to you if you lost them? Why, there isn't really a dollar figure to put on them because they are *priceless*.

If you lost your senses, what would you be willing to pay to get them back? Imagine you had a billion dollars in the bank and were told that after years of not seeing your loved ones, your eyes could be restored through cybernetic surgery?[23] What price tag would you put on being able to do the amazing things you now take for granted? What would you pay for a cancer-free body, for pain-free joints, for a heart that pumped with strength and endurance? I don't know what price tag anyone *could* put on those things. What dollar value would a distant family put on your organs if your life-giving donation could save their child clinging to life in a faraway hospital? Every part of you is worth more than you can possibly imagine.

Consider just the dollar value of your mind. By June 2011, the world's most powerful supercomputer was the Fujitsu "K Computer," which is capable of 10 quadrillion calculations per *second*. At the time of its completion in 2012, it is projected to have 640,000 octo-core processors working around the clock on complex mathematical models. It cost 100 million yen (US$1.25 billion) to build.[24] But it cannot yet generate creative work like symphonies or novels the way a human mind can. It cannot soothe a crying child or demonstrate the courage to stand up to evil. There is no supercomputer that can yet process information and see creative connections the way a human brain can. Computers are incredible at calculating information and solving logical puzzles like a chess game, but they are still just machines. If a computer like that is worth more than a billion dollars, what is *your* brain worth?

I don't believe there is a dollar limit to what any of us would pay for these miraculous gifts. We each have immense value, even if we don't recognize it. If you are a parent, think about your children's lives and how valuable they are to you. They are *priceless* to you. (And remember: a child of God is priceless to Him.)

There is a series of humorous ads promoting MasterCard that describes several different purchases; each ends with an example that is always described as "priceless." For example, a typical ad might have read something like this:

- **Admission to theme park: $100**
- **Junk food throughout the day: $40**
- **Sound of your kids' laughter on the rides:** *priceless*

The MasterCard ads made a great point: the most valuable things in the world aren't easily bought with money. I want to convey this message to you: you are ***priceless***. Here's another version of the MasterCard advertisement you may consider to describe your worth:

- **A functioning mind:** *priceless*
- **Eyes that see the beauty of the world:** *priceless*
- **Hands and arms to hold your loved ones:** *priceless*
- **Ears to hear beautiful music:** *priceless*
- **Taste buds to savor delicious food:** *priceless*
- **Legs to carry you to your destination:** *priceless*
- **A strong heart to power your body:** *priceless*
- **A courageous spirit to stand up for justice:** *priceless*
- **A compassionate heart to help those in need:** *priceless*
- **A spirit of forgiveness to show grace to others:** *priceless*
- **A creative mind to grasp solutions:** *priceless*
- **A burning drive to better the world around you:** *priceless*
- **A joyous sense of gratitude for all these gifts:** *priceless*

My friend, you may not realize how valuable you are. You aren't just worth millions or even *billions* of dollars; please always remember you are *priceless*.

The Touch of the Master's Hand

Awhile back, Orrin Woodward, my mentor and bestselling co-author of *LeaderShift* and *Launching a Leadership Revolution*, shared the following awesome poem at a business conference. It moved me, and I want to share it with you. It describes an auction, a violin, and how we might forget the inherent worth lying within each of us. Sometimes it takes someone else's encouragement and guidance for us to have an opportunity to shine and to remind ourselves how amazing we truly are. I hope you enjoy this poem as much as I did.

"The Touch of the Master's Hand" by Myra Brooks Welch

'Twas battered and scarred, and the auctioneer
Thought it scarcely worth his while
To waste much time on the old violin,
But held it up with a smile.
"What am I bidden, good folks," he cried,
"Who'll start the bidding for me?"
"A dollar, a dollar. Then two! Only two?
Two dollars, and who'll make it three?"

"Three dollars, once; three dollars, twice;
Going for three…" But no,
From the room, far back, a grey-haired man
Came forward and picked up the bow;
Then wiping the dust from the old violin,
And tightening the loosened strings,
He played a melody pure and sweet,
As a caroling angel sings.

The music ceased, and the auctioneer,
With a voice that was quiet and low,
Said: "What am I bid for the old violin?"

And he held it up with the bow.
"A thousand dollars, and who'll make it two?
Two thousand! And who'll make it three?
Three thousand, once; three thousand, twice,
And going and gone," said he.

The people cheered, but some of them cried,
"We do not quite understand.
What changed its worth?" Swift came the reply:
"The touch of the Master's hand."
And many a man with life out of tune,
And battered and scarred with sin,
Is auctioned cheap to the thoughtless crowd
Much like the old violin.

A "mess of pottage," a glass of wine,
A game—and he travels on.
He is "going" once, and "going" twice,
He's "going" and almost "gone."
But the Master comes, and the foolish crowd
Never can quite understand
The worth of a soul and the change that is wrought
By the touch of the Master's hand.[25]

You see, the violin in this poem always had value, but the world had forgotten its worth. I think a lot of us might even feel like that violin: beaten up, dented, and ignored, our talents buried under a layer of dust. Disappointment can make us hang up our gloves and shy away from the ring, with the cheer of the crowds only a bittersweet memory. Sometimes we just need to be reminded of the greatness that lies quietly inside us, waiting for the touch of a "master" to give us the

Sometimes it takes a friend or mentor, someone who is a "master" at building people up, to lift our spirits and show us we were great all along.

energy and confidence to risk sharing our gifts again. Defeat leads to timidity, and soon our feelings of victory are hidden under feelings of regret. Sometimes it takes a friend or mentor, someone who is a "master" at building people up, to lift our spirits and show us we were great all along.

God Memorandum

"I am as my Creator made me and since He is satisfied, so am I."

– Minnie Smith

As a Christian, I believe we are a miracle of creation, unique in the universe. I believe that God made each of us to fulfill our own unique purpose. My hope is that I can inspire you to see in yourself what He sees in you.

In all of history, there has never been anyone exactly like you and never will be again. You are precious and valuable. As Viktor Frankl said, "Everyone has his own specific vocation in life ... There he cannot be replaced, nor can his life be repeated. Thus, everyone's task is as unique as is his specific opportunity to implement it."

I also know that it is the nature of man to look at other people with eyes of envy and wish we were more like them. But God made you as you, not as them. Though every person can always improve, you are already special and amazing just as you are. You might be a proverbial BMW, and the guy beside you at the stoplight might be a proverbial Mercedes Benz. Both are great cars, just different. A Beemer will never be a Benz at its core, but it doesn't need to be.

One of my favorite authors is Og Mandino, and I would like to share a passage from his wonderful book *The Greatest Miracle in the World*, which does a great job of summing up the idea we are discussing here.

Never, in all the seventy billion humans who have walked this planet since the beginning of time has there been anyone exactly like you. Never, until the end of time, will there be another such as you. You have shown no knowledge or appreciation of your uniqueness. Yet, you are the rarest thing in the world. From your father flowed countless seeds, more than four hundred million in number. All of them, as they swam, gave up the ghost and died. All except you! You. You alone persevered within the loving warmth of your mother's body, searching for your other half, a single cell from your mother so small that more than two million would be necessary to fill an acorn shell. Yet, despite impossible odds, in that vast ocean of darkness and disaster, you persevered, found that infinitesimal cell, joined with it, and began a new life. Your life, two cells now united in a miracle. Two cells, each containing twenty-three chromosomes and within each chromosome hundreds of genes, which would govern every characteristic about you, from the color of your eyes to the charm of your manner, to the size of your brain. With all the combinations at my command, I could have created three hundred thousand billion humans, each different from the other. But who did I bring forth? You! One of a kind. Rarest of the rare. A priceless treasure, possessed of qualities in mind and speech and movement and appearance and actions as no other who has ever lived, lives or shall live. Why have you valued yourself in pennies when you are worth a king's ransom?

What are the odds of that? One hundred percent because God designed it that way. How can such an amazing miracle as you be anything less than invaluable? You have tremendous worth. That value is recognized and treasured by many others, if not by you. I hope that you can recognize and accept the inherent value in yourself.

TAKE STOCK OF YOURSELF

"Ninety percent of the world's woe comes from people not knowing themselves, their abilities, their frailties, and even their real virtues. Most of us go almost all the way through life as complete strangers to ourselves—so how can we know anyone else?"

– Sidney J. Harris

Have you ever sat through a bad movie and felt glad when it was over? I know I have. (And I wondered why I didn't leave the theater earlier.) What's amazing is that the human brain functions a little like a movie projector: we replay events over and over in our head and relive not only the memory but also the feelings we experienced.

In our mind, we have a very obedient projectionist. He will search through the database and replay whatever movie we have a desire to view. Most of us have the bad habit of replaying *negative* movies in our head. If we choose to replay movies about moments that caused fear, sadness, anger, or embarrassment, we will relive those defeating emotions again. Remember that time you missed catching the football during the big game? Remember the kids laughing when you forgot your lines in the play? Remember when the neighbor's dog bit you? Remember the last failed job interview? None of those memories fill you with feelings of confidence. They make you feel terrible. And feeling sad, angry, scared, or embarrassed doesn't set you up to have success in anything you do today. Feeling down sets you up for more failure.

There is a great Native American story of a grandfather speaking to his young grandson who is learning his way in the world. The grandfather says, "Imagine two wolves. They are fighting a great battle in your mind. One wolf, the good wolf, represents courage, love, integrity, grit, and compassion. The other wolf represents fear, hatred, dishonesty, weakness, and heartlessness. The fight continues until one wolf wins."

The grandson, curious, asks, "Which wolf wins the battle?"

The grandfather smiles and answers, "Whichever wolf you *feed*."

If you feed your anger and sadness, you will create more anger and sadness. If you feed your love and courage, that is what you will get.

Robert Johnson says, "Measure yourself by your best moments, not by your worst. We are too prone to judge ourselves by our moments of despondency and depression." What we have to do is make the conscious choice to play powerful, inspiring, uplifting mental movies of our *victories*. Remember the time where you kicked the soccer ball past the goalie and scored the game-winning point? Remember when you brought home an A+ in tenth-grade math? Remember when you asked your college sweetheart on a date and she said yes? Remember when you got a big promotion on your job? Those are great memories to replay! When you replay them in vivid detail, you will relive all the amazing emotions. Now you feel invincible. Now you feel as if you will close the sale. Now you feel as if you can conquer the world.

Playing great memories in your mind starts first with identifying those past moments that made you feel proud of yourself. A good way to do this is to ask yourself: "What have I accomplished before? What challenges have I overcome? What victories have I had?" If you've asked these questions in advance, when the time comes to use this technique, you will have several memories ready to go.

Please take a moment and consider: "What have my top five victories been in life?" Maybe you have overcome cancer, raised a child on your own, closed a huge business deal, or gotten a scholarship to college. If you are thinking you don't have any victories or talents to list, I

> *Everyone is capable of showing courage, brilliance, and compassion.*

challenge you to dig deep; ask family, friends, and co-workers for their input.

And by the way, the first thing on your list could be that you are reading this book to better yourself. Most people won't even read a positive book, but you are doing it right now. Give yourself some credit for taking positive action.

Have you ever donated any time or money to charity? Raised a child? Finished school? Gotten a job and stood on your own two feet? Maybe you've escaped a bad situation. Maybe you've had the guts to make it through one more day. Whether the actions are big or small, everyone is capable of showing courage, brilliance, and compassion. Everyone has moments of greatness. So, whatever your victories are, take a moment to stroll down memory lane and arm yourself with some empowering memories.

The Top Five Victories in my life have been:

1. _____
2. _____
3. _____
4. _____
5. _____

Now, consider all your amazing abilities. John Templeton says, "Everyone has special talents, and it is our duty to find ours and use them well."[28] Everyone has something he or she is good at. Perhaps you are a warm, caring person who is always there to help out a friend in need. Maybe you are a detailed, organized person who is excellent at keeping paperwork filed perfectly. Maybe you have a creative flair with music, singing, or writing. Maybe you are the celebrity chef in your family, and everything you cook has your family salivating. Maybe you are a determined, focused person who accomplishes everything to which you put your mind. Maybe you are an outgoing, charismatic person who lights up the room and attracts people like a magnet. Maybe you are good at scaring small children and keeping them in line. (Just kidding.) Maybe you have rock-solid character, and everyone can count on you to do the right thing.

You have gifts and talents no one else can match. Don't diminish or devalue your strengths; you are probably better than you think. Maxwell Maltz, author of *Psycho-Cybernetics*, says, "We react to the image we have of ourselves in our brain. Change that image for the better and our lives improve. Self-image is changed for the better or worse not by intellect alone, not by intellectual knowledge alone, but by experiencing."[29] If you focus on your best qualities, you will realize that you have a lot of wonderful value to offer the world.

My Top Five Talents/Abilities in life are:

1. _____
2. _____
3. _____
4. _____
5. _____

Now that you have listed your Top Five Victories and your Top Five Talents/Abilities, how are you feeling about yourself? We've spent the last few minutes doing something very powerful: focusing on the *good* in you, on what you do *right*. Each of us certainly makes mistakes, and as a Christian I believe each of us is fallen. We are not perfect, nor will we ever be in this life. But I also know that we have a lot of good qualities to celebrate.

Esteem literally means "to value something or to have a high opinion of something." So *self*-esteem means to value ourselves and actually like ourselves. It means that we see ourselves as valuable, worthwhile persons. I can tell you that this is the foundation of confidence. If we don't like ourselves and try to strut around looking or acting confident, we come off as fakes. Other people can see right through

> *Esteem literally means "to value something or to have a high opinion of something." So self-esteem means to value ourselves and actually like ourselves.*

us. But when we genuinely like ourselves deep down and see all the great qualities we have, it's amazing how that inner strength is also obvious to everyone around us.

Becoming successful and having confidence go hand in hand. A person with low self-esteem won't have the confidence to ask for the promotion, make the business contact, or court the person he or she loves. If we don't like ourselves, we turn other people off. It's tough to be a "people magnet" when we repel even ourselves. Learning to like ourselves is a major key to confidence.

It's important to note that the way we think about ourselves is not always accurate. In fact, most people are unusually and unfairly hard on themselves. We tend to notice what is bad and ignore what is good. But sometimes we do the opposite: we ignore what is bad and only see what is good. Either way can be harmful. Maya Angelou said, "Success is liking yourself, liking what you do and liking how you do it." Just as we must learn to show grace to others, we must be gentle and loving toward ourselves. That doesn't mean that we don't hold ourselves accountable for our mistakes or poor decisions; it means that we don't simply focus on what is bad, but we also take the unusual step of noticing what is good.

So grab your pen again, take a moment, and record evidence from each area of your life of why you are a good person.

I am a good person because _____.
I am a good spouse because _____.
I am a good parent because _____.
I am a good employee because _____.
I am a good boss because _____.
I am a good friend because _____.
I am a good neighbor because _____.
I am a good sibling because _____.
I am a good child because _____.
Strangers like me because _____.
I know I am courageous because _____.

I know I am smart because _____.
I know I am trustworthy because _____.
I know I am caring because _____.
I know I am worthy of love because _____.
I know I am worthy of success because _____.
I know I deserve happiness because _____.

Now, go back and reread the completed statements you just wrote. I bet that if you focus on all the good found in those statements, your self-worth and confidence will begin to grow this very moment!

HAVE A ROCK-SOLID FOUNDATION

"If you don't have solid beliefs you cannot build a stable life. Beliefs are like the foundation of a building, and they are the foundation to build your life upon."

– Alfred A. Montapert

Every little kid hears the story of the *Three Little Pigs*. Each pig goes off to build his home, and the big bad wolf tries to blow it down. The first pig builds his house with straw, and it is easily wiped out by the wolf. The second pig builds his house with sticks, and it just as easily collapses by the wolf's efforts. But the third pig takes his time, putting in more sweat equity and long-term thinking, and he builds his house with bricks. And that house stands up against the worst the wolf can offer and protects the little pigs inside.

> *Timeless values and principles hold us up when the storm winds blow.*

It's a childhood story that serves as a warning to each of us: We need to build our homes with construction materials that can weather

47

the storms of life. If we cut corners, build on the cheap, or simply hope that the storms of life will avoid us, we are in for a rude and perhaps even tragic awakening. Buildings constructed using shoddy materials, without a strong foundation or structural support, will collapse easily during an earthquake.

Similarly, wise men and women build a framework for themselves with figurative concrete and steel. As R. C. Samsel said, "Character is the foundation stone upon which one must build to win respect. Just as no worthy building can be erected on a weak foundation, so no lasting reputation worthy of respect can be built on a weak character." Timeless values and principles hold us up when the storm winds blow. If we ignore this principle, we do so at our own peril. Consider the report from a 2011 earthquake in New Delhi, India, in which seven people died and twenty-one were injured:

> The collapse of the apartment block in November was blamed on poor engineering, cheap construction materials and shoddy foundations. For all building types ... ground conditions matter: structures built on rock are likely to be more earthquake-resistant than others.[30]

I was in Haiti a couple of years after the earthquake of 2010 to rebuild a church and an orphanage and help out however possible. When the crew and I arrived, we found the construction workers on location were mixing the material to be used to make bricks. With no scientific or engineering method, no process, and no correct ratios to follow, they were actually just mixing up a pile of ingredients on the ground. The blocks that had cured for several days were so fragile you could pick them up and break them with your bare hands. And those were the cinder blocks that were meant to hold the building together!

I talked to the construction foreman and tried to explain my concerns. I felt we needed to put more cement in there and get the mortar mix correct. He shook his head and said, "No, this is how we've done it for years." I was trying not to be offensive, but that was exactly the problem they had. They had done it that way for years.

This was a major reason why the entire city of Port–au-Prince and the surrounding area were reduced to rubble during that earthquake. With such shoddy materials, it was easy to see why so much damage had occurred. It wouldn't take an earthquake to knock down the building we were constructing.

Just as with the buildings in Haiti, each of us would be wise to ensure we always lay a strong foundation when building anything. To walk through life with confidence, we need to build our character upon granite and our framework with steel and concrete. We need to build our structure with the best materials possible.

What Are Your Priorities?

"Nothing profits more than self-esteem, grounded on what is just and right."

– *John Milton*

Stop and consider all of the things you value. What do you hold dear? What are your highest priorities in life? Knowing clearly what you stand for will give you a better chance to audit whether you are building on granite or sand. As Joe Batten said, "Our value is the sum of our values."[31]

In the checklist below, place a check mark next to everything you value. Feel free to add any additional examples that are not on this list. Then, circle the top five priorities that drive you.

- o God
- o Freedom
- o Charity
- o Power
- o Servant leadership
- o Marriage and your spouse
- o Achievement
- o Watching sitcoms

o   Travel
o   Time with loved ones
o   Courage
o   Health and fitness
o   Truth
o   Popularity
o   Adventure
o   Leisure
o   Fame
o   Career advancement
o   Creativity
o   Recognition
o   Money
o   Children
o   Friendship
o   Solitude
o   Fairness
o   Your sports league
o   Forgiveness
o   Revenge
o   Honor
o   Fun
o   Learning and growth
o   Playing video games
o   Service
o   Material possessions
o   Environment
o   Fashion and looking good
o   Control
o   A favorite possession
o   Order and tidiness
o   Community
o   Making a difference
o   Winning

o   Other: _____
o   Other: _____
o   Other: _____

Now consider whether your priorities are based on Scripture and true principles or indulgent desires and shallow interests. If they are not based on true principles, you might want to consider the long-term effect of holding such ideals as a priority.

> *Be sure you know why you believe what you believe.*

Could your life be better served by reconsidering what you value? Is there something missing from your life that would strengthen your foundation? Could your life be of greater service to others by prioritizing things that have deeper meaning? Could your confidence be eroded by valuing the wrong things? If you don't know what you stand for, you might accidentally accept what someone else values instead of deciding for yourself the best path to success. As the old saying goes, "If you don't stand for something, you'll fall for anything." Take the time to really scrutinize what you value. Be sure you know why you believe what you believe.

Depth Produces Security

In the leadership community to which I belong, we have a saying that empowers us: "Depth produces security." The analogy that we borrow from is found in dendrology, which is the science of wooded plants.[32] The tallest and strongest trees have very deep root systems, including a taproot that burrows far into the ground to find water and provide nourishment to the tree. Additionally, the deep taproot provides structural strength for the tree when strong winds blow; the tree is anchored and held stable by the counterbalance of the taproot. In essence, the depth of the taproot produces security and strength.

Just as the depth of the taproot produces security for the tree, depth can produce security for each of us in our lives. Consider the strength that someone's "roots" in a large, extended family provide when the storms of life hit. Depth in relationships through strong family bonds can shelter a person in times of tragedy, such as experiencing financial devastation or having an ailing relative in need of palliative care. It can also provide support in good times, such as the example of having loving grandparents who "tap in" for the afternoon to watch the newborn baby when the newly minted mommy and daddy are about to drop from exhaustion. But family roots don't provide assistance only when we are busy or overwhelmed; our key relationships from childhood also help form our initial self-respect and self-image.

You create a rock-solid foundation in your life by having several sources of unwavering depth that can provide emotional, psychological, and relational strength. In my life, the depth of my relationship with God produces security for me.

Here are a few critical areas in which to nurture depth that I have seen make a difference for the people in my life:

> **Depth of *mission* or *purpose*.** The late Zig Ziglar, motivational author and speaker, used to say, "Outstanding people have one thing in common: an absolute sense of mission."[33] When something is so important to you that you would lay down your life to defend it, the strength that is built inside you is not easily defeated. Consider Nelson Mandela, the first democratically elected president of South Africa. Mandela was an anti-apartheid activist who spent twenty-seven years in jail in protest against the racist regime of his country. How did he have the strength to do that? He had a burning purpose and mission greater than his personal comfort or even his freedom. His depth of purpose was so great that he led his nation to freedom and ushered in a

> *When something is so important to you that you would lay down your life to defend it, the strength that is built inside you is not easily defeated.*

new era of compassion and equality, relative to the indignities of the past. His work earned him a Nobel Peace Prize in 1993 and the respect of hundreds of millions of people around the world. [34]

➤ **Depth of *duty* or *responsibility* to others.** As Orrin Woodward and Chris Brady teach in *Launching a Leadership Revolution*,[35] true leaders step up not because of the potential perks and benefits they might get from their position but rather because of a sense of duty and responsibility. Consider a young husband who has a history of irresponsible behavior. Even when an unreliable couch potato faces the prospect of fatherhood, the new responsibility and sense of duty can inspire him to grow up and start acting like an adult overnight.

Look at the dramatic example of courage and responsibility shown by German business tycoon Oskar Schindler, whose incredible story is captured in Stephen Spielberg's epic film *Schindler's List*. A savvy entrepreneur who found it profitable to socialize with Nazis and provide munitions for their war machine during World War II, Schindler grew to realize that his Jewish workers were more than just a means to fund his lavish lifestyle; they were human lives that depended upon him for their very survival. Time and again, Oskar risked his freedom, his wealth, and potentially his life in the midst of the chaos of the war, eventually bankrupting his company and losing everything he owned, all to save the lives of more than a thousand Jewish workers. His depth of duty and responsibility made him a hero of World War II and his life is celebrated today by the many tens of thousands of descendants of those that Schindler saved. [36]

➤ **Depth of *values*.** The values you hold dear are the raw materials for your character. Shallow values will produce a shallow character. The late Stephen Covey made this distinction in his book *The 7 Habits of Highly Effective People*. He wrote, "Principles are not values. A gang of thieves can share values, but they are in violation of the fundamental principles...."[37] Some might value lying on the couch, eating junk food, spending money foolishly, sleeping in, gossiping behind people's backs, or showing off. Some might value their reputation more than their character. Some might value watching TV more than playing with their children. Some might value flirting with the receptionist more than romancing their spouse. Some might value lying, cheating, stealing, or even violence. A political dictator might value power more than human life. The simple fact that we value something doesn't make it correct. What we should aspire to is not just to live our values but to live by correct values. Most major religions on earth recognize the same universal truths: Do not lie, cheat, or steal. Do not murder. No matter where your faith lies, moral and rational people around the world recognize that these universal truths are worthy of valuing. (This is why moral absolutes are so important. Otherwise, who says?!)

➤ **Depth of** *conviction.* Brian Tracy says, "The depth of your belief and the strength of your conviction determines [sic] the power of your personality."[38] Depth of values and depth of conviction are two very different things. Depth of values means: how principle-based are the values that you feel (or know for a fact) are important? Depth of conviction means: how far will you go to uphold the values that you feel are important? For example, you may feel that truth is an important value. That's excellent because it is a value of great depth that is principle-based and upheld in Scripture. But how far will you go to defend the truth? One time, I was traveling with a business associate and crossing the border into Canada. The customs agent asked where we were going, and I explained we were going to a business meeting. The leader I was with seemed surprised that I would risk exposing myself to some sort of fine or further scrutiny. I explained that it didn't matter what the cost might be to me in terms of money; telling the truth is always more important than money or power or fame or anything else. As Abraham Hicks said, "Nothing is more damaging to you than to do something that you believe is wrong."[39]

I can tell you that in my own life, I have witnessed incredible courage and conviction. For example, my pastor, Tom Ascol, has served his congregation for more than twenty-five years. He endured a spiritual attack where close friends of his were used by the enemy to try and tear the church apart. He stood strong in what he knew the Lord had called him to do, and the church has been blessed because of his depth of conviction.

Another example of people having depth of conviction can be found in my business partners and friends Orrin and Laurie Woodward and Chris and Terri Brady. They have all been through the fire and had their convictions tested, and they have all passed the test with flying colors. It is no wonder that they have massive confidence; their character is built on a foundation of stone.

FEELINGS DON'T DETERMINE WORTH

"Mankind are governed more by their feelings
than by reason."

– Samuel Adams

"We do not deal in facts when we are
contemplating ourselves."

– Mark Twain

Before we conclude this chapter, we need to definitively answer a very common counterargument. It's entirely possible that despite everything we have discussed so far about your worth, you still have a disclaimer. You might say, "Tim, all this stuff sounds reasonable, but I just don't feel like a worthwhile person." Fair enough. It's entirely possible you feel depressed and down on yourself. You might feel lower than a pregnant ant's belly. You might feel like you have no redeeming value in the world. And what you need to understand is that feelings don't determine worth.

Feelings aren't necessarily connected to facts. Feelings can be completely irrational and disconnected from reality. You might *feel* as if you are in mortal danger in the presence of a Chihuahua, but that little Taco Bell dog isn't likely to go for your jugular. You might *feel* as if you are in mortal danger flying on an airplane, but the guy beside you is happily enjoying a nap on the same flight. On the other hand, some drunken ninny out camping might wander off into the woods and stumble upon a bear. This guy might pound his chest with false bravado and *feel* invincible. But he's not. (Actually, he'll feel a little chewy and in need of seasoning, but that's more from the bear's perspective.) In both cases, how you feel is irrelevant.

Consider making this argument: "I feel like a worthless loser; therefore, I *am* a worthless loser." Can you see a flaw in the logic? Just *feeling* something doesn't make it true. Your feelings might be totally irrational. Imagine walking into a jewelry store to purchase a diamond ring so you can propose to your sweetheart. You select a ring and say to the cashier, "I *feel* like this diamond ring is only worth $100." The cashier doesn't care what you feel. You might *feel* that a diamond ring is worthless, but your feelings don't change the value of the ring by a single penny.

The same goes for real estate. My friend Chris, who is a top realtor in Florida, shared with me that one of his biggest struggles is trying to explain to the owners the worth of their home in this downturned economy. Many people feel their house is worth $500,000, whereas the house is actually only worth $275,000. Regardless of what the owners may feel, the price of the house is determined by what the market will bear. We can take that story and turn it right around to describe our own worth. We might think we are worth a very small amount, whereas in reality we are priceless.

Also, how you treat the diamond ring doesn't change its worth. You can step on the diamond ring, rub it around in mud, throw it down the sewer, insult the diamond ring, call it names, or tell other people it is worthless, but none of that changes the value of the ring. Your feelings about the worth of the ring have no connection to its value.

Perhaps you are like a diamond ring that has been misjudged. Maybe other people have treated you badly. Maybe they actually felt you were no good. Guess what? Their feelings about you don't count either. How your parents, teachers, classmates, boss, or anyone else treated you or felt about you does *not* determine your worth. (We will cover this more in depth in the chapter "Cut Your Anchors.")

By the way, just to play devil's advocate, the opposite is also true. I'm sure Adolf Hitler and Osama bin Laden felt as if they were great guys. They were not; they were as evil as humanly possible. You may feel that you are a great person, but that doesn't make it so. This is another example of why absolute truth is so important. Former Congressman Bob McEwen calls it the "who says" factor. He means if we don't have absolutes, we rely on popular opinion; in other words, we base our moral viewpoint on "who says" something is right or not. If for example your neighbor (or anyone else) says something is okay, that doesn't automatically make it true. Many people have very strong feelings and divided opinions about different topics, but feelings aren't facts.

Henri J. M. Nouwen, a Catholic priest and author of over forty books, had this to say on feelings of self-worth:

> Over the years, I have come to realize that the greatest trap in our life is not success, popularity, or power, but self-rejection. Success, popularity, and power can indeed present a great temptation, but their seductive quality often comes from the way they are part of the much larger temptation to self-rejection. When we have come to believe in the voices that call us worthless and unlovable, then success, popularity, and power are easily perceived as attractive solutions. The real trap, however, is self-rejection. As soon as someone accuses me or criticizes me, as soon as I am rejected, left alone, or

abandoned, I find myself thinking, "Well, that proves once again that I am a nobody." [My dark side says,] I am no good, I deserve to be pushed aside, forgotten, rejected, and abandoned. Self-rejection is the greatest enemy of the spiritual life because it contradicts the sacred voice that calls us the "Beloved."[40]

Learn to Accept Compliments

If we doubt our worth, we find it hard to believe that anyone else would be able to see something good in us. This is made obvious whenever someone offers us a compliment. We can't stomach the difference between their nice words and our lousy view of ourselves. If someone offers a compliment, we may take their words either as:

a. weak attempt to lift our spirits simply out of pity on their part;
b. deceitful attempt at flattery to somehow take advantage of us; or
c. half-baked or ignorant appraisal of our worth because they clearly don't know how rotten we are, or they wouldn't say nice such things about us.

If we have low self-confidence, we can't believe that anyone could think highly of us; instead, we think one of these three reactions must be the truth. However we choose to reject the compliment, the point is that we reject it.

We might think people are saying nice things because they feel sorry for us. They see us as metaphorical shivering puppies caught in the rain and toss us a few scraps of praise. If we see ourselves as pitiful, it's not a big stretch to assume others feel the same.

Maybe they are being nice to trick us. After all, we've watched smarmy salesmen compliment friends and family in order to close a sale, and we can spot those phonies a mile away. It doesn't occur to us that we are worthy of the compliment, so we might see conspiracy behind every kind word someone utters.

The biggest lie we might tell ourselves is that anyone who compliments us clearly hasn't looked under the hood. Such people don't know the lemon they are hitching their appraisal to. Even a cursory examination of our faults would shock other people at how grossly they have overesteemed us. Surely they don't know how we've fallen down in our efforts and integrity in the past, or they wouldn't spout off about how great we are. We think things like, *Surely they can't know how I've just snapped at my kids for no good reason. The only explanation for their kind words must be they don't really know what a lousy jerk I am underneath this polished exterior.*

These are just a handful of examples demonstrating how we will flush a compliment when we have low self-esteem.

One of my good friends and business partners shared a story of this exact experience. Years ago, my friend's business mentor would at times pay him a compliment, saying, "I wish you could see in yourself what I see in you." My friend would think to himself, *Yeah, well, you're just saying that to make me feel good.*

> *The biggest lie we might tell ourselves is that anyone who compliments us clearly hasn't looked under the hood.*

Not much later, my friend innocently overheard that same business mentor complimenting yet another associate. That other associate brushed off the compliment verbally, saying, "Yeah, well, you're just saying that."

My friend jumped up in defense of his mentor's viewpoint, exclaiming, "No! I see those same positive qualities in you as our mentor does!" And then it suddenly dawned on my friend: his mentor had been speaking sincerely the entire time. Every compliment, every kind word was absolutely genuine and accurate.

If someone keeps saying that we have some great qualities, perhaps there is a chance he or she is right. Perhaps we are being too hard on ourselves, and perhaps we might just be better than we think. If someone points out how good we are at something, and we keep knocking ourselves down, there must be a reason for the huge difference of opinion. Is it possible there is a kernel of truth and accuracy in someone else's assessment? Maybe we can cut ourselves some slack and concede that part of the compliment must be true. At the very least, even if we think the other person is ill-informed or exaggerating, we can't be all that bad. The person genuinely sees some good in us.

The only reasonable response to a compliment is to simply say, "Thank you." Don't knock the compliment; accept it. Don't insult someone's opinion by explaining why it is mistaken. Saying someone is wrong is just as offensive and shows bad manners even when that person's evaluation of your virtues is in error. We wouldn't open a gift on our birthday and throw it back in someone's face. We would simply say, "Thank you." Don't explain away the compliment in your mind. If someone says, "You are a great mom," please don't reject the compliment by replying, "Well, I sent them to school with mismatched socks." Simply say, "Thank you."

(By the way, if you are an egotistical self-absorbed prima donna, just say, "Thank you," when you get a compliment, and leave it at that. There is no need to prance around preening yourself and repeating the story all day long to everyone who will listen. Show some class. Whether you suffer from low self-esteem and knock the compliment, or suffer from low self-esteem and crave lots of compliments, just leave it at "Thank you.")

How to Get Down on Yourself

If you want to be your own emotional punching bag, you don't need to reinvent the wheel; people were beating themselves up emotionally long before you were a twinkle in your parents' eyes. Here are some dependable ways to make yourself feel terrible in no time (said tongue-in-cheek):

➤ **Ignore or devalue everything you do well.** Focusing on what you do wrong and ignoring everything you do well is a surefire way to deflate yourself. If you cook Christmas dinner and nineteen people rave about the food, but one person dislikes the mashed potatoes, make sure to ignore all the compliments and just focus on the one criticism. You'll feel terrible in no time.

➤ **Employ "Yeah, but" thinking.** When people say nice things about you, look for reasons why they are incorrect in thinking that way. Clearly they must be wrong, so it's up to you to figure out how they made the mistake of thinking you are worthy of a compliment. If someone says, "You look great in that outfit!" just answer by saying, "What, this old thing? I got it in a rummage sale. It's really not that nice. Besides, Jane down the street has the exact same outfit." If someone says, "Great job on the report!" you can answer by saying, "Yeah, but I made a mistake on page three, paragraph two."

➤ **Point out the smudges.** If someone comes to your home and mentions what a great job you did painting your living room, say, "Yeah, but did you notice the smudge of paint in the corner of the ceiling? I made a mistake. Wait; let me get the stepladder so we can look at the mistake up close. Do you see it yet? I'm amazed you didn't notice it, because it's all I ever see when I walk into the room."

➤ **Call yourself names.** Whenever describing yourself, use terms like *jerk*, *wimp*, *loser*, and any other creative variation to really knock yourself down and feel bad about yourself. Just constantly insult yourself. Did you lose the race in fifth-grade gym class? Then you are a "loser," now and forever, because of that one event twenty years ago. Never mind that it's utterly irrational to base a global evaluation of your worth as a person on an isolated event or action; go ahead and slap that totally unfair label on for the slightest misdeed or error on your part. That seems fair.

➤ **Be unforgiving of any mistakes you make.** Be your own toughest critic. If you get 99 percent on your real estate exam, what happened with the other 1 percent? Just tell yourself that a good, worthwhile person wouldn't have screwed up the way you did. Surely, such a person would have scored 100 percent. Not only that, you should keep a running tally of every mistake you have ever made throughout your life. Remember how you got the answer wrong in the third-grade spelling bee? Surely any other eight-year-old wouldn't have hesitated when asked how to spell *antidisestablishmentarianism*. You were clearly out of your league and had no business competing. Plus, you should make sure to describe your mistakes in your journal every night so that you can review them and punish yourself forever.

➤ **Exaggerate your faults.** While it might be true that everyone has faults, *your* faults are really despicable. If people really knew the terrible things you do, they would never want to be around you again. Why, just last week you got into an elevator after lunch, having enjoyed several Taco Bell burritos and a sparkling soft drink. Needless to say, the combination of carbonated beverage and reheated taco meat produced an unholy combination in your tummy. Thankfully you were alone in the elevator at the time. Then the elevator doors opened, and someone from the third floor stepped on. Unforgivable. (At least you were trapped in an elevator and not in a Smart Car with a hot date. Or maybe you were!)

Hopefully, as you read these tongue-in-cheek examples, you could see that they were unfair. Sometimes the best way to point out something irrational is to ridicule it. If the way you think of yourself is unfairly harsh, perhaps you need to gently poke fun at how irrational that thinking is in order to reconsider how you can be gentle and loving toward yourself.

As you consider the items on the list, please don't think, "I'm such a loser for thinking this way. I always beat myself up. I'm sure everyone notices how I screw up this way all the time. It's unforgivable." If you had that reaction when you read the previous list, please reread the list because you are still beating yourself up unfairly. While it can be helpful to keep us humble, focusing on our weaknesses too often can do more harm than good.

"If/Then" Rules

In computer programming language, "if/then" statements are powerful tools to direct the software on how and when to take action. When certain conditions are met, then the software moves forward. Unfortunately, if there is "bad code" in the software, "if/then" statements in the programming can actually cause the software to hit a roadblock and generate an error message. The programmer might have created an impossible situation, so the software experiences a glitch.

I experienced this firsthand at work. When I was an engineer, we had forty-two robots in the factory. For the most part, each of these robots ran on simple I/O (input/output) programs. If for any reason an input was missed, it would shut down an entire production line, causing backups in other departments and resulting in tens of thousands of dollars of downtime.

Just as the robots in my factory had their version of programming instruction that set the boundaries for what they could and could not do, we each define the limits of our ability using "if/then" statements. In self-esteem language, "if/then" rules take on a whole new meaning. While normally fair and helpful, "if/then" rules might create tough standards for us to live up to. We might be unfairly harsh with ourselves. Consider the following statement, and think about how you might fill in the blanks:

"If I was _____, then I would be _____."

How would you fill in the blanks? The answer is a really powerful way to understand the way that you think about yourself and your life. It shines some light on the way the circuits are wired in your brain. If we've got "bad code" in the way we see ourselves and the world around us, our "if/then" statements will lead us to paint ourselves into a corner. Some answers might include:

➤ "If I was more intelligent, then I would be more successful."
➤ "If I was special, then I would be happier."
➤ "If I was prettier, then I would be married."
➤ "If I was luckier, then I would be rich."
➤ "If I was taller and more athletic, then I would be popular at school."
➤ "If I was the boss's favorite, then I would get the promotion."
➤ "If I was born in January, then I would make the hockey team."
➤ "If I wasn't bald, I would have more confidence."
➤ "If I wore black motorcycle boots, then I'd be cool!"*

Do you notice a trend in all the examples above? Every one of the "if" statements listed describes a quality about ourselves that is *out of our control*. It is totally defeating to connect success to any quality that we have no control over. Worse, it's usually not accurate.

Here is something a little more insidious about "if/then" statements like those listed above: **they let us off the hook for getting results.** They create a convenient "back door" to allow us to make excuses about why we didn't achieve what we desired. Didn't get the promotion? It couldn't have anything to do with my proactivity and leadership skills; it's because I'm not a suck-up like Anderson is. Besides, the boss has it in for me anyway. Not popular at school? It couldn't have anything to do with my people skills, warmth, or caring attitude toward others; it's because Sally's parents are rich and buy

---

* If you have followed the longstanding debate between bestselling author Chris Brady and me, you know that white motorcycle boots are never a display of confidence—or of masculinity!

her nice clothing. Didn't get picked for the hockey team? It couldn't have anything to do with how hard I practice; it must be because I was born in December, so I'm smaller than the other kids. It's no fault of my own, and no responsibility rests on my shoulders.

How do you combat this kind of failure thinking? Recognize that the formula for success is due almost exclusively to factors *within your control*. Life deals you a hand of cards, and then you play the hand you are dealt. Your worth as a human being is not determined by factors outside your control. If people don't like you, it's not because you are worthless; perhaps you act like a thoughtless jerk. (I mean, maybe you aren't very pleasant to be around!) If you didn't get the promotion, it's not because you are worthless; perhaps you are lazy and choose to cut corners.

Your *actions* create your results, and you have the power to change your actions this instant. Don't cop out and blame your parents, your environment, or the kids at school for how you measure up. For my Christian friends: it's easy to fall into the trap of thinking, *God must not want me to be successful*. To quote John MacArthur, "It's amazing to me how many people confuse the will of God with good old-fashioned bad decision making." Take ownership for who you are and how you act, and free yourself of these limiting "if/then" rules.

> *It is totally defeating to connect success to any quality that we have no control over. Worse, it's usually not accurate.*

SUMMARY

We each have value. David A. Seamands, author of *Healing for Damaged Emotions*, says:

...Many Christians...find themselves defeated by the most powerful psychological weapon that Satan uses against Christians. This weapon has the effectiveness of a deadly missile. Its name? Low self-esteem.

Satan's greatest psychological weapon is a gut-level feeling of inferiority, inadequacy, and low self-worth. This feeling shackles many Christians, in spite of wonderful spiritual experiences, in spite of their faith and knowledge of God's Word. Although they understand their position as sons and daughters of God, they are tied up in knots, bound by a terrible feeling of inferiority, and chained to a deep sense of worthlessness.[41]

While it can sometimes be hard to see the good in ourselves, the foundation of confidence is recognizing we each have tremendous worth.

Key Points

1. I am priceless beyond measure. If I ever doubt that, I should just imagine what a disabled billionaire would pay to regain everything I take for granted.
2. I am a miracle of creation, never to be repeated, and my rarity imparts massive value.
3. As a Christian, I know my Lord loves me and sees value in me and in every person.
4. When taking stock of myself, I choose to note all my talents and victories rather than wallowing in memories of my defeats.
5. A worthy life is built upon a rock-solid foundation. I base my life upon my faith, values, depth of purpose, and conviction.
6. My feelings don't determine my worth. This is important to remember because I might be unfairly harsh with myself. I need to stop beating myself up, learn to accept compliments, and be fair and forgiving as a best friend would be.

2

STOP COMPARING

"Until you make peace with who you are, you'll never be content with what you have."

– Doris Mortman

We like to rate things. We like to rate restaurants, offer our review of a book on Amazon.com, or see that a movie got four stars out of five. We rank athletes and guess who will be picked first in the draft. We are fascinated by magazine rankings of which business person is the wealthiest or which celebrity is the sexiest.

Just as we like to rate the world around us, we like to rate ourselves. We like to see how we measure up against the other guy. This is called comparison, and it's a pretty unhealthy mental habit. In fact, it's one of the biggest sources of self-esteem problems for a lot of people. In this chapter, I want to tackle why we do it, why it is wrong, and why we should stop beating ourselves up and knocking other people down.

WHY COMPARE AT ALL?

We start down the path of comparison when we haven't answered the first concept of this book, "Know Your Worth." If we haven't put that question to rest, if we don't see our inherent value as human beings, we feel compelled to search for an answer. We quickly realize that we need some sort of standard of measurement with which to evaluate ourselves. Without a clear sense of Scripture-based or principle-based values to use as a standard of measurement, we tend to pick the next most obvious yardstick: the guy standing next to us. In the absence of an objective standard, our brother, our neighbor, our father, or the guy working in the cubicle beside us becomes the stopgap yardstick until a better one comes along.

> *Without a clear sense of Scripture-based or principle-based values to use as a standard of measurement, we tend to pick the next most obvious yardstick: the guy standing next to us.*

And so the comparison game begins. If we were comparing one person to another, how would we determine who was "better"? What criteria would we use to evaluate everyone involved? Do I decide that I'm a better person than you if I can bench-press two hundred pounds, and you can only bench one hundred? Are you a better person than I am if you have a million dollars in savings and I'm broke? Am I a better person than you are if I can quote Scripture, chapter and verse, by memory? Are you a better person than I am if you actually live the Scripture and go to church four times a week? There are countless ways we could try to measure someone's worth. What I've listed here are examples of attempting to define worth through comparison to others. This is obviously a perilous way to go about it.

Without an *objective* standard for comparison, we resort to using a *subjective* standard even though it is completely arbitrary. Doing this gives us either an inflated sense of self-worth or an unfairly harsh verdict against ourselves. Depending on our mood, we might pick an easy target that is pleasurable to trump, or if we are feeling masochistic, we might select a world-class competitor who crushes us in comparison. Neither is fair. Wouldn't it make sense to measure our worth based on an *objective* standard? I believe Scripture-based and principle-based values are the best—and the only—objective standard. Don't measure yourself against other people. Measure yourself against Scripture.

Plug the Leaky Bucket

Many people believe if they can excel in one area, it makes them inherently better human beings. Some people believe the key to increasing their confidence is to *increase their accomplishments*: to rack up more trophies and accolades and to become "better" than the next guy. You can spot these guys sitting at the Thanksgiving dinner table as they boast about their latest conquest at the office, on the golf course, in the weight room, etc., but no one at the dinner table cares.

Consider this excerpt from *Psychology Today* that discusses overachievement as it relates to a sense of self-worth:

> People driven to overachieve are motivated by an unhealthy compulsion to show they are worthy. "Overachievers have an underlying fear of failure or a self-worth contingent on competence," says University of Rochester psychologist Andrew Elliot. "Rather than setting and striving for goals based on a pure desire to achieve, their underlying motivation impels them out into the world to avoid failure." Overachievers are likely to adopt competitive performance–approach or fearful performance–avoidance goals because of an underlying motivation to "be better than others to avoid rejection," Elliot says.[42]

Notice also that this type of comparison is usually focused on *one* criterion: your physical strength, your bank account, your faith, or something else. Do you really believe that you can measure the complete worth of a person based on one criterion, or ten, for that matter? The worth of a person is vast and unique.

What if someone is a world-class champion in one category and a total failure in another? Tiger Woods is a world-class golfer, yet he is not doing quite so well on the marriage and fidelity front. How do you determine his worth as a person? What if you are a grandmaster chess champion and two hundred pounds overweight? What if you cook an amazing pot roast, but your taxes are totally disorganized? What if someone ran into a burning building to save a child, but later that night his daughter caught him viewing pornography? You can't measure the total worth of a person based upon a single action.

Many rich and successful people have discovered this the hard way: they have achieved fame and fortune and yet wallow in self-loathing and depression. Why? Because worth as a person is not solely determined by accomplishments. As American tennis player Jim Courier said, "It is very dangerous to have your self-worth riding on your results as an athlete."[43] Achievement can be fleeting. You may have won the championship this year, but that doesn't guarantee anything next season. Any fame, fortune, or achievement you earn is certainly *part* of you, but not the sum total of what you are worth as a person.

Picture a leaky bucket that you constantly try to fill. No matter how much water you pour into it, it's going to flow out. That's what is happening when people try desperately to make themselves feel good only through achievement: they are trying to pour in enough accomplishments before the good feelings flow away. The key is to first plug the leaky bucket. Once you do that, you'll realize you have enough wonderful qualities to clearly see your self-worth and develop confidence. Drawing from a famous quote by Blaise Pascal, I believe in every person's heart there is a God-shaped hole that people try to plug any way they can.[44]

Les Giblin says:

The man or woman who realizes that he is "something" not because of what he has done or how good he has been, but by the grace of God in endowing him with a certain innate worth, develops a healthy self-esteem. The man or woman who doesn't realize this tries to give himself significance by making money, gaining power, getting his name in the paper, or in a hundred other ways. Not only is he what we call an "egotist," when we use that word in its worst sense, but his continual unsatisfied hunger for self-esteem is what causes most of the trouble in the world.[45]

Comparing versus Competing

Comparing and competing are very similar in that they involve spending a lot of time thinking about how you stack up against another guy. But in the case of comparison, that's all there is. Comparison tends to devolve into either self-flattery ("Look at how great I am because I'm *better* than Bob") or self-pity ("Look at how terrible I am because I'm *worse* than Bob"). Both these responses involve sitting around and staying the same as you are now. You are either patting your own back or kicking your own butt.

Competition goes one crucial step further than comparison. You don't just think about the other guy; your reflection drives you to take *action*. Comparison merely says, "I hope the other guy isn't very good so I can *seem* better." Competition says, "I hope the other guy brings his A-game so it forces me to *become* better." Comparison says, "Look at where I AM." Competition says, "Look at where I am GOING."

> *Competition goes one crucial step further than comparison. You not only think about the other guy; your reflection drives you to take action.*

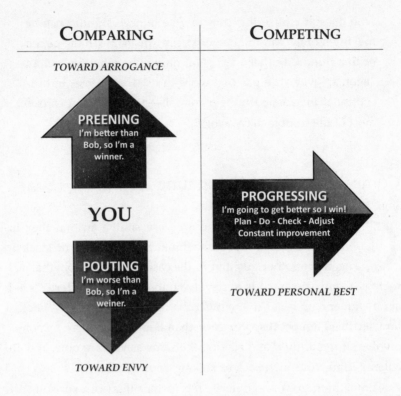

Wallowing in comparison will simply beat down our attitude and our activity; we risk feeling discouraged and might stop sharing our talents with the world. We each have our God-given talents, but we don't need to search very long to find someone who is better than we are at a particular talent. For example, I regularly speak in front of business audiences of hundreds and thousands of people. In one sense, you might say I am an accomplished professional speaker. But I am no Zig Ziglar (who went to be with the Lord in November 2012). He was, in my opinion, the best motivational speaker of all time. He was the Michael Jordan of speaking. But he had a very unique style. I should not try to emulate his style because, unless I was born in Yazoo City, Mississippi, and lived in Texas, I couldn't do justice to his deep Southern drawl.

There will always be someone who is better than we are at something. God created Zig to be Zig, and He created me to be me. Don't try to copy people; be your own unique version of excellence.

Ralph Waldo Emerson said, "Insist on yourself. Never imitate."[46] Don't blindly copy someone else. You are an individual.

Competition helps us strive for greater heights and break through limiting beliefs. If someone else is a champion, it can show us what is possible for us if we apply the same dedication to mastery that the other guy invested. If we can find someone who has conquered a Goliath we are facing, that can inspire us to believe we can also succeed.

Looking at other people's success *should* inspire and motivate you. Maybe I'm just hard-wired that way: I can look past how their amazing performance trounced mine. It's a delicate balance; on one hand, you are okay with the fact that they are winning; on the other hand, it needs to bug you enough to cause you to take action.

I need to be inspired by other people's examples. It's probably the number-one reason people watch the Olympics. I love that several world records were broken in the 2012 Olympics. It's so cool to think that in 2009, Olympic athlete Usain Bolt demolished the world record for the 200 meter sprint, crossing the finish line at 19.19 seconds; then he returned four years later, after battling a back injury, to sweep the London Olympics and claim three more gold medals.[47] Some people went to the 2012 Olympics just to see Bolt rip up the track.

Some people are so inspired by excellence in sports they will actually tear up when they witness humans performing at their *best*. Sadly, this does not always include the well-intentioned but totally misguided little-league parents who want to eliminate keeping score in children's sports. It's ridiculous not to keep score. Besides, without keeping score, we wouldn't be able to celebrate accomplishments like those of Usain Bolt.

Perhaps in the past we might have looked at someone else's amazing performance and felt we needed to make excuses for why we weren't competing at their level. We fired up the "excuse making machine" and said things like, "They must have better genetics." Maybe that's true. And maybe they also had to overcome a brutally abusive childhood. For everyone who believes the path to success was easy for a champion, I'll show you a Michael Jordan who got cut from his high school basketball team. If you catch yourself making excuses, you've got to "pattern interrupt" (more on that later). You've got to reframe the event in your mind and say instead, "If they overcame those terrible obstacles, I'm going to have a much easier road to success.

Without proper success thinking, when some people see others at their best, their confidence spirals downward. This depends a lot on how you view other people. Remember when you see a champion that he or she has undoubtedly worked harder than others for *years*. Recognize if someone is farther along the journey than you. If they have been practicing golf for twenty years and you've been practicing for twenty days, that's an unfair comparison. Also, don't compare the date you both started; compare how many *hours* of practice you've engaged in and the quality of that practice. Maybe you and a buddy have both had a golf membership for ten years. If your friend has been practicing three hours a day, seven days a week for ten years, that's 10,000 hours of mastery. If you only play one game a month, you just aren't going to be playing at the same level. You can't expect to be great without paying the same dues. If you and I are willing to do what champions do, we can be gold medalists in our sport, our marriage, or our business.

> *Rather than wallowing in comparison, a competitive spirit will drive you to improve.*

So get fired up when you see someone performing at a higher level! Rather than wallowing in comparison, a competitive spirit will drive you to improve as you realize that you can follow the same principles of practice over time.

When Comparison Slips Down into Envy

When comparison motivates us to compete, we honorably want to take *action*. But when comparison makes us envious of others, we merely want to take their *stuff*. Envy is basically comparison that has slipped down into greed and coveting. We might look at someone whom we feel is "ahead" of us in some way and say to ourselves, "I feel jealous and want what they have."

Let's suppose someone you know has just purchased a Mercedes Benz. Here are the different reactions brought about by comparison, competition, and envy:

- **Comparison** says, "Wow, this person is better than I am because he has a Mercedes Benz, and I don't. I feel bad about myself."

- **Competition** says, "Wow, it's amazing that this person has a Mercedes Benz. I don't have one yet, but I am fired up and believe that it's possible for me to get one too!"

- **Envy** says, "I am ticked off that he has a nice car, and I don't. It's not fair. I want what that guy has."

There is no limit to what we can envy. We can envy how easily someone makes friends. We can envy people for their house, their six-pack abs (or small thighs for the ladies), their career, and even their spouse. We want what they have and are upset they've achieved something we haven't. Thinking these thoughts is obviously sinful.

My advice is this: When you see successful people, don't covet what they *have*; aspire to be what they *are*. Aspire to develop their courage, their compassion, their drive, their focus, their people skills, their frugality, their loving heart, and their discipline. Aspire to develop the qualities of character they possess

> *When you see successful people, don't covet what they* have; *aspire to be what they* are.

that have attracted the success they enjoy today. Aspire to have those qualities, or else let it go.

Once you start to envy someone, it's a slippery slope downward. Sadly, I have personally seen too many tragic examples of lives destroyed by envy. Envy poisons a person's heart and can open the door to incredibly immoral behavior, including lying, cheating, stealing, adultery, and even murder. Feeling envy and bitterness toward someone is like drinking poison and expecting the other guy to die. Envy is a small crack in your moral armor that can rot your soul if you don't notice it and squash it quickly.

In our business community, we host massive leadership events, and one goal my business partners and I set is to see how many people we can bring to the event. In fact, we actually have a formal competition and awards for this exact focus. Years ago, I was competing to win this sought-after award, called the "Top Gun Award." I ran like crazy to win this competition. I worked as hard as I could and left no proverbial stone unturned in my hunt to win this contest. On the big day, I arrived at the event filled with the confidence that I had a really good shot at winning.

Well, just as I was about to step up on stage with the four other people competing to win, I learned to my dismay I had come in second place. In fact, I learned that I was literally seven points away from winning this prize. I had wanted to win. I had wanted it badly. I forced a smile on my face and walked out on stage for the award to be handed out. I looked at the other guy holding the trophy and thought, *That should have been me*. In fact, the thought crossed my mind for just a moment, *I could have just purchased the seven points and won this trophy*.

> *If you cheat in a contest and "win," you are not outrunning or outperforming your competition; you are out-lying them.*

But I thank God I didn't do that, because then I would be selling out my character for a twenty-five-dollar bowling trophy and thirty seconds of applause. The fact is, plain and simple, I didn't work hard enough to win, and I didn't earn it.

Celebrated college basketball coach John Wooden always taught that if you did your best, you won, no matter if the other guy got the trophy or not. I'd rather know I gave it my all and lost honorably than lied in order to claim a false victory. Please understand, and never forget: *appearing* to win is meaningless; *actually* winning is everything. If you cheat in a contest and "win," you are not outrunning or outperforming your competition; you are out-*lying* them. If you ever even *think* of doing this, I want you to imagine the announcer's voice over the speakers saying, "And the award for the laziest, most cowardly liar with the least character in the room is *you!*" Then everyone looks right at you. They see right through you and know what you've done. Please don't do this to yourself. You'll be up all night sick with guilt, and the trophy will feel meaningless. Sadly, a lot of people would have chosen to allow their character to fall because they coveted something like winning a contest. As Jon Huntsman says in his book of the same title, "Winners never cheat."[48] This is true if you fudge the numbers in car sales, if you're in manufacturing and you doctor up the efficiency numbers, or if you cheat on your taxes. Cheating is cheating, and your conscience knows it. Your self-esteem will pay the price if you cheat.

One former business associate of mine really experienced the disastrous effect of envy, coveting, and cheating. This guy was fudging his business numbers all the time in order to make himself look like a winner. But on the inside, he knew he was lying. His whole life crumbled because of it. His wife realized what was happening and completely lost faith in him. In her disgust and anguish at her husband's fraudulent behavior, she literally went behind his back and committed an even bigger sin by having an affair. All of this happened because this guy was too scared to take a good look at himself and do the hard work of changing. He wanted to *look* rich in performance rather than *be* rich in performance and character.

Envy will rot your soul. Envy will tempt you to falsely win empty victories. Envy will take the focus off of improving yourself. Don't be envious of others; celebrate their accomplishments, and let them drive you to take action.

How Our Conscience Affects Self-Esteem

Many people cut corners, cheat on taxes, fudge the numbers just a teensy bit, and think they are going to get ahead of the competition. They feel that looking successful will make them successful. You should know, however, that your conscience will call you out for doing it.

We all have a conscience; the internal feeling that we are doing right or wrong. One of the reasons we might lack confidence is that we might have violated our conscience. In fact, some people do it so often they become incapable of even seeing it. For instance, those who commit a crime may feel guilt the first time or two, but after a while, they might start to feel they have a "right" to commit the crime.

Here's how I know we all have a conscience: everyone knows it's wrong to murder someone. Even murderers (usually) know that. Well, everyone reading this book right now knows they would never commit murder. But ask yourself: "Did I ever lie, cheat, or steal?" And this train of thought goes all the way down to asking if we ever stole a pack of gum. If we know we have done something wrong, our conscience will beat the stuffing out of us. We might have lashed out at our kids, looked at an attractive co-worker and had improper thoughts, or broken our vow of sobriety. It doesn't matter how many self-help books we read; if we don't tackle the sin and guilt of broken moral absolutes in our lives, we will never have the self-esteem and confidence we desire.

Recently I was mentoring a guy about managing his finances. He and his wife wanted to buy a new house but were not in a financial position I felt was strong enough to justify the purchase. I encouraged him to pay off debts first and then save a certain amount of money; that would put him in a better position to move into a new house. He moved houses anyway. He knew it was wrong. He was emotionally and spiritually off track. When you know you are doing something wrong, stop it. If you are fooling yourself, you'll try to fool others.

I would encourage you to tighten up your moral filter. What's that? Imagine that every deed, every action you take, has to pass through a filter that weeds out the immoral actions. Some people have a fine mesh filter on their actions that even a grain of silica sand wouldn't slip through. Other people have a moral filter with holes so wide that bad behavior the size of a Volkswagen would have no problem getting through with both doors open! We need a small mesh filter that stops the bad behavior. We need to tighten up our moral filter. Martin Luther wisely said, "I cannot and will not recant anything, for to go against conscience is neither right nor safe. Here I stand; I can do no other, so help me God. Amen."[49] When we do what we know is right, we rightly feel good about ourselves and can stand firmly upon it.

The False Pride of Credentials

One final way that people compare themselves is regarding the difference in career success based on years of schooling. For instance, younger brother Bob is a successful accountant, but older brother Doug is a successful neurosurgeon. Bob spent five years getting his college degree but Doug spent twenty years getting his MD. And to make matters worse, older brother Doug has a bad habit of reminding Bob of this at every family gathering. Being a neurosurgeon is definitely a commendable accomplishment. Being a boastful, arrogant, ego-driven neurosurgeon is much less impressive. By reminding everyone of his supposed superiority, Doug is placing too much pride in his credentials.

In their new bestselling book *LeaderShift*, authors Orrin Woodward and Oliver DeMille give an example of someone who ties a lot of pride and self-esteem to his career. They call such people "credentialists."[50] A "credentialist" is someone who cares about—you guessed it—credentials. All that matters to these guys is what sheepskin from which school you've got hanging on the wall.

There is nothing wrong with education; in fact, I'm all for it. I strongly believe in living a life that pursues continuous, never-ending education. But please don't get a degree just because the world around you has told you to. Instead, decide what you want to accomplish, learn from those who have accomplished the goal you seek, and do what they have done. Sadly, many people put too much emphasis on where they have been and their past victories, such as a degree they have earned. While they would never admit it, credentialists live in the past, reliving the glory of graduation day when they earned their master's degree.

Now I can understand from their point of view why this stuff is so important to them. Hey, if you worked your guts out through college or university to achieve your degree, it's noteworthy, and you deserve to feel proud of your accomplishment. I personally took night school to pursue my engineering degree while working a full-time job, and I admit that managing to find the time and energy to study and focus mentally at the end of a long day is something I can be proud of. Some people have poured so much time, energy, and money into getting their degree that it hurts to imagine their efforts as anything less than heroic.

I would gently suggest that credentialists need to step back and take a look at the larger world around them and ask: "What value do my credentials actually bring?" A degree doesn't guarantee you a job. In fact, it doesn't even guarantee an interview. It probably gives you a bit of a competitive edge in your career-seeking journey, as long as your goal is to work for someone else. But what if you have no desire to work for other people? There are so many billionaires that only have high school diplomas that we can easily lose count of them.

When people realize how much work is involved in self-improvement, they can become fearful and retreat to focusing on past accomplishments. It's easy to look at your credentials. You can look at "I'm a doctor, look at how far I've come." But we should also be looking at where we need to grow. We should never feel content with where we are. If our last and best victory was twenty years ago in school, then brother, we need to step up our game and accomplish something more current.

DON'T COMPARE APPLES TO ORANGES

"Too many people overvalue what they are not and undervalue what they are."

– Malcolm S. Forbes

When it comes to comparison, we have an amazing ability to measure ourselves *unfairly*. We fall into one of two categories when it comes to how we view ourselves:

1. We measure our weaknesses against other people's strengths. We usually compare our exaggerated and incomplete view of others, seeing mostly their gifts and achievements, to our full knowledge of all our blemishes and defeats.

2. We measure our strengths against other people's weaknesses. We ignore our faults, see only our positive qualities and focus our attention on someone else's imperfections in the shallow attempt to make ourselves feel superior.

Both ways of thinking are wrong, and we should challenge ourselves to elevate our thinking.

When we compare ourselves to others and highlight what we feel are the attributes that make them "better" than us, often the attributes we are in awe of don't even apply. For example, we might have a friend who has a degree in mathematics and mistakenly assume that guy must be better than we are at business. That's nonsense. Some of the most successful entrepreneurs have only graduated from high school!

> *We usually compare our exaggerated and incomplete view of others, seeing mostly their gifts and achievements, to our full knowledge of all of our blemishes and defeats.*

Another example would be famed basketball player Shaquille O'Neal. While he has achieved massive success in basketball, a man of Shaquille's size would be a total failure as a horse jockey! It would be foolish to evaluate Shaquille based on his ability to win the Kentucky Derby. If I haven't yet sold you on the error of comparing to begin with, hopefully I can convince you to at least compare apples to apples. Don't compare your weaknesses to another person's gifts; at least shine light on the highest virtues of both parties.

The Grass Is *Not* Greener on the Other Side

"If the secret sorrows of everyone could be read on their forehead, how many who now cause envy would suddenly become the objects of pity."

– *Italian Proverb*

If you are looking at others thinking they've got it all together, understand that the grass is *not* greener on the other side of the fence. This is as true in lawn care as it is in personal excellence. (As a matter of fact, I've been on the other side of the fence, and sometimes there is no grass there at all!)

People don't tend to broadcast their weaknesses; instead, they usually try to put their best foot forward. We tend to see their "marketing brochure" at first rather than all their hidden faults. We see they got the big promotion at work but overlook their cold and dying marriage. They show off their fancy new car but not the failed cholesterol report from their physician. They boast of high school victories on the gridiron but hope no one asks about their drug-addicted teenager. The grass usually just *looks* greener on the other side. I've heard it said that if we put all of our problems and all of the problems of other people in

> *The grass is not greener on the other side of the fence. This is as true in lawn care as it is in personal excellence.*

a pot, stirred it up and pulled out someone else's problems, we would likely want to have our problems back.

One exceptional organization that has gone a long way toward giving young people the experience that "the grass isn't greener on the other side" is challengeday.org. Their work has been featured on *Oprah*, and they hFad a documentary crew film their sessions for a reality TV series. They go into high schools across North America with the goal of creating a great culture in schools for all the students by eliminating bullying, harassment, and abuse and giving kids an opportunity to see the value in themselves.

One particularly powerful exercise in their seminar occurs near the end of the day. They begin with several icebreaker activities to get the kids comfortable and starting to open up and share. Next they lay a long piece of tape down in a line that stretches the length of the gymnasium and ask all the kids to stand on one side of the line. Then they start to ask a series of questions—questions that get deeper and tougher and really reveal what might be going on in someone's life experience. Each time they ask a question, they'll say, "Everyone who fits into this category, step across the line." They ask questions like these:

- "Step across the line if you've ever felt afraid."
- "... If you ever felt humiliated."
- "... If you or anyone you know has ever been bullied at school."
- "... If you or anyone you know has hurt or bullied someone else at school."
- "... If you or anyone you know has divorced parents."
- "... If you or anyone you know suffers an addiction."
- "... If you or anyone you know has ever suffered abuse at home."
- "... If you or anyone you know has ever been raped."
- "... If you or anyone you know has attempted suicide."

The statements get tougher and tougher. But the most amazing part of the experience is how the bullies see the kids they taunt step across the line, and the agony they've inflicted is really shown to them. The weaker kids look up and see the "cool" kids they've idolized step across the line

> *Everyone sees that everyone else is hurting just as much as they are.*

saying they've endured terrible things in their lives. Everyone sees that everyone else is hurting just as much as they are.

The end of the day is a truly cathartic experience. Kids stand up to take the microphone and share their thoughts on the day and what they've learned. Many times the talks are highly emotional. Often, a kid who has bullied others will step up to the microphone, sobbing, stand in front of the school, apologize to the kids they've taunted, and beg for forgiveness. They commit to making a change.

The whole culture of the school shifts after these programs. Bullying and violence drop like a rock. Kids step up and have the strength to hold the line against alcoholism, drugs, and sex. Lives are transformed because the kids can see the pain each other has suffered. Jealousy, intolerance, and anger are replaced by compassion.

Everyone faces fear, self-doubt, sadness, and tragedy. No one is immune. Always remember that the person you think has everything going for him has also likely faced terrible tragedy and sadness.

Don't Fear Other Men; They Are Just as Scared as You

We often look at someone we admire and feel small in such a presence. We are scared to walk up and introduce ourselves. We feel intimidated by the person's accomplishments and think they've got it all together.

The truth is no one has it all together. Everyone has some insecurity, some fear that lingers just below the surface. The more famous people are, the more they usually hope to hide their fear from the public.

Stephen Richards, author of *Releasing Your Fear*, says, "Fear can make a moth seem the size of an elephant."[51] People are people, whether they are successful or not, and everyone is scared of something, rational or otherwise. In fact, when you get to really know someone you think has it all together, you'd be surprised at what scares them.

Barbara Streisand is one of the most decorated singers in history. She has won two Academy Awards, eight Grammy Awards, and a Tony Award, among other accomplishments. Despite being an acclaimed concert performer, she suffered crippling stage fright for twenty-seven years, brought on by forgetting the lyrics to a song in front of 135,000 people in Central Park, New York. She couldn't bring herself to sing on stage again until the invention of the TelePrompTer.[52]

Famed Canadian music producer and composer David Foster has a crippling fear of riding in elevators. He takes the stairs, even if it means climbing fifty-seven flights and risking a heart attack to reach a rooftop party.[53]

Howie Mandel, actor, comedian, and host of *Deal or No Deal* and *America's Got Talent*, suffers from crippling mysophobia, or a fear of germs. He cannot shake anyone's hand, including excited guests or even other cast members, without wearing a latex glove. He was once interviewed on TV and declined to shake the interviewer's hand. The interviewer shook his hand by surprise and Mandel screamed, running off camera. On *America's Got Talent*, Mandel has run off camera several times, once when someone's act involved sneezing and another time when someone dropped a piece of used dental floss near him. He is terrified of public bathrooms and can only use his own. He details his fears in his book *Here's the Deal: Don't Touch Me.*[54]

I try to have compassion for anyone who faces such an overwhelming fear of anything. My research for this book uncovered some other famous people with phobias, some fears that seemed quite legitimate (such as a fear of water when you can't swim) and a few that seemed a little silly.[55]

- Madonna is afraid of thunder.
- Kim Basinger and Daryl Hannah fear wide, open spaces.

- Carmen Electra, who starred in *Baywatch*, is actually scared of water because she can't swim.
- Matthew McConaughey is scared of tunnels and revolving doors.
- Johnny Depp, Daniel Radcliffe, and Sean "Diddy" Combs are frightened of clowns.
- Orlando Bloom is scared of pigs.
- Country singer Lyle Lovett is terrorized by cows.
- Scarlett Johansson is frightened of cockroaches.
- Nicole Kidman fears butterflies.
- Christina Ricci is afraid of indoor plants.
- Billy Bob Thornton is afraid of antique furniture and bold colors.
- And I, Tim Marks, am afraid of being trapped in small places (claustrophobia). And as my closest friends know, I am also afraid of kryptonite. And white boots!

It's easy to see someone's outer confidence and forget the invisible anxiety that trips them up in private. Successful people are scared of their own personal bogeyman[†] just like you and I. They have phobias that would seem silly to us if we only knew; their personal kryptonite is probably something you've easily conquered long ago. So the next time some "big shooter" walks into the room with his chest puffed out, remember that he is not invincible and should not be stared at in awe. Don't fear other men; they are just as scared as you.

Every "Idol" Is Still a Fallen Man

"Let every man be respected as an individual and no man idolized."

– Albert Einstein

[†] Don't believe in the bogeyman? Then why did you run up the stairs of your grandparents' spooky basement after shutting off the lights? Admit it. It's the bogeyman!

Wment you catch yourself imagining someone is unattainably better than you, please remember he or she is simply a man or woman who has also fallen before. Sometimes we look up to someone to the point of idolizing them. Remember that everyone has failed, sinned, lied, broken a promise, and gone against their own values at some point. No one is immue.

It's wrong to deify people. Strangely, in North America we tend to deify sports stars and movie stars over all else. Celebrity is held in higher esteem than character. For instance, the pastor of my church, Tom Ascol, is a respected Christian

> *Be careful whom you admire; their rock-hard abs might be built on a moral foundation of sand.*

author, speaker, and preacher. When he walks into a room, Christians will merely say, "Hey Tom, how are you?" In contrast, if Bono were to walk into the room, people would freak out and start cheering and begging for autographs and pictures. As the front man for the band U2, Bono is a world-class musician and is celebrated for having done a lot of humanitarian work. Without doubt, these are admirable accomplishments. The Bible teaches, "Pay ... honor to whom honor is owed" (Romans 13:7). But the contribution Bono has made in my life is a speck of dust in comparison to the contribution my pastor has made. (As an aside, when people get a chance to meet a movie star or the president of the United States, their palms get sweaty, they blush and go all tongue-tied. Why aren't we like that in prayer in the presence of God? Just a thought.)

The media gives a twisted worldview of people we should deify; skinny women and guys with six-packs are somehow more worthy of our attention than missionaries. Personally, I'm not ever going to have a six-pack, and I'm not even going to try to match up to that. It's admirable to be in shape and value your health; my business promotes fitness and believes in having success in that area. But be careful whom you admire; their rock-hard abs might be built on a moral foundation of sand.

87

Be cautious about putting anyone on a pedestal; even though you may see accomplishment in one area, that doesn't mean he or she is a person worth following. For example, I used to look up to one particular business leader in the early days of building my business. I went to a convention one weekend, and this guy was on stage in front of thousands of people. He was one of the best speakers I had ever heard, and I was absolutely inspired by him and his example. I said to myself, "I've got to meet this guy and get to know him." Years later, I was really let down to discover that he was doing a lot of very unscrupulous things behind the scenes. I was disheartened. This guy was all about personal glory and ego. He had unplugged from his mentor and was taking his own advice. As with many fallen "idols," his arrogance was his downfall. I learned not to lose faith in all men just because one man let me down.

> *Be cautious putting anyone on a pedestal; even though you may see accomplishment in one area, that doesn't mean he or she is a person worth following.*

> *I learned not to lose faith in all men just because one man let me down.*

But I don't idolize any man. It should be noted that any man who lets you put him on a pedestal shouldn't be there anyway. Sadly, this theme repeated itself several times in my business journey. Because of my hard work and many blessings, Amy and I achieved some pretty big goals fairly quickly. I was excited about meeting many of the other inspiring speakers I had seen on stage. Like the previous example, sometimes I would meet leaders whom I had admired and I discovered they weren't living the same values they were preaching. In a way I had been idolizing these guys and hadn't realized it; I was making them out to be better than many of them actually were.

> *Any man who lets you put him on a pedestal shouldn't be there anyway.*

One leader I remember specifically was someone who spoke on stage against adultery. A while later, both this leader and I had earned a reward trip to Hawaii from the vendor we worked with. I saw this guy and walked up to him asking if I could get a picture with him. He surprised me by turning me down, saying, "No, you don't want a picture with me." It turns out the lady accompanying him was not his wife; she was his mistress. He had fathered three kids with his office secretary; he was drinking and smoking and not even trying to act like the man he once pretended to be.

Again, I was disheartened that a man I had looked up to had fallen so far. I wrongly put my faith in a man. There has only been one perfect man: the God-man, Jesus Christ. When "man" becomes the standard, we grow disillusioned because the standard always fails. So be careful not to put people on a pedestal. No matter how good they look, no one is perfect.

All People Have Something about Themselves They Don't Like

No one has it all together. Everyone you look up to has some flaw, some blemish that is like a stubborn stain; it just won't go away, no matter how hard they try to overcome it. Successful people have qualities they would probably prefer to be rid of. Oprah Winfrey has struggled for years with her diet and weight. Tom Cruise is dyslexic,[56] as am I. Sylvester Stallone suffered complications at birth resulting in partial paralysis to his face and slurred speech.[57] Elisabeth Hasselbeck, co-host of the TV show *The View*, suffers from a painful digestive condition due to celiac disease.[58] President Roosevelt was paralyzed from the waist down and confined to a wheelchair but did his level best never to be seen that way in public.

We all have things about ourselves we may want to improve; some things we can, and some things we can't. And we need to be able to discern the things we can and can't change, the "low-hanging fruit" that can be changed quickly and the matters that will take a while. For instance, I am completely bald today (well, I have the "Caesar ring"). When I started to lose my hair at age twenty, it really bothered me. I was self-conscious around others with a full head of hair. (Since then I have come to realize that God made a few perfect noggins, and the rest He covered with hair!)

In all seriousness, if you are bald or balding, and you don't think properly about it, it can mess with your self-image. I know some people are really affected by it and get down on themselves. For every story of a head going bald, there is a story of a bruised ego trying to cover it up in some way. As I travel around and meet different people, I am witness to a lot of different attempts to cover up a balding head:

- People dye their hair
- Cut their hair
- Grow bangs
- Cut bangs
- Get a perm
- Get it straightened
- Get it moved, or transplanted
- Buy wigs
- And my personal favorite: the blessed comb-over. (My close friends all know this one guy who only has hair on the sides and the back. He grows the sides about nine inches long and then combs it toward the top and uses lacquer to hold it in place. Not a good look. Also, disaster strikes for this guy whenever it's time to swim or go outside when it's windy.)

In the past, losing your hair was a sign of a loss of virility or masculinity. Interestingly, society is changing what it thinks looks masculine and powerful. Think Michael Jordan. No one thinks he isn't masculine. In a *Wall Street Journal* article on how bald men can have an advantage in business, a recent study out of the University of Pennsylvania's Wharton School shares that men with shaved heads are perceived to be more masculine, dominant and, in some cases, better potential leaders than those with longer locks or with thinning hair. [59]

Author Seth Godin, who has sported a bald look for two decades, says at least you are taking action by shaving your head when your hair starts to thin. Godin says, "These are people who decide to own what they have, as opposed to trying to pretend to be something else."[60]

My point is this: if we go through so much trouble for the sake of appearance, it must be important to us. But should it be? If you are balding, I would encourage you to focus on the things you *can* change, emphasizing the things that actually matter in terms of one's value and worth as a person. Let's start on the inside, shall we? We will come back to more on personal appearance later in the book.

YOU ARE EQUAL TO THEM

"Live as if you like yourself, and it may happen."

- Marge Piercy

In order to build our confidence, we need to see other people as equals, neither more nor less than ourselves. This stops the deadly game of comparison in its tracks. How can we see other people as equals? First, we need to remember the other guy isn't perfect. Second, we need to remember we have many strengths they don't have. In the words of Glenn R. Schiraldi:

> Wholesale self-esteem is the conviction that one is as worthwhile as anyone else, but not more so. On one hand, we have a quiet gladness to be who we are and a sense of dignity that comes from realizing that we share what all humans possess—intrinsic worth. On the other hand, those with self-esteem remain humble, realizing that everyone has much to learn and that we are all really in the same boat. There is no need to be arrogant or boastful, no need to think that we are more worthwhile as a person than others or more skilled or important than we really are.[61]

Sadly, many people struggle with this.

When my wife Amy was in high school, she dreamed of being a fashion model. She actually did a few shows and got paid for her time. However, she has moved away from her dream, and I am thankful that God closed the door on that career. On the occasions when I went to shows with her and met the people in the industry, I began to feel something wasn't right. I had a strong feeling that these were not the people I wanted my future wife hanging around. I don't mean to say that everyone in the industry is like this, but the people I met when Amy was working seemed to have their priorities wrong. People's worth as human beings, it seemed they were saying, was based on one criterion: how they looked. Everything else was secondary. Sometimes they viewed the runway models as objects, as pieces of meat, not as people with feelings. In fact, some of the people running the shows even seemed "slimy" to me, for lack of a better word.

The entire culture of the fashion industry seemed shallow. There is a movie, *The Devil Wears Prada*,[62] starring Meryl Streep, which presents the fashion industry in an unflattering light. People depend on the approval of others complimenting them on their looks and style. They reason that if they don't look good on the outside, they feel worthless on the inside. If someone wears the latest "in style" colors and someone else doesn't, one person is superior, and the other is inferior. Each spring they announce a certain style is "in," and a certain style is "out". Why is the style no longer cool? Who knows?! The popular style changes without notice and seems absolutely arbitrary. If you are "in the know," you'll be wearing the new style and be better than other people. It all just seems ridiculous to me.

In his book *When People Are Big and God Is Small*, author Edward T. Welch shares this amazing insight:

> Do you know what happened the last time we came home from a party where I tried to dance with my wife? My mind began to roam; I began to fantasize that I was a great dancer.‡ My fantasy was that I walked casually out onto the dance floor, just

‡ By the way, that's another fear of mine: dancing in public. I said for years as a joke, "I can't fast dance; I have a trick knee." Guess what? I just had knee surgery a few months ago ... and it's still not right. The good news is ... I can't dance on it.

a regular guy, and all of a sudden I was John Travolta. People were amazed, my wife thought I was great; you get the idea.

It was funny or pitiful, depending on how you look at it. My point is that the relatively harmless fantasy is filled with fear of man, shame, and pride. It is fear of man because I am consumed with what other people might think of my klutziness. It is shame, especially the more secularized version, because I'm not feeling too good about myself. I'm feeling exposed before other people, believing that only a real jerk would be that hopeless on the dance floor. It is pride because I want to be perceived as great—at least in something.

That's the paradox of self-esteem: low self-esteem usually means that I think too highly of myself. I'm too self-involved, I feel I deserve better than what I have. The reason I feel bad about myself is because I aspire to something more. I want just a few minutes of greatness. I am a peasant who wants to be king. When you are in the grips of low self-esteem, it's painful, and it certainly doesn't feel like pride. But I believe that this is the dark, quieter side of pride—thwarted pride.[63]

Your worth as a person is not based on your ability to dance. You aren't worth *less* if you are a bad dancer, and you aren't worth *more* if you can dance like John Travolta. For your self-esteem and self-confidence to flourish, you have to understand you are as worthwhile a human being as those sitting next to you. You aren't superior to them, and you aren't their doormat. Looking fashionable doesn't make you better or worse. Being rich doesn't make you better or worse. Having a happy marriage doesn't make you better or worse. These are things to aspire to, *not measurements of your worth as a person*. To stop the comparison game in its tracks, we need to drop the envy, idolizing, and self-deprecation and accept ourselves for who and what we are. We must judge ourselves fairly, on an objective scale of worth. And we must remove from our eyes the things we mistakenly see are reducing our worth and our confidence.

All people have unconditional worth. If you are a parent, you can appreciate what I'm about to say: a new parent loves her young child, no strings attached. The child has accomplished nothing. It doesn't have good grades or a fancy car, hasn't thrown the game-winning touchdown, and hasn't brought home an *A* in algebra. A parent's love for the child is not conditional on the child's status or accomplishments. If you found your child sobbing in her bedroom because she felt as if she were worthless, you would know in your heart this just wasn't true. You would see her worth through your loving eyes. Likewise, we need to see ourselves as intrinsically worthwhile beings who are loved.

> *A parent's love for the child is not conditional on the child's status or accomplishments.*

List Your "I Can'ts" and Then Demolish Them

Motivational author and speaker Les Brown said, "If someone else has done it, it's possible I can do it." When we struggle with self-esteem and compare ourselves to other people, we might focus on what they "can" do and what we "can't" do. We think, "Sure, that guy is successful, but I'm not able to be as successful because of this certain quality I have." We start making excuses to ourselves because of our perceived weaknesses. The things we think we "can't" do become the bars on our self-made prison cell, trapping us from achieving our full potential.

I want to encourage to dig up your "I can'ts" and stomp them into the ground. How do we do that? First we list the barriers that we think are holding us back. Then we look for someone who has faced that same exact challenge (or worse) and managed to succeed in spite of it. Here are some typical "I can'ts" I have

> *The things we think we "can't" do become the bars on our self-made prison cell, trapping us from achieving our full potential.*

had people share with me to explain why they weren't able to be successful. They've said, "Tim, I would be more successful, but I can't because ..."

- **I'm too old.** So was a seventy-two-year-old Japanese woman, Tamae Watanabe, who ignored her age to become the oldest women to scale Mount Everest.[64]
- **I'm too young.** So was twelve-year-old Craig Kielburger, a Toronto schoolboy who read the story of another twelve-year-old who was assassinated for speaking out on child labor in Asia. Craig traveled to Asia, still just twelve years of age, interviewed kids in child labor camps, met with the prime minister of Canada, and launched a charity called Free the Children. Today, Free the Children has built over 450 schools in third-world countries and has been featured on *Oprah Winfrey* and *60 Minutes*. Craig has won the Order of Canada, the highest award possible for a civilian.
- **I'm too short.** So is Tom Cruise at 5'8", Martin Luther King at 5'7", Ryan Seacrest at 5'7", Napoleon Bonaparte at 5'6", Joe Pesci at 5'5", Elton John at 5'4", Michael J. Fox at 5'4", Martin Scorsese at 5'3", Prince at 5'3", and Dudley Moore at 5'2". Their height never stopped them from becoming wildly successful.
- **I'm bald.** So are Sean Connery, Bruce Willis, and yours truly. Didn't stop us.
- **I speak poorly.** So did James Earl Jones, the baritone voice of Darth Vader in the *Star Wars* movies. Most people don't know that Jones had a stutter so severe as a child that he refused to speak and was functionally mute for eight years. He gives credit to his English teacher for forcing him to recite poetry every day in class, knowing that being encouraged to overcome this stutter through public speaking would help build his confidence.[65]

- **I'm not educated (enough).** President Andrew Johnson received no formal education and grew up in poverty. Working as a tailor's apprentice, he developed a love of learning as visiting citizens came to read to the tailors from great books in the shop in which he worked. They generously lent him books. Despite those humble beginnings, he became the most powerful man in the country.[66]

- **I've got a disease.** So does Michael J. Fox, actor in the *Back to the Future* movies. He suffers from Parkinson's disease. Since being diagnosed, he has continued acting and doing voice work in movies such as *Stuart Little* and is a passionate advocate for Parkinson's research and fundraising. In 2009, he wrote the bestselling book *Always Looking Up: The Adventures of an Incurable Optimist*, which chronicles his journey with the disease. [67]

- **I'm paralyzed.** So is Rick Hansen, paralyzed from the waist down at fifteen years of age when the pickup truck he was riding in the back of flipped over. Rather than wallow in self-pity, Rick became the first handicapped graduate of the University of British Columbia and a Paralympian in volleyball. He also launched the now famous "Man in Motion" tour where he wheeled himself around the world. He was a torch bearer at the 2010 Winter Olympics. He credits his paralysis as the greatest thing that ever happened to him.[68]

- **My father was in jail.** So was the father of Olympian Hope Solo, US women's soccer team goalkeeper. Her father was in jail for embezzlement, and Solo was actually conceived during a conjugal visit. She grew up with a father who was a criminal and succeeded despite her roots.[69]

- **I've been in jail.** So was Frank Abagnale, one of the world's most famous imposters and the focus of Steven Spielberg's film, *Catch Me if You Can*. After five years of jail time, Frank became a celebrated fraud consultant, working with the FBI and banks to create currency that could not be forged.[70]

Use other people's success as an example to build your confidence, not as something to be discouraged about. Look at what someone has accomplished and remind yourself, "If I think I'm not successful because of such-and-such quality, and someone with this very same quality has become successful, maybe it's not such a big deal. Maybe I can win. Maybe there is greatness within me."

Focus on What You *Can* Do

So many people beat themselves up for what they *can't* do, they fail to recognize and celebrate the good that they *can* offer. Celebrating the good you can do is a key to a strong sense of self-worth and ultimately confidence. You might say to yourself, "If I can solve world hunger, I will feel good about myself." That's a noble aspiration. It's also not likely to happen. Why? Because there are too many factors that are simply outside of your personal control. Do what you can, where you are, with what you've got. If you are passionate about feeding hungry people, set a goal that is within your control. A better example might be "If I volunteer at a soup kitchen, I will feel good about myself." Another variation might be "If I donate food to a local charity during the holidays, I will feel good about myself."

Can you clearly see the difference here? People who beat themselves up sometimes have a bad habit of setting a benchmark for success that is impossible to reach. Instead, have a simpler list of ways to show excellence in your life.

> *Do what you can, where you are, with what you've got.*

The key is that these actions need to be *completely within your control.* For example, you might say, "If I show kindness to someone today, I deserve to feel good about myself." That is totally achievable. How about "If I show discipline in getting out of bed when my alarm clock goes off and demonstrate 'mind over mattress,' I should feel good about myself"? What about "Someone was gossiping in the office about another co-worker today. I gently suggested that this wasn't professional and asked them to change the subject. I feel proud of myself for showing some courage and doing the right thing"? Finally, consider this: "I was at the gas station, and the clerk handed me back too much change. I noticed and returned the extra money. I feel proud of myself for being honest."

All these examples are things in daily life over which we have total control.

Rebut the "He's Better than I Am" Thoughts

As we drift into the negative habit of comparison, we need an alarm to go off in our head that shouts, "Hey, stop it. You're starting to compare yourself." You can usually spot this a moment after you feel emotionally a little down or discouraged after having seen someone else's success. Someone steps up to the plate and swings his bat at the baseball, tagging a home run. A moment later you feel down on yourself. In your head, you started to compare. Your negative self-talk started trashing you out, saying, "This guy is so much better than I am...I could never do that...I'm a loser." That alarm in your head needs to be shut down. Stop comparing.

When you catch yourself doing this, you need to rebut the negative thought. You are just as good as that guy. You need to replace the critical thought with an affirming thought. For example, let's suppose someone reaches a goal in business faster than you. Maybe you've been struggling for weeks, months, perhaps even years to hit that goal. And some guy just reaches the goal like it's nothing. You might feel upset. You might feel jealous. You might envy the rewards and recognition he is receiving. You might start beating up on yourself and saying, "What's wrong with me that I haven't accomplished that?"

You need to replace the critical thought with an affirming thought.

When this happens, you've got to catch the thought, kill it, and rewrite a new, positive, affirming thought. Maybe you say instead, "Hey, that guy has spent the last twenty years reading personal development books. Maybe he has received special technical training in our field. When he launched his business, he had already invested decades of time in his personal development. It only looks like he has achieved the goal faster. In reality, his overnight success took twenty years to accomplish. I'll probably achieve my goals even faster than he did!"

If someone drives up in a nice car, you might feel upset and then envious, and then you might get down on yourself. Perhaps you say to yourself, "That guy drives a Lamborghini, so he must be better than I am." If you have that thought, stop it! Rebut the negative thought. Say instead to yourself, "I'd rather *be* rich than *look* rich. Most people drive leased cars to look good. My mentor is teaching me how to live responsibly by purchasing cars with cash and paying off debt. Many people get their expensive cars on a lease; odds are this guy is one of them. I'll bet he would be grateful to meet my mentor and achieve even greater success."

You are not worth less than the other guy with a nice car, and you are not worth more if you are better at managing finances. If you catch yourself thinking those thoughts of comparison, stomp them out. Net worth does not determine self-worth.

> *Net worth does not determine self-worth.*

Compliment High Achievers

"People place themselves on a level with the ones they praise."
– *Johann Wolfgang von Goethe*

When someone does something that impresses you, offer a genuine compliment. Doing this forces you to *take action*, and often you will see that the person is nice and will likely compliment you in return. Also, at least you'll break the pattern of feeling bad because paying the compliment will make you feel good. That short-circuits the negative feelings of comparison. It takes *guts* to speak up and approach a stranger, it takes *courage* to express *humility*, it takes a spirit of *service* to lift up another person, and these are all admirable traits.

It also takes the other person down off any pedestal when they interact with you, because now it's just another person you are chatting with. Besides, you probably made somebody's day, because most people never receive compliments. That way, your value to the other person just went up; you had the special ability to make another feel good.

A friend of mine was at the gym, and a bodybuilder was leg-pressing a thousand pounds. My friend was doing much less. Although it takes a lot of guts to speak up and say hi to a stranger, he complimented the bodybuilder, who responded with a friendly word of thanks. My friend saw that the bodybuilder was a really nice guy and not at all stuck up or arrogant. By engaging more successful people in conversation, we normalize and humanize them rather than put them up on a pedestal. You are just as good a person as they are, and paying them a compliment can help you remember that.

THEY ARE EQUAL TO YOU: ## STOP LEVELING PEOPLE

"He that undervalues himself will undervalue others, and He that undervalues others will oppress them."
– *Author Unknown*

Everyone wants to feel worthwhile and valuable. All of us want to feel some good inside ourselves. But when we start comparing, the only way to feel good is to beat the other guy. There are only two ways to be the biggest building in town: make yourself bigger, or knock everything else down. Sadly, that's what a lot of people with low self-confidence do. They spend their time criticizing, correcting, and embarrassing other people, pointing out their mistakes and showing where they went wrong.

The age-old advice is as true today as ever: if you can't say anything *nice*, don't say anything at all. Ephesians 4:31 says, "Let all bitterness and wrath and anger and clamor and slander be put away from you, along with all malice." I'd encourage you to make it your goal to lift people up rather than knock them down, even if you think they deserve to be knocked down a peg or two. Les Giblin, author of *How to Have Confidence and Power in Dealing with People*, says, "[Knocking down an arrogant jerk] doesn't work, because we know that the self-centered, egotistical person is not suffering from too much self-esteem, but too little."[71] If you're on good terms with yourself, you're on good terms with others. You'll find that lifting people up elevates you more than your criticism ever could. Each time you catch yourself about to knock someone else down, just freeze, take a breath, and say something complimentary—or say nothing at all.

> *[Knocking down an arrogant jerk] doesn't work, because we know that the self-centered, egotistical person is not suffering from too much self-esteem, but too little." – Les Giblin*

Stop Embarrassing Other People

"To belittle, you have to be little."

– Kahlil Gibran

Les Giblin makes the point that when criticism is for the purpose of helping the other person, it is valuable. He cites the example of air traffic controllers guiding a plane safely in for a landing. If the plane is off course, the controller is going to correct the pilot. He doesn't make it a personal attack by saying, "Hey, dummy. Where did you learn to fly? Turn it to heading 270°, or you're toast!" The air traffic controller simply lets the pilot know what to correct. Any corrective suggestions are to help the plane land safely.

When criticism is for the purpose of ego satisfaction, it is destructive. Giblin asks, "Do you criticize an employee only when you have an audience? Do you 'correct' your husband's table manners in the presence of company? If so, the chances are very good that your real purpose in criticizing is not to help the other person, but to derive ego satisfaction out of humiliating him."[72]

If you find yourself criticizing people in a way that embarrasses them in front of others, ask yourself why. Really dig deep to figure out if you are getting any pleasure in doing so. If you are, may I gently recommend that you *knock it off*! (Said with love.)

> *When criticism is for the purpose of ego satisfaction, it is destructive.*

It's just another example of tearing other people down to try to build yourself up, and it carries with it a tinge of schoolyard viciousness. It comes from having low self-esteem, and frankly, you might benefit from sometime reading a book on the subject. (Oh, wait…you are.)

A friend of mine is a corporate trainer and likes to make the audience laugh. A few years ago, he got into the habit of cracking a joke when someone walked into his session a few minutes late. He would joke loudly upon their entrance, "Well, at least we aren't teaching time management today!" The audience would laugh at the expense of the latecomer, and the tardy one would sheepishly slink towards a seat, face red. After a while, my friend realized that he was embarrassing the late employees and that he was placing his own need to be funny above the feelings of that one employee. He realized he could still be an entertaining speaker without being mean-spirited and dropped the joke.

Stop Correcting People

"Don't find fault. Find a remedy."

– Henry Ford

W hy do people feel the need to point out other people's mistakes? Well, it could be that they genuinely want the other person to improve. It could be that they want to help. Or it could be that they are trying to knock the other person down a few pegs to make themselves feel powerful in comparison.

For some people, their self-esteem and identity are tied to "being right" and "being knowledgeable." They feel that they are worthwhile only if they are correct—and, more important, if other people know it. If you derive your self-esteem from being right, the question to ask yourself is *why? Why* is that your source of self-esteem? Do you feel embarrassed being wrong or making a mistake? Does that seem rational to you? Surely you must realize that you

> *Compulsively correcting people is purely an ego game, and "one day, you will come to understand that in a pretentious game of gratifying your ego, you have auctioned the inner beauty of your soul."*

can't be right *all the time*. If you were only right 51 percent of the time, you would make a billion dollars on the stock market this year. If someone was right *all the time*, they'd have easily developed the cure for cancer, brought peace to the Middle East, and found a solution to world hunger. Since these haven't been accomplished, you may want to lower your estimation of yourself as being "all-knowing" a notch, Scooter. Compulsively correcting people is purely an ego game, and "one day, you will come to understand that in a pretentious game of gratifying your ego, you have auctioned the inner beauty of your soul."[73]

I have a family member whom I love very much who is, and has always been, right about everything (in his own eyes). It's a sad condition, because it holds him back from learning. Why

103

would someone bother learning when he thinks he already knows everything? It might be true we have some expertise in a certain area, but imagine the vast ocean of knowledge we *don't* have. Also, is it possible that our suggestion is correct, but someone else's idea might also have merit? There might be two different solutions to the same problem. 2+2 equals 4, but so does 1+3. And even if we are correct, remember that no one wants to hear about it if we come across as an arrogant know-it-all! (No one except us.)

The world is filled with people who will tell you what you do wrong. Your friends, family, and colleagues are constantly told by everyone around them what they do wrong. Even if your heart is genuinely in a good place, and you want to help the other person by correcting them, may I suggest you reconsider? As Dale Carnegie wrote, "When we are wrong, we may admit it to ourselves. And if we are handled gently and tactfully, we may admit it to others and even take pride in our frankness and broad-mindedness. But not if someone else is trying to ram the unpalatable fact down our esophagus."[74]

If someone is about to make a tiny mistake, consider letting them know gently. Please don't come across as a know-it-all. You may want to say, "I could be wrong, but have you considered this? Perhaps there is another way of looking at this problem." Or "This is only my opinion, and I certainly am not an expert, but what about this option?" Using language like that leaves a back door for the other's ego to remain intact. Throw a little uncertainty into your language in order to gently introduce a suggestion. You may also try asking permission to offer a suggestion—perhaps something like "Bob, if I noticed something I felt could really help you, do I have your permission to offer a little tip?" By virtue of having given their permission first, they are probably more open to hearing what you have to say. I learned from my mentor that it matters less to the other person whether you are right than it does that you care and that their ego and feelings are intact.

Finally, stop yourself and ask, "Who am I to criticize this other person?" Consider all the mistakes you have made throughout your life. It can be pretty easy to feel self-righteous when considering our strengths in comparison to another, but what about our flaws compared to their flaws? In John 8:7, Jesus said, "Let him who is without sin among you be the first to throw a stone at her." I know all my flaws. Who am I to judge another person?

Now, naysayers will point out that avoiding correcting people doesn't count for landing airplanes, brain surgery, or running a nuclear power plant. Of course there are times when you point out a mistake. If your spouse is driving the car and about to run a red light or crash into someone, don't *avoid* pointing it out in order to dogmatically follow this principle. (My wife Amy is really good at this and has saved us from terrible car accidents a few times.) Use discretion. However, the three extreme examples I just gave are situations where a person is in *mortal danger*. Only one time in a thousand are we in mortal danger, so the exception almost never applies. You still need to avoid offering criticism most of the time.

Stop Upstaging People with a Bigger Fish Story

"True heroism is remarkably sober, very undramatic. It is not the urge to surpass all others at whatever the cost, but the urge to serve others at whatever the cost."

– *Arthur Ashe*

We've all experienced it: you've had a great day at the office, or fishing, or playing sports, and you share a fun story of your accomplishment. Most of your friends and family enjoy the story and feel happy for you. But maybe one or more listeners can't just enjoy the tale; they've got to top the story with one of their own. It's the "Yeah, me too" disease. If you caught a three-foot fish, they caught a four-footer. If you threw a football thirty yards, they threw it forty. If your daughter got an *A* on her report card, their kid got an *A+*.

Why do people do this? Because in their mind, if you are having success, it means they *aren't*. They feel diminished if someone else gets

105

ahead of them. It's the scarcity mentality versus abundance mentality; they feel there is only so much success to go around, and when you succeed, you are taking from their share of the pie. It's really a sure sign of a low self-image.

I share this with you because I want you to consider whether you might be doing this. When someone in conversation shares a story of their success, do you squirm a little and feel the need to share a story of your own? If your brother-in-law gets a promotion, do you need to let the family know about the important project you are working on? Someone once said, "If you wish your merit to be known, acknowledge that of other people." Imagine the self-confidence it takes to *not* share your "bigger fish" story. On the other hand, bragging is a sure sign of a low self-image and a great way to keep it low.

> *Imagine the self-confidence it takes to not share your "bigger fish" story.*

A few years ago, my dear friends and business partners and I had just returned from an amazing Mediterranean cruise. We had stopped off in some of the world's most beautiful cities, including Naples, Italy, to enjoy the food and some shopping and to see the sights. We walked the streets of Rome, visited Greece, drove little Italian cars, and actually ate pizza in Napoli where pizza was first invented. How amazing is that?! It was a real blast for us and birthed a love of Italy for many of us.

When we got back from the trip, not surprisingly a lot of people asked us how it was and to please share the stories. Well, one of the guys standing in the group was a real "Better-Story Bob." He always had to upstage everyone else. As my wife Amy and I were describing eating pizza in a quaint outdoor café in Naples, it was basically the most amazing pizza eating story humanly possible. When he heard our story, "Better-Story Bob" actually said something along the lines, "Until you've eaten at Jet's Pizza in Flint, Michigan, you haven't eaten pizza." Amy and I were just stunned. We were simply answering someone's honest question, and we weren't bragging. At first we just laughed it off, but then later we actually felt a little sorry for the guy. How could anyone think that local pizza guy would compare to pizza in Naples? "Bob's" self-image was so low he always had to top everyone's story with one of his own.

Another way of "topping" someone is showing off for the purpose of upstaging them. If they can do something well, you might feel you have to show everyone you can do it *better*. Instead of giving in to that negative impulse, I would encourage you to let them have their chance to shine. For example, a friend of mine is a pretty good piano player and was at a dinner party when one of the other guests sat down to play the piano. The other guest was a good player, but not as good as my friend. When the first guy finished playing, he received some polite applause. Someone then asked my friend to play afterward, but he politely declined. My friend knew he was a much more experienced player than the first guy and felt it would make the previous player feel diminished if he played. He didn't need to top the other guy and show off.

You shouldn't feel threatened when someone else succeeds, and you don't need to prove you are better than other people. Let other people enjoy some accolades and applause. And if they're excited they've caught a twelve-inch fish, smile and congratulate them. It's a great way to show confidence.

SUMMARY

A confident person is not shackled by a need for comparison. Your worth isn't determined by how you measure up to the guy beside you. As Woodrow Wilson said, "All the extraordinary men I have known were extraordinary in their own estimation."[75] Recognizing your inherent worth as a person and setting aside the need to compare yourself to others are the first two steps in building your self-confidence.

Key Points

1. If we don't know we are intrinsically worthwhile, we tend to look for another yardstick against which to measure ourselves. The most convenient yardstick tends to be the people in our lives.

2. You can't plug the leaky self-esteem bucket with accomplishments and accolades. Most people have a God-shaped hole in their heart that can only be filled by Him.

3. Comparison merely says, "I hope the other guy isn't very good so I can *seem* better." Competition says, "I hope the other guy brings his A-game so it forces me to *become* better."

4. Envy will rot your soul. When you see someone who is successful, don't covet what they *have*; aspire to be what they *are*.

5. If you violate your conscience to try and look superior, your self-esteem will suffer.

6. Don't compare your strengths to another's weaknesses, and vice-versa. You are being unfair with yourself either way.

7. When you see someone you think has it all together, I promise you they've got something about themselves they don't like. And you probably don't know about it.

8. Don't idolize anyone. Any man who lets you put him on a pedestal shouldn't be there anyway.

9. You are just as worthwhile as the person beside you, neither more nor less, because all people have intrinsic worth.

10. If you think you don't deserve to walk into a room with confidence, remember that whatever you think is holding you back has already been overcome by someone else.

11. Compliment high achievers. People place themselves on a level with the ones they praise.

12. If you knock other people down in order to build yourself up, knock it off! It's one of the surest signs of a low self-image. Stop embarrassing people, pointing out their mistakes and showing how you would have done it better. Your fish story does not need to top theirs.

3

MANAGE YOUR
SELF-TALK

"We cannot always control our thoughts, but we can control our words, and repetition impresses the subconscious, and we are then master of the situation."

– Florence Scovel Shinn

When we see people who carry themselves with confidence, we're looking at their outward behavior. We watch them walk into a room with a smile to welcome everyone. We see how they stand, how they make eye contact, how they radiate energy that draws other people in. We watch them extend a hand to greet other people and make fast friends. We watch their behavior the way we might look at a high-performing sports car and marvel at how it looks on the outside when it drives by and takes a corner.

But the real magic is under the hood. It's in the engine and the onboard computer and how it communicates with all the systems in the car. The real magic of confidence is in the *way we talk to ourselves*.

Consider the following story:

An old blind man was sitting on a busy street corner in the rush hour begging for money. On a cardboard sign, next to an empty tin cup, he had written: "Blind – Please help."

No one was giving him any money.

A young advertising writer walked past and saw the blind man with his sign and his empty cup, and also saw the many people passing by completely unmoved, let alone stopping to give him money.

The advertising writer took a thick marker-pen from her pocket, turned the cardboard sheet back-to-front, and re-wrote the sign, then went on her way. Immediately, people began putting money into the tin cup.

After a while, when the cup was overflowing, the blind man asked a stranger to tell him what the sign now said,

"It says," said the stranger, "'It's a beautiful day. You can see it; I cannot.'"[76]

What we realize is that no matter how great our challenges may be, there is always a better way to look at the world. When we speak this positive thought into existence using our words (written or verbal), it's amazing how we connect with other people. And when we do, we will attract success in all that we do.

HAVE AN INVINCIBLE ATTITUDE

"Nothing can stop the man with the right mental attitude from achieving his goal; nothing on earth can help the man with the wrong mental attitude."

– Thomas Jefferson

Here's something I've discovered about life: each of us faces wonderful days, and we each suffer through tragic days. We feel joy at the sight of our newborn baby, and we feel broken as we bury our parents. Our heart soars when we marry our child-hood sweetheart, and our heart aches when we sit with him or her in the doctor's office when the bad news is given. We swell with pride as we cut the ribbon to our new business, and we choke back tears as we struggle to make a week's payroll. We jump for joy as we get the keys to our new home, and we stare in numb silence as the fire burns our home to the ground.

Everyone enjoys victory, and everyone suffers defeat; no one is immune. Life is up one day and down the next. It's like a proverbial roller coaster, and you ride your emotions wildly from peak to valley. As Orrin Woodward says, "Attitude is the ability to reframe the experience to empower you to future victories."[77] What I've learned from being on this wild adventure called life is that when you are down in the dumps, and everything feels like it's going against you, you just need to have the faith to believe that things will turn around. And not surprisingly, they always do. It's when the night is darkest that the stars come out. As the late Ernest Reisinger said, "Never forget in the darkness what you learned in the light."

Confident people understand that life brings setbacks and disappointments. In fact, they know that if things have been going well for a while, it's time to brace for some sort of unexpected calamity. By knowing and accepting this, we can handle it when the tough times hit and keep standing strong.

Romans 8:28 says, "And we know that for those who love God all things work together for good, for those who are called according to his purpose." Please note the verse doesn't say all things are good. It says "all things," which means all things both good and bad, *work together* for good.

> *Having a positive attitude simply means no matter the situation, we choose to view it from a "solution" viewpoint rather than a "damnation" viewpoint.*

Some people might think that having a positive attitude is denying the facts of a situation. That's not true. If you have a car crash but then stick your head in the sand like an ostrich and pretend nothing happened, that isn't positive; that's delusional! Having a positive attitude means that you acknowledge reality, but you don't blow it out of proportion. A positive attitude says, "Wow, we had a fender bender. Luckily, no one was hurt, and the insurance will cover it." Compare this to a whiny, negative attitude that says, "Oh no. We had a fender bender. That means that today is going to be terrible. I'll be late for work. I'll probably get suspended and then fired; then we'll lose our house and end up living in a van down by the river!"

Wow, that was a little melodramatic.

Having a positive attitude simply means no matter the situation, we choose to view it from a "solution" viewpoint rather than a "damnation" viewpoint. Zig Ziglar said this about a positive attitude: "Positive thinking won't let you do anything, but it will let you do everything better than negative thinking will."[78]

Years ago when I was transitioning from being an engineer to a real estate investor, and later into the leadership/life coaching business, I faced some massive financial and personal struggles. I gotta tell ya, Zig's words served me well. If Charles Swindoll is right, "Life is 10% what happens to you and 90% how you react to it."[79]

It's true that we can't always control our circumstances. I know it stinks when we are going through massive financial, health, or relationship challenges. Despite that, let's ask ourselves an honest question: does it help to have a bad attitude when we lose our job or a business fails? The answer is *no*. It also doesn't help to stick your head in the sand and pretend the tough times aren't happening. You see, when we have to make a choice to have a positive attitude, the decision may be easier said than done, but it is still our decision.

> *When we have to make a choice to have a positive attitude, the decision may be easier said than done, but it is still our decision.*

Some people mistakenly think that certain individuals just randomly won the "lottery of life" (as Al Gore mistakenly calls it) by being born with a positive attitude or that a positive environment creates a positive attitude. By this reasoning, only the "lucky few" born into a great family situation might be positive. That's a load of nonsense! It might be nice if you were born to parents who were doctors or lawyers and they packed your lunch each day while you walked to school through your upper-middle-class neighborhood. It might be awesome if your dad came to all your football practices and your mom helped you with your homework, always providing a shoulder to cry on. While some people reading this book might have experienced that, for others (like me) that sounds like a fantasy family only seen on *Leave It to Beaver*. The fact is that most people with invincible positive attitudes probably had their proverbial teeth kicked in by life a bunch of times along the way. They have the emotional and sometimes physical scars to show for it.

Our circumstances don't determine our attitude; we must *choose* to see things in the best possible light. Author John Maxwell shares a story of Snoopy, the dog in the *Peanuts* cartoon. Snoopy is feeling down because it's Thanksgiving. He says to himself, "How about that? Everyone is eating turkey today, but just because I'm a dog, I get dog food."

Snoopy thinks for a moment and considers, "Of course, I could have been born a turkey!"[80]

Manage Your Automatic Negative Thoughts

"If you want to test your memory, try to recall what you were worrying about one year ago today."

– E. Joseph Cossman

One of the hallmarks of unconfident people is how quickly their thoughts drift toward the negative. A simple example would be when a person's manager comes to his desk at work and says, "I'd like to talk to you. Please see me in my office at 5 p.m."

Most people aren't going to think, *Wow! I'm finally getting that promotion I've been hoping for.* Instead they probably are going to assume that something bad will happen at 5 p.m. and say to themselves, *Oh no, at 5 p.m., I am dead meat.*

This knee-jerk reaction toward assuming the worst-case scenario is called an "Automatic Negative Thought" or ANT. ANTs invade your thinking when you aren't being careful. They infest your brain and chip away at your defenses. They burrow tiny holes in your mental foundation. These are destructive invaders and need to be dealt with swiftly with the heel of your boot. You need to stamp out your ANTs with enthusiasm!

So how do you do it? How do you train your brain not to drift on autopilot toward whatever might be wrong in the world? First of all, you need to notice the ANTs. The way we spot the ANTs is by looking for telltale signs of their destructive presence: we pay attention to our emotions. Most particularly, we notice our negative emotions.

Let's suppose we notice we are feeling a little down in the dumps.

> *One of the hallmarks of unconfident people is how quickly their thoughts drift toward the negative.*

A simple philosophy to spot an ANT is to assume "where there's smoke, there's fire." What that means is, "Where there are negative emotions, surely there was first an ANT." Notice that when you feel any sort of negative emotion, almost certainly your thinking contributed in a big way toward the feelings. Try to figure out when you started to feel down. Was it when you arrived at the office? During your coffee break? When you returned from lunch? "Aha!" you might say. "I started to feel lousy when I got back from lunch."

Next, think about what specifically happened at that time that might have tripped a "bad feeling" switch. You think to yourself, *Did I feel bad this morning?* Nope. *Did I feel bad when I left for lunch?* Nope. After carefully checking everything out, you realize what set you off was getting a phone call from another partner who apologized that they had lost the ABC account and the project was now cancelled. You realize that *this* is what really set you off.

With some further questioning, you realize that receiving that message set you off, and you feel beaten up because of it. The critical question to ask is, "What did I say to myself to cause such a negative emotional reaction?" You see, you likely had to tell yourself an ugly story about why something happened in order to get angry.

Whenever someone does something that doesn't exactly fit our mold of what we think should happen, we tend to assume they did it for a malicious reason. Basically, our imagination runs wild, and we see hurtful conspiracies everywhere. In order to stamp out our Automatic Negative Thoughts, we need to re-write the words we say to ourselves that our mind blurts out so quickly.

Going back to the example of the project getting cancelled, what words did you likely tell yourself about why this terrible injustice occurred? You might have said something negative:

"This isn't fair. That project was my only shot at impressing the big boss. Now I'll be on the sidelines for another year for sure. How come all the good-looking, popular people are getting promoted past me? Man, I'm never going to get out of the job rut I'm stuck in."

While this might be a normal reaction, it certainly isn't a very *positive* reaction. Let's try coming up with a more positive reaction than this Automatic Negative Thought:

"It's true the project got cancelled, but there will be many other opportunities to showcase my talent. I've already impressed the big boss, and they know I'm interested in a promotion. I will schedule time with my manager to discuss my career options. I'm sure all of this will turn out for the best."

These are two very different reactions to the same situation. The biggest question is this: will you catch yourself when you drift into an Automatic Negative Thought, and will you consciously prune the negative thoughts out, leaving only the good thoughts? This is a powerful ability you have under your control. When you start pruning the ANTs out, you'll only have remaining the thoughts worth keeping. And you'll be on your way to becoming a much more secure, self-confident individual.

People Notice What They Look For

When learning to manage our positive self-talk, many people honestly believe they have a good attitude. But the fact of the matter is that most of us are deceived. We each struggle in some way with maintaining a positive attitude, whether the situation is a major global crisis or a minor irritation around the house. The power of attitude affects whether we notice opportunities right in front of us or ignore them completely. Let me give you an example.

In our home, occasionally something mysterious seems to happen to our kids' clothing. Those of you with children may relate. Their clothing literally disappears from sight. One minute it is right where they left it, and the next minute it has vanished from view. Upon further investigation, we've discovered that the issue of the missing clothing has more to do with who is doing the searching. It seems that our kids are sometimes temporarily afflicted with a terrible type of blindness when it comes to finding a piece of clothing. They literally can't see it!

This usually involves a yellow basketball shirt or white football pants. In fact, I've seen what happens if the favorite football pants aren't easily found; the conversation quickly shifts to blaming a brother. I guess it's easier for the victim to point fingers and announce that someone must have stolen his pants out of their bedroom in the middle of the night than admit to himself that the pants might be misplaced.

> *It's easier to notice when someone else isn't looking at a situation correctly than it is to notice when our own thinking is off track.*

Well, after thirty minutes or so of searching all over the house, miraculously, the missing garment was discovered by the pool where my son or daughter had an evening swim right before bedtime the night before. When confronted with this, the offending kid might say, "Hey, who put my pants there?!"

You might shake your head at this example, but we all can deceive ourselves and be blind to the truth that is staring us in the face. It's easier to notice when someone else isn't looking at a situation correctly than it is to notice when our own thinking is off track.

Here is what I have discovered: we tend to notice what we look for in life. We see blessing when we look for it, or we see tragedy. The opportunity lies in deciding where we want to direct our focus.

> *We tend to notice what we look for in life. The opportunity lies in deciding where we want to direct our focus.*

I once heard author and speaker Tony Robbins give a great illustration of this point. He shared how we can't seem to see things unless we are deliberately focused on finding them. Here's how this works: wherever you are, I want you to put this book down for a moment and look around the room. As you do, notice everything that is *blue*. Try it for ten seconds. Go ahead and take a moment to do this.

Have you done that?

Okay, now that you've looked around the room, in a moment I want you to put the book down, close your eyes, and name everything that is *red!*

Notice you probably weren't paying a lot of attention to anything red, since you were looking for everything blue. Something very interesting has happened here. Most people have a tough time recalling anything they saw that was red, because *they weren't looking for it*. Now, take a moment and look around the room and consciously spot everything that is red. Isn't it amazing that you surprise yourself and manage to spot a lot of red that previously you didn't recall?

Here is another way of trying this experiment: look around the room, and imagine you are a firefighter. Look at the room you are in through the imaginary eyes of a firefighter. What do you see? If you are sitting in an office, you might notice the sprinklers in the ceiling, the emergency lights, the fire alarm on the wall, the exit signs, etc. If you are sitting in your home, you might notice a fire extinguisher on the wall, a smoke detector on the hallway ceiling, anything flammable, and the fire exits from the room.

Now, try this experiment: imagine you are looking at the room you are in, but this time pretend that you are an interior decorator. What do you see? You probably don't notice things like sprinklers or emergency lights. You probably notice things like the colors in the room, how the furniture is laid out, the fabric on the sofa, etc.

My point is that we tend to see what we are looking for. What is especially powerful about this is that we can actually train our brains to notice what we want.

Scientists have actually identified a certain part of the brain that is really involved in everything I've described. It's called the RAS, which stands for Reticular Activating System.[81] That's quite a mouthful to say, so let's call this part of your brain the "noticer." Your "noticer" is a pretty cool tool that you can use to your advantage once you are aware of it and how it works. In fact, it's such a powerful tool that if you don't take conscious control over it, it can also really hold you back from success.

Here's how your "noticer" works: imagine you've got a file folder in your brain of all the things that you have decided are important to pay attention to. It doesn't matter whether the stuff in your file folder is of major significance or of no real importance; if you've decided this stuff is significant, your "noticer" is going to spot it every time it crosses your path. That's why firefighters notice the sprinklers when they walk into a room and why an interior decorator notices the drapes.

Here's an example of your "noticer" at work: whenever we buy or rent a car. Have you ever experienced buying a new car, and as soon as you buy it, that same make and model appears everywhere around you? Years ago I bought a new red GMC pickup truck. All of a sudden, I noticed red trucks all around me everywhere I went. That's a pretty big coincidence, don't you think?

Here's what was happening: those red GMC pickups had *always* been driving beside me on the road, but I hadn't decided they were important enough for my "noticer" to pay attention. So I basically ignored them. My eyes saw them, but my "noticer" couldn't have cared less, so my brain flushed the images, and it seemed as if those trucks were invisible.

The great part about this is you get to choose what your "noticer" pays attention to by deciding what *you* consider important. How important is this in helping you become successful? It's a game-changer.

Imagine you are in real estate sales. Everything about real estate opportunities and potential prospects is incredibly important to you. (At least, it should be important to you, assuming you are a hungry and ambitious real estate agent.) Anytime you are driving through a neighborhood, you'll zero in on real estate signs. Whenever someone mentions that he is looking at buying or selling his home, your ears will perk up. Whenever someone asks you what you do for a living, you'll shift gears and see an opportunity to promote yourself and your services.

Do you see how this works? If you weren't in real estate, other people around you might be talking about wanting to sell their homes, and it might go in one ear and out the other, because it's of no great importance to you. But if it's your career, your "noticer" will zero in on any opportunity important to you.

Ask Yourself Positive Questions

How do you take conscious control of your "noticer," your Reticular Activating System, and use it to help you become more confident and ultimately more successful? Simple. You start asking yourself positive questions. If you've read Vince Poscente's excellent book, The Ant and the Elephant,[82] you know that every conscious thought triggers two thousand neurons (a fancy word for brain cells, basically). However, what's really powerful is that every subconscious thought triggers four billion neurons. That is a multiple of two million! The subconscious mind is incredibly powerful. Orrin Woodward has spoken about how he used to employ the power of his subconscious mind in solving complex engineering problems when designing fuel pumps for GM trucks (designs which eventually earned him four US engineering patents and benchmarking awards). Orrin would think deeply about the problem he was trying to solve right before he went to sleep. He would literally dream about the inside of the fuel pump and see how it would work. When he awoke, he wrote down every detail he could recall from his dream into his planner. Orrin asked himself a positive question, "How do I solve this engineering problem?" and his subconscious mind looked for and found the answer.

> *Whatever question you ask yourself, your subconscious mind is going to look for and find an answer, so make it a good one.*

Just as the subconscious mind is a powerful ally in finding the positive answer to a question, the opposite is also true. Whenever you listen those who are down in the dumps, who clearly don't attract success in their direction, it's amazing how you will hear them constantly ask themselves *negative* questions. Here are some examples of questions to be on the lookout for, both in yourself and others:

- "Why does this always happen to me?"
- "What did I do to deserve this?"
- "How come I never get any breaks?"
- "Why am I so clumsy/forgetful/broke/unsuccessful?"
- "What's wrong with this?"
- "Why do they keep bugging me?"
- "How come I never have a turn?"
- "Why do I always get left behind?"
- "How did I get myself in this dumb mess again?"
- "What's wrong with me?"

Here's the amazing thing about your "noticer": whatever question you ask, your subconscious mind is going to look for and find an answer—so make it a good question. It doesn't matter if the question you ask is reasonable or even rational, let alone positive or negative; it only matters to your subconscious that you've asked a question. When you ask a question, your subconscious starts chewing away on it, searching for an answer. So, what questions are you asking yourself each and every day?

Here are some examples of questions I would recommend that you should ask yourself in order to notice the positive in every situation and have a more positive mental outlook on life:

- "What is *great* about this?"
- "What did I like the *best* about this?"
- "How am I so *fortunate* to have such an amazing spouse as you?"
- "Why am I so *blessed* to be alive today?"
- "What is *funny* about this situation?"
- "What can I *learn* from this?"
- "How does this setback make me *stronger* and *wiser*?"
- "What are my *strengths*?"
- "Why am I just as good as or *better* than the competition?"
- "How awesome is it that, because I'm bald, I'll save thousands of dollars on hair products?!"

When you get into the habit of asking positive questions, you'll be amazed to find that you discover positive answers.

Go on a Mental Diet

When you look at someone who is totally ripped and able to run marathons, do you ever think, *Wow, that guy or gal must chow down on pizza, beer and candy bars*? Not likely! When you're looking at a high-performing athlete, he or she has poured quality food and nutrients into that body in order to get the best from it.

What about a world-class sports car like a Ferrari or a Lamborghini? Do you think the owners ever water down the gasoline or use regular grade? No chance. They are pouring the highest-quality octane into that engine in order to get superior performance. The same is true of our brains. Orrin Woodward once commented, "Your brain is like a billion-dollar computer. If you had paid a billion dollars for something, would you take care of it?" I hope the answer is yes. Jim Rohn said, "Formal education will make you a living; self-education will make you a fortune."[83] So what sort of brain food do we need?

> "Formal education will make you a living; self-education will make you a fortune."
> – Jim Rohn

Ask successful people, and they will tell you that they are lifelong students of success information. This information comes in the form of ABC: association, books, and CDs (and other audios). It also comes from mentoring and worship. If you want to develop a positive attitude and build your confidence, one of the fastest, simplest, and easiest steps you can take is to start pouring positive information into your brain.

> **Association**. M. Hulburd said that "character is so largely affected by associations that we cannot afford to be indifferent as to who and what our friends are."[84] I couldn't agree more. One of the most important steps in creating a positive attitude is hanging around positive winners who are going places. Why? Because we start to act like them. We start to think like them. We start to become like them.
>
> Don't believe me? Just picture a little boy or girl who comes home from public school. All of a sudden he or she starts using a lot of profanity. Where did that come from? From hearing the other kids use those words. What if the other kids are talking back to the teacher, being rude and disruptive, or throwing

little temper tantrums? You can bet your child will pick up on that and start acting that way.

The same is true for us. We pick up the attitudes and behaviors of the people with whom we hang around most often. If there are people in your life who are habitually negative, may I gently suggest that you try to limit the time you hang around them? If someone is spouting off some negative, perhaps try counteracting it with positive. At the very least, your ears will hear what your mouth is saying, and it will give your ears a balanced perspective. Will Rogers said, "A man only learns in two ways, one by reading, and the other by association with smarter people."[85] So choose wisely those you are hanging around, because you're always learning from them.

> **Books.** Socrates said, "Employ your time in improving yourself by other men's writings so that you shall come easily by what others have labored hard for."[86] Reading a book is an incredible way to learn in hours or days what another person labored for a lifetime to discover. Books allow you to have a conversation with great minds at a distance of space or time. It's been said that CDs and audios can "pump you up," but books change you. Sir J. Stephen said, "Every man has in himself a continent of undiscovered character. Happy is he who acts as the Columbus to his own soul."[87] Books open a powerful doorway to personal improvement. Take time every day to read. Set an initial goal of fifteen minutes every day, and go from there. Lower-level learners will read a book a month. A serious reader will read one to two books a week. These days, we have smartphones and tablets that carry downloadable

> *"A man only learns in two ways, one by reading, and the other by association with smarter people."*
> *– Will Rogers*

> *Reading a book is an incredible way to learn in hours or days what another person labored for a lifetime to discover.*

versions of books. We can carry a whole library in our back pocket. This way, we can catch a few moments of reading even when waiting in line. Read every day. (I would recommend that, whatever books you choose, you should also include the Bible in your reading list. If you aren't familiar with the Bible, may I suggest the English Standard Version, the ESV? Start with the Gospel of Mark; then make your way through Proverbs and finally the first three chapters of Genesis.)

➤ **CDs/Audios.** Do you spend time in your car? As author Stephen R. Covey once said, "The key is in not spending time, but in investing it."[88] How are you investing those minutes behind the wheel? May I make a powerful suggestion that has made a huge difference in my life? Rather than sit idly in traffic to and from work, decide to pop in a leadership or self-development CD. In fact, don't just listen in your car; put the MP3s on your smartphone, carry it around in your pocket, and listen to them while you cook, clean, do laundry. You can even put the device in a speaker "dock" and listen while you shower. Make use of those tiny fragments of time by listening to CDs and learning. Imagine how much you will learn over the course of a year by gathering up the scraps of time here and there, it all adds up. Listen to CDs to improve your mental attitude.

TALK TO YOURSELF LIKE A WINNER

"They told me I couldn't. They told me I wouldn't. They told me I shouldn't. That's why I WILL. That's why I AM. That's why I DID."

– Michael Jordan

There's a story of a young boy who was drawing at the kitchen table. His mom asked what he was doing. Without looking up from the table the young boy replied, "I'm drawing a picture of God."

124

His mom, trying not to burst his bubble, tried to let him down gently. "But sweetheart," she said, "no one knows what God looks like!"

The little boy, reaching for another crayon, replied without hesitation, "They will when I'm finished." Now that's how champions talk to themselves.

Boxing legend Muhammad Ali knew this fact cold. He was famous for referring to himself as a champion. He once boasted, "I'm so fast that last night I turned off the light switch in my hotel room and was in bed before the room was dark!"[89] Now, Ali was a little on the boastful side, which I'm not recommending. I do want to point out the difference between the way Muhammad Ali spoke to himself and the way a lot of other people speak to themselves. Ali was dripping with confidence. There was no doubt that he was going to dominate in the ring. The crowd knew it. His opponents knew it. And Ali told himself he was a winner so often that *he* knew it.

If people could hear the words you say to yourself, could they tell if you were a winner?

How do you talk to yourself? If people could hear the words you say to yourself, could they tell whether you are a winner? Could they tell that you are going places in life? Could they tell that your dominant thought is focused on victory, on being the best person you possibly can, on living the life you've always wanted? I hope so.

Become Aware of Your Self-Talk

"It's not what you say out of your mouth that determines your life; it's what you whisper to yourself that has the most power!"

– Robert Kiyosaki

125

Words have power. Words can move mountains. When used by Winston Churchill, they could motivate an army to defend the world against tyranny and declare to the world that their aim was victory at any cost. When used by President John F. Kennedy, words could inspire scientists to land the first man on the moon within the decade, not because it was easy but because it was hard. When used by Martin Luther King Jr., words could cast a vision of a land where little black boys and little black girls could play with little white boys and little white girls. Words can change the world. If words are so important to victory, to achievement, to unity, why are some people so careless with the words they use?

Words are our tool to describe the world around us. Words not only *represent* the way we see the world, but the right words can actually *change* the way we see the world, for better or for worse. What words do you use to describe your world? Ludwig Wittgenstein said, "The limits of my language mean the limits of my world."[90] If we are careless with our words, we might describe the weather as "crummy," our job as "dead-end," and our life as "fair to middling." If we are deliberate with our words, we will describe our spouse as "gorgeous," our career as "amazing," and our life as "an adventure." Our words define our experience of our world.

> *Words not only represent the way we see the world, but the right words can actually change the way we see the world, for better or for worse.*

What's interesting about this is that you might actually be *feeling* crummy, but when you choose to use a positive word rather than a negative word to describe how you view your world, it changes how you think and feel. In a recent article in *Psychology Today* entitled "Choosing Positive Words Improves Mindset and Performance," columnist Christopher Bergland related how researchers can actually see the spark of activity go off in our brain through a brain-imaging MRI when we use action verbs such as "Go. Jump. Attack." The same reaction cannot be seen when we make negative statements such as "Stop. Sit. Surrender."[91] Quite literally, our choice of positive or negative words can motivate us to take action or paralyze us to stay sitting on the bleachers.

So how are you communicating with yourself? Most of the time we have almost no idea which words we are using to describe the world around us. In fact, our subconscious mind describes the world so quickly that we can barely notice it. It's like background music in a movie: we don't notice the music, but we do notice how it makes us feel. The same is true of the words we say to ourselves. As I mentioned before, we don't notice them, but we notice if we feel discouraged, depressed, anxious, embarrassed, frustrated, or furious.

Notice how the following negative words make you feel:

- Grief
- Fear
- Loneliness
- Suicide
- Murder
- Poverty
- Sadness
- Disease
- Failure

Now notice how these positive words make you feel:

- Joy
- Inspiration
- Happiness
- Birth
- Creation
- Wealth
- Warmth
- Victory
- Love
- Success

Can you feel a difference? Words can actually change our mood. We must make a conscious choice to use positive, empowering words. Our words can act like fuel on a tense situation or like water to put out

> Our words can act like gasoline on a tense situation, or act like water to put out a proverbial fire.

a proverbial fire. If you are stuck in traffic, you might say, "These other drivers make me so *furious!*" But is the choice of the word "furious" really the wisest option? What if you were to say, "These other motorists are super goofy"? I dare you to stay angry when you use ridiculous word choices like "super goofy" to defuse your upset feelings.

Now that's just how you describe other drivers to yourself; how do you describe *you* to yourself? Do you get frustrated and say, "I'm such a *loser!*" or "I'm such a *failure*"? These word choices are probably not fair or accurate, and they are certainly demotivating. Do you always lose? Always? In every single interaction since birth? Is that really fair? Perhaps it's more accurate to say, "I'm a work in progress," or "I have so much still to learn, but I am willing to learn." (I know it's true you want to learn because you are halfway through this book!) Try shouting those statements with a rage-filled voice. It will be tough to stay angry.

Be aware of the words you use. As science fiction writer Philip K. Dick said, "There exists, for everyone, a sentence—a series of words—that has the power to destroy you. Another sentence exists, another series of words, that could heal you."[92] It is up to us to seek out and meditate on those healing and uplifting words.

Silencing the Inner Critic

Many people who lack confidence are unfairly harsh and critical of themselves. If we are against ourselves, how can we expect to attract people to our cause and lead people in business, at church, in our homes, or in our community? People are attracted to those who feel good about themselves. If you are constantly beating up on yourself, pointing out what you have done wrong and ignoring all that you've done right, you'll struggle with confidence.

In her article entitled "Silencing the Voice That Says You're a Fraud," *Wall Street Journal* columnist Melinda Beck stated: "Unrelenting self-criticism often goes hand in hand with depression and anxiety, and it may even predict depression."[93] So what's the answer? We need to catch the negative thoughts swirling in our head and put a stop to them. How? By noticing how we are being unfair or unreasonable in our estimation of ourselves. An entire field of study, called Cognitive Behavioral Therapy or CBT, is devoted to helping people rewrite the words they say to themselves and elevating their moods while reducing depression. In his bestselling book on CBT *Feeling Good*, David D. Burns, MD, shares a story of a counseling session with a depressed mother. She was beating herself up unfairly because she felt she was a bad mother. Here is an excerpt from the conversation. Notice how the patient, Nancy, defines her ability as a mother with standards that are impossible to meet.

Dr. Burns:	Okay. What's wrong with this statement, "I am a bad mother"?
Nancy:	Well…
Dr. Burns:	Is there any such thing as a "bad mother"?
Nancy:	Of course.
Dr. Burns:	What is your definition of a "bad mother"?
Nancy:	A bad mother is one who does a bad job of raising her kids. She isn't as effective as other mothers, so her kids turn out bad. It seems obvious.
Dr. Burns:	So you would say a "bad mother" is one who is low on mothering skills? That's your definition?
Nancy:	Some mothers lack mothering skills.
Dr. Burns:	But all mothers lack mothering skills to some extent.
Nancy:	They do?

Dr. Burns:	There's no mother in this world who is perfect in all mothering skills. So they all lack mothering skills in some part. According to your definition, it would seem that all mothers are bad mothers.
Nancy:	I feel that *I'm* a bad mother, but not everybody is.
Dr. Burns:	Well, define it again. What is a "bad mother"?
Nancy:	A bad mother is someone who does not understand her children or is constantly making damaging errors. Errors that are detrimental.
Dr. Burns:	According to your new definition, you're not a "bad mother," and there are no "bad mothers" because no one constantly makes damaging errors.
Nancy:	No one...?
Dr. Burns:	You said that a bad mother *constantly* makes damaging errors. There is no such person who constantly makes damaging errors twenty-four hours a day. Every mother is capable of doing *some* things right.
Nancy:	...If I paid more attention to him and gave him more help, he could do better at school and he could be a whole lot happier. I feel it's my fault when he doesn't do well.
Dr. Burns:	So you are willing to take the blame for his mistakes?
Nancy:	Yes, it's my fault. So I'm a bad mother.
Dr. Burns:	And you also take credit for his achievements? And his happiness?
Nancy:	No—*he* should get the credit for that, not me.
Dr. Burns:	Does that make sense? That you're responsible for his faults but not his strengths?
Nancy:	No.
Dr. Burns:	Do you understand the point I'm trying to make?
Nancy:	Yep.

Dr. Burns:	Yes, there are all degrees of effectiveness at parenting skills. And most everyone has plenty of room for improvement. The meaningful question is not, "Am I a good or bad mother?" but rather, "What are my relative skills and weaknesses, and what can I do to improve?"
Nancy:	I understand. That approach makes more sense and it feels much better. When I label myself "bad mother," I just feel inadequate and depressed, and I don't do anything productive. Now I see what you've been driving at. Once I give up criticizing myself, I'll feel better, and maybe I can be more helpful to Bobby. [94]

Notice: with each thought, Dr. Burns gently pointed out to Nancy how she was being unfair or unreasonable with herself. That's the greatest trick of self-criticism: we simply aren't being fair. We would not likely judge people with the same impossible standards by which we tend to judge ourselves. By stating them out loud or writing our thoughts in a journal, we can notice where we have been unreasonable and use the next technique, rewriting our thoughts, to overcome our negative feelings and create a more positive attitude.

Keep Asking "Why?" to Reveal Your Root-Cause Thinking

Many people just let fear and lack of confidence run their lives. If you are hesitating to take action on something you feel is worthwhile, do a "5 Why" analysis, which means ask "Why?" up to five times to dig down to discover your underlying thinking.[95] Each time you make a statement to yourself, ask, "Why?" Answer that. Then ask "Why?" of the answer. As you dig deeper, many times you may be shocked at your irrational thinking. Once you discover your underlying thinking, rewrite what you say to yourself. Describe the situation in fair and rational terms. But you first must do the digging to discover what you actually think.

Here are some simple examples of how this line of questioning may be approached:

- "I'm scared of calling someone to book a sales appointment."
- WHY?
- "Because the other person might say no."
- WHY does that matter?
- "If they say no, I'll feel really hurt and disappointed."
- WHY?
- "Because if one person says no, I think it will mean that everyone else will probably say no."

Now what follows is a positive and empowering way to speak to yourself instead.

Positive Reframe: "One person's bad reaction isn't the end of the world. There are plenty of other fish in the sea. And it's a really big exaggeration to think that *everyone* will respond the same way. It's likely that I may need to ask a few people, but I need to see that many times the person isn't saying no to what I'm saying, but rather *how confidently* I am saying it. Once I get my confidence *up*, more people will say *yes* to me."

- "I'm scared of starting my own business."
- WHY?
- "Because I might fail."
- WHY is that important?
- "Because if I fail, my family and friends and neighbors will laugh at me and think I'm a loser."
- WHY is that important?
- "Because it will mean I *am* a loser."

Positive Reframe: "I don't know for sure that my family will think I'm a loser; I am just guessing that. After all, I'm not a mind reader. I can't perfectly predict how they will react to something. Besides, my family's opinion of me doesn't make me a winner or a loser; it's just their opinion. I am choosing to give their opinion power over me, and I have the power to revoke that power any moment I choose. Other people shrug off criticism, and I can too. Finally, everyone fails. In fact, any millionaire will tell you failure is a necessary part of the success formula. The only people who don't fail are, as Roosevelt said, 'Those timid souls who know neither victory nor defeat.' I have the guts to try to go after my goals, and the snickering peanut gallery doesn't have the guts to go after theirs. Why would I value the opinion of a Monday-morning armchair quarterback when I have the courage to step onto the gridiron and take the hits? The glory goes to the man or woman who reaches for the brass ring."

Now you try it. Consider a situation that is causing you worry, fear, anxiety, guilt, embarrassment, frustration, etc. Name the situation and how it makes you feel. Then ask yourself "Why?" Answer that on the line below, and then ask "Why?" again. Continue asking "Why?" until you find the root cause of the thinking.

UPSETTING SITUATION:

Why is that?

_____

Why is that?

_____

Why is that?

_____

Why is that?

_____

Why is that?

_____

Now, rewrite a positive statement to rebut the negative thought.

Positive Reframe:

_____

_____

_____

Stop Replaying Memories of Failure

Our memories are a powerful tool. They allow us to shift the car into first gear while planning our route to the grocery store. They remind our fingers where the buttons on the keyboard are while we're thinking of the next word to type. And they store every good deed and every dumb mistake we've ever made.

When you replay a memory of an event in your head, if it was a particularly *emotional* event, the emotions become attached to the memory. That's why we can recall exactly where we were the morning of September 11, 2001, but not the morning before. Recalling the event means you also relive some of the emotions. If you pull up a memory of a joyous time, you will bask in a moment of happiness. If you pull of a memory of a terrible failure, you will probably dredge up some of those old yucky feelings that went along with that memory. The problem for some people is they replay movies in their head of all of their defeats, over and over, and when they do, they relive the bad feelings, too.

Let me ask you: when you are feeling down, are you a more loving spouse, caring parent, effective businessperson, diligent worker, and proactive leader than when you feel empowered and confident? Of course not. So if you want to be more confident, replay movies in your head of great moments rather than movies of defeats. Replay memories that make you feel great, moments when you were proud of yourself, moments that make you smile when you think about them. If you catch yourself starting to replay old movies of bad memories, press "pause" on your mental Blu-ray player. Say, "I'm not thinking about that stuff right now." Change the channel on your mental TV set and immediately play a video of one of your victories.

Choose to remind yourself every day of what you did right, rather than beating yourself up for what you did wrong. If you had a critical friend who only pointed out what you did wrong and rarely pointed out what you did right and was unwilling to change this habit, you would (or at the least, you should) drop that friend. Be a good friend to yourself, and replay movies of victories.

DEVELOP MENTAL TOUGHNESS

"Mental toughness is to [the] physical as four is to one."
– Bobby Knight

Whether you are an athlete on the gridiron or in the board-room, a certain quality is always found in the guys who remain standing when the storm winds blow. When rejection hits these guys, its bounces off them like spitballs off a battleship. They chuckle at groundless criticism. They bounce back quickly from setbacks. They feel energized to try even harder after a defeat. The special quality these warriors are showing is something called "mental toughness." Wikipedia defines this as "a term commonly used by coaches, sport psychologists, sport commentators, and business leaders - generally describes a collection of attributes that allow a person to **persevere through difficult circumstances** (such as difficult training or difficult competitive situations in games) and **emerge without losing confidence**"[96] (*emphasis added*).

At some point in our lives, each of us will receive a gut shot that knocks the wind right out of us. It's not a matter of *whether* you will be struck by disaster, but *when*. In my book, *Voyage of a Viking*,[97] I describe in detail many of the challenges I faced through my life. I've faced my storms,

> *It's not a matter of whether you will be struck by disaster, but when.*

and I know that I have more storms awaiting me. I also know that you do as well. Rather than sitting around moaning and complaining when we are being pelted by chunks of hail the size of golf balls, we can put on a suit of armor to deflect whatever life throws at us. That suit of armor is your mental toughness.

You can't measure mental toughness; you measure its *effect*. You can't measure what's going on inside a leader's head, but you sure can measure his behavior. You see it when he loses his biggest customer one month, and it ticks him off just enough to make him go smash a sales record

> *You can't measure mental toughness; you measure its effect.*

the next month. You see it when someone is totally exhausted, yet she keeps throwing hundreds of shots into the basketball hoop to perfect her free throw (like my awesome daughter, Mya). You can see mental toughness when someone is running a marathon and he is gasping for breath, and the only thing keeping him putting one painful foot in front of the last is strength of will. Mental toughness is courage in action. When you've got it, you cope better than your opponents with the demands you face.

How do we develop mental toughness? Here are a few principles to get you started:

136

Principle #1: Realize Mental Toughness *Can* Be Developed.

Some people might be born with a certain personality, like a "Choleric" or "D" personality type, and maybe this personality type handles adversity a little more effectively than others. But that's not always the case, and either way, anyone can develop this side of their personality. Don't cop out on yourself by selling yourself any victim thinking, like "That's just the way I am." Brothers and sisters, you can *change*. How do you build mental toughness? The same way you build muscles in the gym: by pushing yourself to new limits and increasing the pressure or resistance you are pushing against.

Principle #2: Mental Toughness in the Gym Correlates to Mental Toughness in *Life*.

The gym is the ultimate proving ground for "tough guys" and "tough gals." You really find out what you're made of when you're doing hack squats or leg extensions. Many people get into the gym, start doing bicep curls, and as soon as it starts to get uncomfortable, they say, "Okay, I've done enough for now," and they stop exercising. This is actually the exact *wrong* thing to do, *if* your goal is to develop your muscles. You see, when it starts to hurt, that's the lactic acid burn in your muscles saying, "Great job. Keep going. You're making progress." But when many people start to feel discomfort, they choose to ease off.

You don't become successful at *anything* by letting your foot off the gas pedal when the going gets tough. This includes the gym, it includes your marriage, and it includes your business. When it hurts to do even one more rep of an exercise, that's when the real muscle development starts. (By the way, I'm not talking about pushing through pain when you are actually injured; I'm referring to the normal discomfort we feel when we are tearing down our muscles during a workout.)

If you throw in the towel on the bench press, you train your brain to quit when things get tough. When you force yourself to keep pushing the weight even when you want to give up, you are training your brain to keep pushing. Some people on my business team "run for the tape," as my good friend Chris Brady says. That means that when there is a fast-approaching deadline to hit a business target, and things look grim, they keep pushing and fighting right up to the last minute. They don't give in just because it looks unlikely or difficult to accomplish; instead they pull a rabbit out of the hat by persevering despite all odds against them.

Principle #3: Champions Fall in Love with Discomfort.

Winners know that the path to success is steep and rocky, and the path to defeat is like a sign pointing at a waterslide that says, "Slippery, Fun and Easy to Reach the Bottom in a Jiffy!" Bad habits are easy to slip into, like a warm bed when you're exhausted. Good habits are pretty much guaranteed to feel tough because they may force you to deny

> *Bad habits are easy to slip into, like a warm bed when you're exhausted.*

yourself luxuries and pleasures. You must learn to do what is uncomfortable. To develop the psychological edge, you must have extreme discipline to give up the comfort zone in which you train and live. Delaying immediate satisfaction is the ultimate sacrifice that all warriors must choose.

Orrin Woodward recounted a story of arriving home one day in the wee hours of the morning. He had been driving for hours from a business meeting, and had to get home to get to work the next day. It was so early in the morning that he knew he would only get a few hours of sleep. But Orrin's viewpoint of this was a feeling of pride. He actually said to himself, "I'm losing sleep. I'm fighting harder to help my family than my neighbors, who are all getting a nice sleep right now." His brain naturally connected feeling tired with unhappiness, but now his brain connected fatigue with a feeling of honor. That's what winners do.

Principle #4: Our Mental Weakness Is Our Greatest Enemy.

We tend to think that our biggest "Goliath" is a big hairy obstacle that is outside us. It's true that sometimes we face external challenges that can be overwhelming. The challenges can be financial, relational, from business competition, or that amazing boss at work with whom you get to deal. Whenever we are running a race, our competitors serve an important purpose: they raise our standards of excellence. They force us to perform, even pushing ourselves past where we thought we could go. We should thank our competitors whenever they throw down a challenge. I know I really get into gear when someone suggests he might whup me, my family, or my business team. Whenever someone proclaims, "I'm going to kick your butt," he had better pack a lunch, because it's going to be a long day for him!

But my competitors aren't the real problem. The biggest Goliath that threatens us is not our competition; it is a pipsqueak little voice in our own head that chips away at our confidence. This voice is whispering and teasing, "Take a break. You don't have the energy today. You don't really think you have what it takes, do you? You're not a leader. Who would want to follow you? Come on, the other guy is so much sharper than you. Give up; it's too hard. No one really expected you to succeed, anyway."

That negative self-talk is crippling, and there really is only one response to that garbage: knock it off! Your biggest competition is the erosion of confidence through self-sabotage. Your naysaying voice is like water seeping into the cracks on a bridge and then freezing in the winter: it weakens the structure by fracturing it from within.

> *Your biggest competition is the erosion of confidence through self-sabotage.*

As you embark on a conscious battle of the mind, you will be tested every time you put up a fight. Your mind will look for an escape route every time it perceives unnecessary pain. Hours before I work out, I'm already fighting a mental battle. Just the thought of the grueling exercise regime ahead has me mentally drained. But I recognize that. I know it's all in my head. And so I force myself to perform and push past those limiting voices.

Principle #5: Mentally Tough People Are Motivated Intrinsically.

If you were to ask anyone on the street, you'd find that most of the masses are motivated by extrinsic factors. When outside forces push them, they respond. They jump out of bed in the morning because the *boss* will be angry if they're late. They remember to take out the garbage so their *spouse* won't nag them. They rush to file their taxes so that the *government* won't be after them.

World-class performers are very different. They jump out of bed in the morning because *they* are excited to work on a project. They clean their house because *they* love serving their spouse. They keep their paperwork organized because *they* feel compelled to exhibit excellence in their business. World-class performers are driven by intrinsic motivators; they drive themselves.

> *World-class performers are driven by intrinsic motivators; they drive themselves.*

Extrinsic positive motivation is short-lived. It's like the sugar rush from a candy bar that causes your energy to spike and just as quickly crash down. It's like motivating yourself to hit a goal by getting a new toy. Is that completely wrong? Nope; earning my Donzi fishing boat was highly motivating, and I used it to push myself to accomplish a major business goal. But most adults have the same psychological reaction to "toy" motivation as kids do: after you play with the toy for a while, the excitement wears off. Just watch any kid at Christmas when he gets a new toy. For the first few weeks, he carries the toy everywhere. Then by February, it's forgotten and left under the dirty clothes in his closet.

World-class performers are primarily motivated intrinsically, by their dreams, desires, and passions. Although *extrinsic* motivation is short-lived, *intrinsic* motivation is nearly impossible to exhaust until the goal is achieved. If you doubt this, just picture two scenarios. In the first situation, you are hanging by one hand off a cliff, and in the other hand you are holding a heavy briefcase filled with one million dollars. In the second scenario, you are also hanging off a cliff, but your other hand is holding your child. Here's the question: Would your arm get tired faster holding the briefcase filled with money or when your child's life is on the line?

Exactly.

In terms of motivation, your purpose and passion will always trump a payout, every day of the week. World-class performers and leaders know that the secret to motivating themselves and others is discovering what they will fight for when the going gets tough. In fact, the truly great performers move away from logic-based motivators ("This makes sense; I *should* do this") and toward emotion-based motivators ("Thinking about this accomplishment brings tears of joy to my eyes"). Mentally tough performers know the key to finding the true power of the individual lies in the deep recesses of the psyche.

> *In terms of motivation, your purpose and passion will always trump a payout.*

If we don't refresh ourselves mentally by refocusing on our passion and purpose, we can expect to lose our edge. In their book *Mentally Tough: The Principles of Winning at Sports Applied to Winning in Business*, authors Loehr and McLaughlin describe this decline:

> This "de-motivation" happens to athletes who lose their spark—they've accomplished whatever they have set out to do in their sport, and they can't get fired up about it anymore. If they play, they just go through the motions. They aren't hungry anymore. It happens to entrepreneurs when they succeed—they're motivated by the challenges of starting an enterprise; the day to day necessities of keeping a business

going depress them. It's often called "burnout" and it happens to everyone from time to time.[98]

When you need to give a proverbial booster jump to your motivational engine, there are a few tried and true techniques you can use. One merely *okay* way to recharge yourself is to depend on motivational pep talks such as those from seminars or audio recordings. These can be fun and exciting and are definitely a massive improvement over listening to the radio. In fact, I recommend you listen to four or five positive CDs/audios a day. But remember that the rah-rah, jump-up-and-down pep talks are like the electric paddles on a defibrillator during cardiac arrest: You only receive a momentary blast of electricity to simply jolt you back to life. That one jolt doesn't keep your heart beating; the electrical impulses to do that come from within *you*. You need the lasting fire that emotional motivators generate.

To discover your emotional motivators, the best coaches and leaders use a process that involves very little jumping up and down or fist-pumping rah-rah speeches. Rather, their elite and transformational process is actually a little boring; it's tedious, time-consuming, and deceptively simple: They ask questions. They do an investigative search just like Detective Columbo, and they don't stop asking questions until they have discovered your emotional hot buttons.

If you don't have a world-class mentor or coach to work with directly, you can do a lot of the heavy lifting yourself by asking the following five critical thinking questions. I've left space for you to jot down your own responses to each. Knowing your answers to the following questions can literally kick-start your momentum toward massive results in business and in life:

1) What am I willing to fight for?

2) What values do I hold dearest to my heart?

3) What values would I be willing to die for?

4) If I could achieve a single thing, what would make all my hard work worth the struggle?

5) If I had thirty minutes left to live, what would I tell my children are the three most important things I learned about how to live a happy and worthwhile life?

Your answers to these questions reveal a lot about what drives you emotionally. Your answers are your suit of armor for when the going gets tough. Business and life always bring setbacks, disappointments, heartache, and discouragement. If you are really going to win, it's inevitable that you're going to get your rear end kicked—by your enemies, your customers, your boss, the economy, and even sometimes your family. But when you know what drives you, what you will fight to the end to defend and uphold, you are wearing emotional Kevlar. Now you will fight even when it's hard and the odds are against you. Now you possess Olympic endurance and stamina. Now you have graduated from merely "fired up" into true mental toughness.

SUMMARY

"When you are joyful, when you say yes to life and have fun and project positivity all around you, you become a sun in the center of every constellation, and people want to be near you."

– Shannon L. Alder

A confident person radiates a positive attitude. He believes that things will work out. He sees possibilities coming together. He has a warm energy that is attractive to others. But without a positive attitude, we lose all of that. Honoré de Balzac said, "When you doubt your power, you give power to your doubt."[99] Believe in your power. Once you know you are worthwhile and you've stopped comparing yourself to other people, your positive attitude will be a beacon attracting other people to you.

Key Points:

1. Have an invincible attitude. We don't always choose our circumstances, but we always choose our response. Your positive response can open the door to more opportunity.

2. Manage your ANTs. Automatic Negative Thoughts sneak in without warning. Now that you know about them, you can catch them and stomp them out.

3. People notice what they look for. Your brain's "noticer" will find whatever you ask it to. Ask it to find the good in each situation.

4. Ask yourself positive questions. The questions you ask are the fastest way to direct your brain to find a powerful answer.

5. Go on a mental diet. Olympians fuel their body with the proper nutrients. Your mind needs positive brain food. Remember ABC: Association, Books, and CDs/Audios.

6. Become aware of your self-talk. Words have power. The words you choose can empower you or drain you of energy. Choose words that uplift your spirit.

7. Silence the inner critic. People who lack confidence are unfairly harsh with themselves. Cut yourself some slack. Be realistic and fair about what you can do. If you catch your mind beating yourself up, reconsider.

8. Keep asking "Why?" By digging down to the root cause of your concerns, you will unearth your real fears. Once you know them, you can rewrite what you say to yourself.

9. Stop replaying memories of failure. Bad memories can dig up disempowering emotions. If you want to walk into a room feeling confident, replay videos of past victories.

10. Develop mental toughness. Most people give up on their dreams too easily. The Goliath you face isn't usually some big giant; rather, it's a tiny little pipsqueak voice nagging you inside. By developing mental toughness, you'll have the tenacity to push through challenging situations.

4

TAKE ACTION!

"The way to develop self-confidence is to do the thing you fear."

– William Jennings Bryan

When we see someone who carries himself with confidence, we're looking at outward behavior. Confident people don't seem afraid to do what scares other people. But the truth is sometimes different: sometimes, people who seem quite confident are actually feeling a little nervous. The people you think have it all together might be sweating bullets inside, but they choose to take action despite their fear. They know if they give in to fear, it only grows in strength and makes it harder to take action next time.

The first three chapters of this book, "Know Your Worth," "Stop Comparing," and "Manage Your Self-Talk," have all been about managing the internal experience of confidence. This chapter deals with how we will carry ourselves so the world around us can sense the confidence we now carry within ourselves. We're now going to discuss how to act and look confident.

ACT YOUR WAY INTO A FEELING

"Anyone can do something when they WANT to do it. Really successful people do things when they don't want to do it."

– Dr. Phil McGraw

When we lack self-confidence, we might hesitate to take action. We might still be learning how to manage our self-talk, as we discussed in the last chapter. We might imagine everything that could go wrong and talk ourselves out of even trying. But confident people take action even knowing they will probably stumble along the way. As Henry C. Link says, "While one person hesitates because he feels inferior, the other is busy making mistakes and becoming superior."[100]

Confident people are the doers in life, not the Monday-morning quarterbacks who nitpick how the doer slipped up while they were nestled safely on their sofas. Basketball superstar Michael Jordan explained, "I've missed more than 9000 shots in my career. I've lost almost 300 games. 26 times, I've been trusted to take the game winning shot and missed. I've failed over and over and over again in my life. And that is why I succeed."[101]

> *The opposite of success isn't failure; failure is part of the success journey. The opposite of success is quitting.*

Don't worry about failing in life; every successful person does. The opposite of success isn't failure; failure is part of the success journey. The opposite of success is quitting. Whether you quit at the starting blocks or along the road, whenever your feet stop moving toward the goal, you're done.

> *While confident people may experience negative emotions, they certainly don't take advice from them.*

The reality is that almost everyone from Donald Trump to a paperboy has lacked confidence in some area,

148

even if it's been so long they can't remember it. Successful people will tell you that they didn't wait to feel confident; they took action, and then the confidence grew. People who lack confidence tend to be held hostage by their emotions. They ask themselves, "Do I feel like taking action? Do I feel like saying hi to that stranger, making that important business call, or speaking up in the sales meeting?" And the answer that comes back is a resounding *no*. However, while confident people may experience negative emotions, they certainly don't take advice from them. Pearl S. Buck said, "I don't wait for moods. You accomplish nothing if you do that. Your mind must know it has got to get down to work."[102]

When I built my business, I was in the midst of a massive financial crisis. I described this story in detail in my first book, *Voyage of a Viking*, but I'll share a brief recap: I had purchased more than thirty-three rental properties, my property manager had cooked the books, and overnight I found myself nearly $1.4 million in debt. We didn't have money to pay our bills. It got so bad that some days, Amy didn't have money in the checking account to buy groceries. I was in the fight of my life and felt as if I was drowning. As the provider, I felt I had failed my family. I was so overcome with emotion that there were moments I would sit at my desk in the basement of our home weeping.

With all this pressure, most other people would feel overwhelmed. They would wallow in self-pity, get depressed, and say, "How can I possibly go build another business when so much negativity is surrounding me?" Frankly, I didn't have an option. I couldn't allow those feelings to take root in me. I had to get up, put on my suit, pick up the phone, and set up business meetings. I had no choice. I was running from a nightmare. I had to act.

You will face desperate times in your life. You can allow fear to win, or you can take action and claim your victory. Aristotle wrote, "Men acquire a certain quality by constantly acting a certain way. You become just by performing just actions. You become temperate by performing temperate actions, brave by performing brave actions." If you don't feel confident, take action. Your action will create a feeling of confidence in you.

Say Yes to Life More Often!

Opportunities for a rewarding life are always being presented to us. Your friends may call and invite you to dinner. Your family may arrange a camping trip. Your boss may tell you at the meeting that he is setting up a new project team and is looking for someone to lead it. Your pastor may praise how much you have grown in your faith and leadership ability and suggest you become a deacon. Your child's school may be looking for parents to volunteer to be chaperones for a field trip. There are always opportunities to say yes to life.

What you will find is that generally, confident people say yes to opportunities far more often than others do. They grab life by the horns and jump on for the ride. When someone is offering a plate of hors d'oeuvres at a party, they say, "Sure, I'd love to try one." When a friend invites them on a social outing, they say, "I'd love to join you." When a presenter asks for a volunteer from the audience, they say, "I'll be happy to help." When their boss asks the boardroom if anyone has any questions about the presentation, they do not hesitate to speak up.

Confident people are go-getters. They are bold. They are movers and shakers. They have a zest for life and want to experience everything. They are not timid. They are not afraid of embarrassing themselves trying something new in front of a crowd. They volunteer, jump in, climb aboard, ride along, and leap into action. And remember, they likely were not born that way.

A study in the UK by a palliative care nurse came out in February 2012 sharing the top five regrets of her dying patients:

1. I wish I'd had the courage to live a life true to myself, not the life others expected of me.
2. I wish I hadn't worked so hard.
3. I wish I'd had the courage to express my feelings.
4. I wish I had stayed in touch with my friends.
5. I wish that I had let myself be happier. [13]

You see, in the final days of life, most people regret what they *didn't* do more often than what they tried. The word *no* carries an awful burden. It shuts the door to opportunity. It tramples on potential happiness. It erodes friendships. It can close our hearts to love and fulfillment.

> *The word* no *carries an awful burden. It shuts the door to opportunity.*

Bear in mind that you must discern when it is appropriate to say no, for there will be times when you should. I would recommend you say no to anything destructive, illegal, or immoral. There are times when *no* is the only responsible choice. (For example, don't go parachuting at a less-than-reputable place!) But these aren't the examples I'm talking about

> *I'm not concerned you won't say no to life when you* should; *I'm concerned you won't say yes to life when you* could!

here. I'm not concerned you won't say no to life when you *should*; I'm concerned you won't say yes to life when you *could*.

So when a long-lost friend wants to reconnect, say yes. When your spouse risks sharing her feelings, be open to it. When you see a path toward the career you've always wanted, have the guts to pursue your dreams. Say yes to life.

Use the Magic of Momentum

You've had days in your life when everything seemed to be going your way. All the traffic lights turned green. You closed every sales call you made. Every crucial confrontation was resolved in a way that strengthened the relationship. Every step had a bounce in it. Your spirit felt lighter, food tasted better, the sun was shining, and you were on fire for life.

When we are feeling good, we become people magnets. Opportunity comes out of the woodwork. People want to work with us. If we are coaches or leaders, our team responds to our guidance.

151

Things just click. We feel like we are on a roll. It's such a simple concept, but so often ignored: When you've had a victory, use that positive feeling to your advantage. Take action right away, push the gas pedal down even further, and create even greater results.

One teacher used the power of momentum to transform his students' belief in themselves and ultimately their results. In 1974, a Bolivian-born mathematics teacher named Jaime Escalante took a job at Garfield High School in East Los Angeles, an area more commonly known for producing gang members than math whizzes. However, Escalante was not your average math teacher. He had a ferocious love of teaching the subject and inspiring young minds. He also had a rock-solid belief that these kids were smarter than they, their parents, or even the school administration thought they were. Most people had written them off simply because they lived on the wrong side of the tracks. Escalante knew better.[104]

One of the first things Escalante did was raise the bar of excellence for his students. He would demand they answer a math question just to be allowed into the classroom. He made them do a test at the beginning of each day. And he didn't just offer basic math; he offered advanced placement calculus. You can only imagine the reaction these C, D, and F students had toward this, let alone the status-quo principal of the school. But Escalante started talking to the students about getting jobs in engineering and science. He began to cast a vision that they would make it into university, that they could be at the top of their class, and they could change the entire direction of their lives. He started to breathe belief into them that they could do something extraordinary.[105]

After a few years of teaching, he laid down a challenge: The school would have students take the difficult Advance Placement calculus exam. This was a very demanding exam, and no one wanted any part of it. But this man was on a mission to change the culture of his school and to make a breakthrough for his students; he knew that he just needed a small victory to get the ball rolling. He knew that if he could show the students that some of their peers were capable to taking the AP calculus test and passing, the other students would begin to believe in themselves a little more.[106]

And so Escalante rigorously pursued that first victory. In 1978, he convinced five students out of three thousand to take the test. Two of them passed. This was the first small victory that Escalante could leverage. Building on that victory, he won over the minds of a few more students the next year. In 1979, he convinced nine students to work with him and take the test; seven of them passed. Word of his students' growing success began to spread through the school. Kids who thought they never stood a chance started to believe that if their friends could do it, maybe they could as well. The ember of belief had been nurtured into a small flame under Escalante's guiding care.[107]

In 1981, Escalante attracted fifteen students, and fourteen passed the AP calculus test. In 1982, eighteen students passed the test. In 1983, his class size doubled overnight, as did student success: thirty-three students took the AP calculus test, and thirty of them passed. And in 1987, seventy-three students passed the test. Escalante wasn't just inspiring the students at Garfield; he was inspiring the entire country. Everyone wanted to know what this guy was doing.[108]

A book about his remarkable achievement entitled *Escalante: The Best Teacher in America* was released. This inspired the 1988 movie *Stand and Deliver*, starring Edward James Olmos as Escalante. Not surprisingly, having a Hollywood movie made about your high school math teacher is unusual for most students; it only added further fuel to the fire. By 1991, the momentum Escalante had created attracted 570 students to take the AP math exams.[109]

Never squander a victory; use the confidence it produces to take further action and build momentum.

What was Escalante's secret? Momentum! Lowell Thomas said, "Do a little more each day than you think you possibly can."[110] By pushing yourself a little farther, by stretching for that 'impossible' goal and attaining it, you can create a tiny victory. Each victory builds your belief and confidence that you can reach greater heights. Never squander a victory; use the confidence it produces to take further action and build momentum, just as Escalante did with his remarkable students.[111]

HAVE CONFIDENCE WITH PEOPLE

"You wouldn't care so much about what people think about you if you knew how [seldom] they did."

– Dr. Phil McGraw

Learn to Say "Hi" to a Stranger

The old saying is true, both in business and in life: it matters who you know. I heard a leader say that in order for someone to become successful, he needs an army of people behind him who want to see him succeed. Whether it is an Olympic athlete, a pastor who is planting churches and spreading the gospel, a manager getting buy-in for a new idea, an innovative entrepreneur raising venture capital, an aspiring musician looking to build a following, or a family struck by cancer on a crusade to raise funds for research, success at anything requires the support of other people, often *many* other people. The more people who want to see you win, the faster your ascent toward your goal. You must build a team of encouragers, supporters, coaches, lieutenants, collaborators, teammates, suppliers, and ultimately *customers* of your message to the world. And in every instance, without exception, having other people on your side begins with first *meeting* them.

"A stranger is just a friend you haven't met yet" is the best philosophy to live by as you begin to assemble your "army for success." And if you can think about people this way, as friends you haven't met yet, your entire spirit toward them will change. Winners don't look at people as objects to manipulate or obstacles to overcome; they look at people and see an opportunity for friendship. Your spirit toward people will come through loud and clear in your tone of voice, body language, and choice of words. People can spot a con man or a charlatan a mile away, just as they can spot sincerity and warmth and are drawn toward it like a magnet. So what is your spirit toward people?

> *Winners don't look at people as an objects to manipulate or obstacles to overcome; they look at people and see an opportunity for friendship.*

In my line of work, my business associates and I are always meeting new people. In fact, we have a *stated goal* of meeting people and making new friends.

Let's consider a familiar situation: You are standing in line at the grocery store, a coffee shop, or the bank. People are shuffling slowly forward on their feet, looking and feeling a little bored. Many people are playing with their smart phones, texting or playing video games. And they are most certainly ignoring everyone standing next to them.

And then there is you.

You have an altogether different frame of mind, knowing that *you* are going to turn this normally boring experience into a lot of fun.

One of the guys on my business team loves to walk into a crowded elevator and, once inside, keep his back to the door! The elevator doors close behind him, and he stands there smiling right at the ten other people and says in a big, friendly voice, "Good morning, everyone!" Now this usually produces a few different reactions from the crowd. People tend to:

a. Stare in stunned horror that anyone would break the accepted code of silence on an elevator;

b. Quickly look away, sheepishly avoiding eye contact and think, "Wow. That guy is so weird"; or

c. Smile with amusement that someone actually spoke and say, "Hi," back to him.

You see, connecting with other people involves taking a *risk*. Leo Buscaglia says, "Risks must be taken, because the greatest hazard in life is to risk nothing."[112] When meeting new people, you risk other people thinking you are strange. You risk other people not responding well, and perhaps, you might feel a little silly. You risk feeling rejected. However, you do not risk any physical harm. It's highly unlikely you face any imminent physical danger from saying, "Hi," to people. (Unless, guys, you unwisely try to strike up a conversation at the urinal in the men's room while standing next to a big guy dressed in leather from a biker gang; he may not respond favorably! I would suggest some discretion when applying this strategy.

So, aside from rare (and hopefully obvious) situations that may not be appropriate, saying "Hi" to other people really risks nothing of consequence. In fact, I would suggest that if you don't say "Hi" to people, you are taking a bigger risk because you are closing the door on new relationships. The rewards for saying "Hi" to people, and doing it consistently, could literally change your life. You could meet, and I believe you will, some of the most amazing people in the world. You will meet people who could become business partners or friends for life.

> *The rewards for saying "Hi" to people, and doing it consistently, could literally change your life.*

Eight Rapid-Fire Tips to Start a Conversation

So, with the goal of helping you kick-start your progress toward meeting new people and creating new and amazing relationships, here are some tactics you can apply today to take action and get the ball rolling:

1. **Think *I Like You* in Your Head *First*.** People can tell if you have warmed up to them and if you are feeling friendly toward them. If you are arrogant or stuck up, good luck on making new friends. Who would want to be around you? And who would want to stare up your nose at you while you are

staring down your nose at them? (Especially if you haven't trimmed the old nose hairs lately and need a hedge trimmer to clear out the forest growing in there.) So when you look at people, literally think to yourself, *I like you*. Your whole spirit toward them will change, particularly if you are a Christian, see the other people as God's creation, and want to bring a little joy into their day. (If the other person is grumpy, all the more reason. Remember, hurting people hurt people.)

2. **Believe that Other People Will Like *You*.** Les Giblin talks about this in his great book *How to Have Power and Confidence in Dealing with People*.[113] Assume they are warm and friendly and will respond in a positive way. So much of success is expectation. If you expect the conversation will go well, you're halfway there. Will people always respond positively? Nope. But you sure can tip the scales in your favor by having an expectant mindset. If you've faced a cold shoulder before, don't let a couple of bad experiences shape your whole view of meeting new friends.

3. **Be Cool**. Don't come across as too anxious, overeager, or desperate, or you will make them feel uncomfortable. (It helps if you aren't actually *feeling* anxious or desperate to begin with.) If you're eyeing someone like a piece of meat or a meal ticket, they'll quickly sense that you have an ulterior motive, and things will soon become weird. Don't come on strong or push hard. Take it slow and easy. If you're overeager, you'll scare them away.

    A good way to visualize this is to imagine feeding pigeons in the park. Pigeons want bread crumbs. However, if you run into the park waving your arms and screaming, those pigeons will fly away in fear, even if they are starving. If you play it cool and take a sincere interest in others, you'll have greater success in attracting them.

157

4. **Take a Chance!** A great leader in our business community really pioneered this phrase a while ago. Take a chance. All of life involves a little risk, and that includes making new friends. The great thing about chances is that they can pay off with huge rewards. Take a chance on the stranger next to you. Make the first move. Be bold. Have a backbone. Stand tall. Pursue victory. Refuse to give in to fear. Resolve to be a person of courage and character. Take control of the fearful little voice that is whimpering inside you making excuses as to why you shouldn't try to say "Hi." Squish that voice like a bug under your heel, and take a chance.

5. **Play "Smiling Chicken."** It takes some effort just to make eye contact, smile, and say "Hi." When I first started doing this, I thought my face would crack. It's not normal for a choleric (a personality type which is hard-driving and dominant) or for an engineer to smile and "be nice," and I still need to work at it today. In fact, to practice this, I used to literally drive down the road and "smile talk" to myself in my rearview mirror before speaking engagements. (It sounds crazy, but it looks even worse, particularly to people passing by.)

   Although these are pretty simple steps, they can feel overwhelming. Just look right at other people and let your face break into a big friendly smile. Smiling breaks the ice and opens the door to getting them to say "Hi" back to you. Smiling tells people you are friendly, positive, and approachable, and these are all attractive qualities.

   If you are not used to doing this, you might want to try a fun game called "Smiling Chicken." You've all heard of the game "Chicken." With that game, you drive your car toward your competitor at full speed, and whoever flinches first and turns the car off the road is declared the "loser." (This is obviously a terribly dangerous game that I absolutely do not condone; I'm simply offering an illustration.)

Now here is the "Smiling Chicken" game: As you approach a stranger, your goal is to catch the other person's eye, break out in a smile, and provoke a smile in return. Try doing this with ten strangers and see how many people you can get to smile; it can become a lot of fun. (Don't, however, try this with members of the opposite sex, or you might end up with a restraining order!)

Now, offer a **Comment, Compliment**, or **Question**.

6. **Make a *Comment* about Your Shared Situation**. When in line at the bank, you can simply look for an opportunity to break the ice by stating out loud how you think or feel. You might say, "Wow, it's a good thing I'm not in a rush right now," or whatever you feel is appropriate for the situation you're in. In fact, you might even crack a joke about where you are. This is especially appropriate if you are standing in line for a sandwich; perhaps you could comment, "This line is so slow, I think I might have had a birthday while I've been waiting." Or maybe you could say, "Well, at least we have a sandwich line to wait in. In Haiti, they would be willing to wait for three days just to have this food." If you do crack a joke, be sure not to make racist, sexist, vulgar, or hurtful statements. I recommend you use clean and positive humor rather than anything negative. (My good friend and business partner Chris Brady is a terrific speaker and master of clean humor.)

   Another way of making a comment is to point out your similarities. For example, if they have a young child with them, you might ask, "How old is your little boy?" and follow up by sharing, "Oh, that's such a great age. My little guy is seven now." By showing you are similar, you quickly build rapport.

7. **Pay the Other Person a Sincere *Compliment***. When you meet people, look for something about them that you can speak

159

kindly about. If they have a child with them, you might comment, "What a cute little guy you've got with you." If they pull up in a Mercedes-Benz, you might say, "That's a great car you've got there." It's pretty easy to pick out things to compliment, like their clothes, etc.

Even more impressive is to pay a compliment to their character. If you see someone do something kind or generous, stop them and point out, "I just wanted to say I saw what you did, and I feel it was very thoughtful of you." If someone provides great service at a restaurant, a compliment is clearly called for. Compliments are a powerful way to connect with people.

Use caution: Be very careful when complimenting someone of the opposite sex, particularly if *you* are married or if you notice the other person is. I would err on the side of caution and avoid any compliment that could be misinterpreted as a come-on, like "You've got beautiful eyes and a gorgeous smile." Rather, focus on very safe things to compliment, such as "You handled yourself very well in that situation."

8. **Ask the Other Person a *Question*.** This is a really powerful strategy for striking up a conversation. In fact, one of the most natural conversation starters is to simply ask strangers, "Excuse me; can you help me?" Then fill in the blanks with something relevant about where you are or what you need. For example, if you are in a store, say to someone, "Can you help me? Do you know where the such-and-such is?" or "Can you help me with directions?" Please understand that in Western civilization, it is socially acceptable for an absolute stranger to strike up a conversation asking for directions.

If you are standing in line at the grocery store, you might point out something others have in their grocery cart and say, "You know, I've never had any of those; are they any good?" If you are back in line at the sandwich shop, you might say, "You know why it's going so slowly, don't you? These are 'sandwich artists.' Remember that old commercial?" By asking a few questions, you are more likely to get a conversation started. The point of all this is to break the ice in getting other people to talk to you but also to break the ice for *you* in learning to get really comfortable striking up a conversation. Even if the conversation is over in a moment, you've chatted with one more person and lived to tell about it. You now have a little more experience and a little more confidence.

Building on that, once you develop rapport, you can shift to asking questions about the other person. Dale Carnegie talks about this in detail in his landmark book *How to Win Friends and Influence People*.[114] It's simple to keep a conversation going. Just get other people talking about themselves. After all, they are usually their favorite subject.

How to Develop Courage in Making Phone Calls

Part of success in business and life is that you must learn to pick up the phone and connect with confidence. It doesn't matter if you are phoning for a job interview or to ask someone out to the prom or on a first date, the day will come when you have to make an important call. And boy oh boy, does this scare a bunch of people.

When you need to call someone for something like a job interview or to set up a business meeting, that phone can look pretty scary. Sometimes it all but grows fangs and becomes a hairy little monster sitting on your desk, ready to bite your hand if you come near it. The phone can be pretty intimidating if you don't have your confidence in check. So let me give you some tips on making those tough-but-important calls when the need arises:

1. **Determine the *Exact* Time and Place You Will Make the Phone Call**. What happens for many people is that they think they will make a phone call, but they don't develop a plan of action to execute this goal. So they go through the following

mental gymnastics. They say, "I'll make that important phone call at lunch." Lunchtime comes, and they're hungry. So they say, "I'll just run out and grab a bite to eat." Next thing they know, they've run out of time at lunch. So they shift the goal again and say, "I'll make that important call when I get home." So they slog their way through rush-hour traffic and arrive at home exhausted. Then they say, "I just need to recharge my batteries; I'm going to grab some dinner and watch my favorite TV program to relax and unwind first." So they do that, and then one child asks them to throw the football around in the backyard. Then another asks for help on math homework. Then the spouse asks if they'll tidy the kitchen. Suddenly, it's 9:45 p.m., and they say, "Oh, it's too late to call; I'll just do it tomorrow."

If any of this sounds familiar, you are not alone. Just about everyone goes through these mental and emotional hoops. What's happening is simple: we are procrastinating. Why? Because subconsciously we believe that making the phone call will result in immediate discomfort. We believe that it will be difficult or unpleasant. So we con ourselves into believing we will take action, but really we are just avoiding it. We are giving in to fear. And when we are fearful, we are easily distracted by urgent tasks rather than important ones. Our family is shouting at you to take action now on a task, and the phone isn't shouting at us to do anything. So we rationalize away our inactivity.

In their excellent book *Switch: How to Change Anything When Change Is Hard*,[115] authors Chip and Dan Heath share a powerful strategy called an "action trigger." They discuss a psychology study where university students were given the option of getting extra credit by writing a report. Half the students in the test group were given an additional instruction: decide in advance exactly when they were going to write the report (what dates and times) and where they were going to sit to do so. Literally, they would set the goal by stating, "I am going to write this report on December 3 at 2 p.m. while sitting at the dining room table." In this study, of the students who had not defined exactly where and when they would write the report, only 33 percent ended up doing it. Of the students who clearly defined where and when they would take action, an amazing 75 percent wrote the report.

To apply this strategy, state exactly where and when you will make phone calls. Literally decide, "At 7:20 p.m. Monday night, I will sit at my desk and dial this number." Schedule that appointment into your calendar, and build your schedule around it. As you arrive home, and the distractions hit, say: "Absolutely, I'll be happy to throw the football/tidy the kitchen/help you with your homework/etc., but at 7:20 p.m., I need to sit at my desk and make a telephone call." That is how specific you need to be. If you do this for a few months, it will start to feel normal and natural.

2. **Have the Phone Number Right in Front of You**. Don't sit down at your desk at 7:20 p.m. Monday and then say, "Now where did that telephone number go?" That is an excellent way to dissolve all your mental and emotional momentum. Confirm in advance that you have the number ready to go. Glance at the number several times in advance of 7:20 p.m. You may even want to have the telephone number preprogrammed into your phone for ease of calling. One of my business partners uses a Blackberry phone (we'll get him switched over to an iPhone soon enough), and he sets his calendar to generate an appointment at 7:20 p.m. When he sets the appointment in his calendar, he programs the person's name *and telephone number* into the appointment title. That way, at exactly 7:20 p.m. Monday night when he is sitting at his desk, the appointment pops up on his phone with the telephone number already programmed, ready to go, and he just clicks on it with his thumb, and the phone dials. No time to chicken out, no way to be disorganized; he has removed

all the potential distractions so that he can't chicken out or make excuses and say, "Darn, I've misplaced that number. Oh well, I guess I'll call that important person tomorrow." Be organized with your phone numbers.

When you are dialing *dozens* of telephone numbers from a smart phone, another great strategy is to copy the list of names and telephone numbers and paste it into an e-mail and then send this information to yourself. This is particularly effective if you are a salesperson and need to reach a number of people quickly and efficiently. When you open the e-mail on a smart phone, all the telephone numbers appear right there on the screen, and you can click on them easily to place your calls. This makes your phone calling more efficient and doesn't give you time to chicken out and procrastinate.

3. **Take a Deep Breath and Calm Down**. If you get nervous before an important phone call, you are literally going into what's called the "fight-or-flight" response. There are many excellent books on the subject, but basically it is your body overreacting to what you perceive as a threat. Your heart starts pounding, your hands get sweaty, your stomach starts gurgling with nausea, and you find it suddenly hard to breathe. When that happens, the fastest way to get control of your nerves is to slow your breathing down. Taking long, slow, deep breaths short-circuits the stress response, and you can actually feel your heart rate slowing down. If you are feeling nervous about a call, you may even want to start this process a few minutes before you expect to call so that you feel more relaxed. If you get on the phone and get nervous, you might easily become short of breath. That makes it hard to sound confident, let alone feel confident. If you are calling about a job you saw posted online, it's tough to get the other person excited about you if you sound like a

> The fastest way to get control of your nerves is to slow your breathing down.

wheezing little schoolgirl in distress. Get control of your physical reactions when you are feeling stressed, and the call will go much more successfully. And if you are still nervous, listen to some music that fires you up, like "Eye of the Tiger" or some *Jock Jams* music—whatever works for you. If that still doesn't work, pray!

4. **Visualize the Phone Call Being a Tremendous Success.** In his remarkable book *RESOLVED*, Orrin Woodward describes the power of using visualization to help you accomplish your goal.[116] All Olympic champions first visualize achieving their performance goals, hearing the roar of the crowd, and feeling the gold medals going around their necks. They visualize success in such vivid detail that their subconscious mind literally starts to believe that it *is* true. Amazingly, this simple trick actually helps make it a reality.

   Since this is good enough for Olympic athletes, it will be good enough for you. To have power and confidence when making calls, first visualize the people being happy to hear from you when they answer. Imagine the warmth in their voice and how receptive they feel to what you are saying. Imagine them enthusiastically wanting to hear more. Imagine them being excited about your cause and wanting to buy in. Imagine them being eager to meet with you in person and learn more about you and your project. Imagine yourself smiling at your success as you open your calendar and secure a successful appointment. Imagine feeling proud of yourself as you hang up the phone. Imagine success vividly in your mind, and watch with satisfaction as it starts to come true.

5. **Champions Pause to Engage the Person in the Conversation.** When telemarketers call your number, they launch into a rapid-fire script and don't come up for air. This is a huge turn-off, and most people respond by simply hanging up the phone. If you are calling for sales or business, it certainly can

help to have a script that you've developed and practiced, but please don't just talk *at* the person; talk *with* the person. Telemarketers barrage the listener with words and end up sounding like "clanging cymbals." Experts pause to engage the other person in the conversation.

What do I mean? Consider a tennis match with a friend. You can certainly slam balls at him and have him ducking for cover, but if it's just a friendly game you are enjoying for the pleasure of each other's company, you may want to slow down your swing. Lob the ball gently, and then let your friend return the ball. Begin a slow back-and-forth exchange that extends the life of the game. When people are rushed or frantically trying to pepper the listener with words, it's like slamming tennis balls at a competitor, trying to crush him and claim victory. Slow it down, Scooter. You can certainly fire off info about who you are and why you are calling, but make sure at some point that your ears hear the voice of the person replying.

Again, asking questions is the best way to keep the other person engaged. You can say, "Hi, John, it's Tim Marks calling. I've actually never spoken with you before, but Fred Jones referred me to you. Am I catching you at a good time?" This question shows respect and immediately distinguishes you from a telemarketer. (Have you ever noticed how some telemarketers have a keen sense of timing to call just as you are sitting down to dinner or turning on the shower?) Then you might ask another question. In my case I might say, "I am a local businessman looking to expand my company. I understand from Fred Jones that you are a very successful accountant. Did I hear correctly?" Other great questions might include, "How long have you been doing that? What made you get started? What do you enjoy most about your work?" I try to build pauses into my conversation and get the other person talking. It helps me learn more about the person and gets him engaged in the conversation rather than feeling verbally overwhelmed by me.

Have Confidence In Front Of an Audience

Comedian Jerry Seinfeld once joked that most people fear public speaking more than death, which would mean at a funeral they'd rather be in the casket than giving the eulogy! One of the most obvious outward signs of a confident person seems to be his or her ability to stand in front of an audience and deliver a speech. Why is it so frightening for so many people?

Fear of public speaking is a learned fear; we aren't born with it. In fact, babies are born with only two natural fears: the fear of loud noises and the fear of falling. Every other fear is learned, and because of that, each fear can be unlearned. In the case of public speaking, each of us was probably made to stand up in front of our classmates at school and deliver a presentation at some point. And most of us faced a threatening, jeering mob that snickered whenever we tripped up on our words. The sting of that embarrassment cuts deep into most people, and we carry it into adulthood. When we are afraid of speaking in public, we're just afraid of reliving those feelings of embarrassment.

So how do we combat this fear? There are a lot of great books on *how* to speak well, but I'm not focused on technique here. What I'm going to cover in the section is how to keep your confidence up when you finally hit the stage. Here are some tips on managing fear and staying confident for public speaking:

1. **Take Your Focus Off Yourself.** You are there to serve your audience, not to have them serve you with their applause and accolades. You are there to give, not to take. Daniel Goleman, author of *Social Intelligence*, says, "Self-absorption in all its forms kills empathy, let alone compassion. When we focus on ourselves, our world contracts as our problems and

preoccupations loom large. But when we focus on others, our world expands. Our own problems drift to the periphery of the mind and so seem smaller, and we increase our capacity for connection—or compassionate action."[117] Most nervous speakers are simply too focused on themselves. They are asking themselves, "How am I going to look? How am I going to sound? Will they like me?" All of those questions are self-centered, not audience-centered. Here are some better questions: "Who in this audience is hurting? Who needs inspiration? How can I lift their spirits and bring hope and joy into their lives?" Before I started public speaking as a career, I was terrified, to say the least. When I started to pray before I gave a speech and asked God for clear thoughts, peace in my heart, and to give glory to Him, I found my ability to connect with the audience skyrocketed.

2. **Meet the Audience Before You Start**. Will Rogers said, "Strangers are just friends I haven't met yet."[118] Take the time to walk around the room and meet some or all (if possible) of the people attending. Introducing yourself and building rapport allows you to break the ice and work off some of your nerves. Also, you can get a better read on the personalities and backgrounds of the audience as you make small talk with them. That way, you'll have some friendly faces in the audience, and you might be able to refer to meeting these people when you stand up and speak. Finally, it is edifying to hear some of the people you meet say, "I am so excited to hear you speak today." That's a great pat on the back to send you onstage with a smile.

3. **Visualize the Audience Smiling and Applauding**. Just as an Olympic athlete visualizes winning the gold medal, it will help calm your nerves if you can imagine doing well and having everyone enjoy your speech. Not only is it critical to do this, but it is also critical to stop visualizing failure. People

who fear speaking in front of an audience have a bad habit of visualizing failure. They imagine the audience looking bored, checking their watches, or texting on their phones. Instead, imagine the audience hanging on your every word. Imagine them smiling up at you, excited to hear you speak. Imagine them cheering for you and laughing at your every joke. You must squash any negative images of failure and see the audience enjoying themselves.

4. **The Story Trumps the Details.** Many people worry they will forget the details when they speak. Don't sweat it too much; the audience won't remember them either. In fact, if you quiz the audience as they walk out of the meeting room and ask them to repeat the details of your speech, *very few* people can do so. However, if you ask them to repeat the *story* you told, most of them can, especially if the story is emotional or dramatic and you painted a vivid picture for them to imagine. For example, consider the two following announcements, one very dry and one very dramatic. Which one is easier to remember?

Announcement A:

In July, 2012, physicists at the Large Hadron Collider ended a 5-decade-long search when they announced the discovery of the Higgs boson. This long-sought particle is responsible for giving all other subatomic elements, such as protons and electrons, their mass, and was the final piece in the Standard Model, which describes the interactions of all known particles and forces. While LHC researchers were cautious, only calling their results a "Higgs-like" particle until more data and analysis is available, the finding was widely hailed as the most important fundamental physics discovery in more than a generation.[119]

169

Announcement B:

On January 15, 2009, [US Airways Flight 1549] struck a flock of Canada Geese during its initial climb out, lost engine power, and ditched in the Hudson River off midtown Manhattan.

The bird strike, which occurred just northeast of the George Washington Bridge about three minutes into the flight, resulted in an immediate and complete loss of thrust from both engines. When the crew of the aircraft determined that they would be unable to reliably reach any airfield, they turned southbound and glided over the Hudson, finally ditching the airline near the USS *Intrepid* museum about three minutes after losing power. All 155 occupants safely evacuated the airliner, which was still virtually intact though partially submerged and slowly sinking, and were quickly rescued by nearby ferries and other watercraft. The incident became known as the "Miracle on the Hudson."

The entire crew of Flight 1549 [including Capt. Chesley B. "Sulley" Sullenberger] was later awarded [for its bravery.] The award citation read, "This emergency ditching and evacuation, with the loss of no lives, is a heroic and unique aviation achievement." [It has been described as] "the most successful ditching in aviation history."[120]

Why are we able to remember most of the second story? Because our brains don't remember information in a neat and tidy way like a computer file; we need mental "coat hooks" to hang the ideas on in order to remember them. As Carl W. Buechner puts it, "They may forget what you said, but they will never forget how you made them feel." Emotions and vivid images are the most powerful and enduring coat hooks for our memory. That's why details are so much easier to remember, for both the audience and for you as the speaker, when they are shared inside a story. As long as you can remember the story, you are gold. And the easiest story to remember is your own.

5. **Passion Always Trumps Polish.** John Ford said, "You can speak well if your tongue can deliver the message of your heart."[121] Don't concern yourself as much with sounding like an expert or an experienced orator. Chances are you're not, and the audience already knows that. You can be forgiven for being inexperienced; what is less forgivable is to sound bored. Speak with passion! Let the audience know you care about your topic. How? Increase your volume, make larger gestures with your body, and learn by reviewing audios and videos of passionate speakers who inspire you. In his book Public Speaking for Success, Dale Carnegie remarked, "In oder [for a speaker] to appear natural, he has to use much more energy in talking to forty people than he does in talking to one, just as a statue on top

> *Let the audience know you care about your topic.*

of a building has to be of heroic size in order to make it appear of lifelike proportions to an observer on the ground."[122] When you are talking to someone over coffee and you are only a few feet away, your energy only needs to radiate a few feet outward. But when you are in a room with a dozen, or a hundred, or a thousand people, your energy level needs to be amped up. Your energy needs to fill the room and reach the back row. The audience will forgive your lack of polish when you come across sounding passionate.

6. **Practice.** Richard Kline said, "Confidence is preparation. Everything else is beyond your control."[123] Most people worry they will forget their words, offer a flat delivery, bore their audience, and embarrass themselves. There is one practical

solution to push aside this fear: you must rehearse your speech. You must practice in private to master your delivery. Practice while you drive. Practice in front of your bathroom mirror. And practice in front of your kids at dinner and their stuffed animals in the toy room. Then, much like riding a bike or throwing a football, as your performance improves, you will gain confidence. In his book *The Art of Public Speaking*, Dale Carnegie said:

> Face an audience as frequently as you can, and you will soon stop shying. You can never attain freedom from stage-fright by reading a treatise. A book may give you excellent suggestions on how best to conduct yourself in the water, but sooner or later you must get wet, perhaps even strangle and be "half scared to death." There are a great many "wetless" bathing suits worn at the seashore, but no one ever learns to swim in them. To plunge is the only way.

7. **Have a "Plant" in the Front Row**. If possible, get a friend, spouse, co-worker, or trusted ally to sit in front and maintain eye contact with you throughout the presentation. Their job is to keep smiling. Whether you are delivering a speech at a wedding or a PowerPoint presentation at work, having someone on your side can help calm your nerves. When you feel nervous, glance back at this person; his or her smile will be shouting "Hey, you're doing great. Keep rocking!" And amazingly, this will help calm your jitters in front of a crowd.

8. **Be Proud of Your Courage.** It takes a lot of guts to stand up in front of any audience. If you're thinking that the audience will criticize you or mock your presentation, remember that you've got more courage than they do to even step up to the podium. Zig Ziglar said, "Don't be distracted by criticism. Remember—the only taste of success some people have is

when they take a bite out of you."[124] You are already a winner for stepping up to speak. Have a strong sense of pride in yourself.

Walk like a Winner

"The way you treat yourself sets the standard for others."
– Sonya Friedman

People tend to judge us based on the value we place on ourselves. If we hold ourselves in high esteem, other people will think positively toward us. Unfortunately, that door swings both ways. If you walk with your tail between your legs, the world will look down on you too. The first impression people have of us is almost always what they see, followed quickly by what they hear us say. Just as we must work on feeling confident, we must also dress and look confident. First impressions count. Act confidently, walk with confidence, and look confident, and your confidence will soar.§

- **Smile**. Self-assured people tend to enjoy life as a rule; more often than not, they've got good things coming their way. They attract success. Smiling is a billboard that says, "I feel good about myself and my life. I am enjoying this moment." When you feel good, people are attracted to you.

  Not only is smiling a thermometer of your attitude, it can act as a thermostat. Smiling elevates your mood when you are down. If your attitude is in the dumps, you can choose to force yourself to smile, and it tells your brain to be in a better mood.

---

§ I naturally walk with a swagger, in large part due to back problems I have been blessed with my entire life. I do my best to compensate for a pinched nerve in my back, but I end up looking like John Wayne when I walk.

When you greet people, greet them with a smile. A real smile comes from within. For years, I worried about the color and look of my teeth. They weren't perfect (they still aren't), and they were a little coffee stained. If your teeth are badly discolored, you can always have that fixed by the dentist in extreme cases. But remember that the smile is as much about the attitude you are showing as it is about your teeth. Even today, I still have to remind myself to smile when I walk into a room or meet someone for the first time. Thankfully, I have a bunch of friends around me who smile and serve as reminders to me to flex my face and get some air on my teeth.

- **Make Eye Contact.** When you watch people who lack confidence, they tend to look down at their feet, afraid to look another person in the eye. Lack of eye contact can be a sign of insecurity, shame, or inferiority. The cure for this: make eye contact. Nicholas Boothman, author of *How to Connect in Business in 90 Seconds or Less* says:

  In social and workplace situations, subtle differences in eye contact can speak volumes. For example, when someone's eyes are narrowed and his head is lowered and turned slightly to one side, and he is still maintaining eye contact, that can signal an invitation to discuss something private, even intimate. The eyes can signal a feeling of superiority (when the head is raised) or hostility (when a gaze is level and unwavering). Conversely, looking away can imply weakness and avoidance. [125]

  To improve eye contact, Boothman has the following suggestion: Check the other person's eye color. There is no way to do this without making eye contact. In fact, he says that clever customer service managers will ask their staff to take an informal survey of how many clients have brown eyes or blue eyes. The result? Staff members make eye contact. So try playing that game as you meet people. Make a point of noticing their eye color, and see how you develop the habit of confidently looking people in the eye.

- **Dress for Success.** Actors frequently make mention of how the costume they wear actually puts them into character. Their personality changes. Their tone of voice, body language, and demeanor shift as soon as they slip on the costume. The same is true of those in business. When people are searching for work, outplacement agencies will recommend they dress up in business attire, not only for job interviews, but even when making phone calls from home. Why? Because, as the old saying goes, "The clothes make the man." When you are dressed professionally, you actually feel professional. It doesn't matter that the people on the other end of the phone can't see what you're wearing; you feel professional, and they can hear it in your voice. In fact, people who are depressed report that getting out of bed and getting dressed up can simply do wonders for their spirits. If you want to feel more confident, dress like a confident, successful person.

  People who are depressed report that getting out of bed and getting dressed up can simply do wonders for their spirits.

  If you look back in time, say to the Roaring Twenties or the 1950s, people dressed up for everything. Why? Well, obviously, it was a part of that day's culture. Suppose you were an immigrant landing in America with only the shirt on your back. You'd wear the same clothes every day, and they would naturally begin wearing out. As you started to earn some money and enjoy your newfound freedom, even enjoying some prosperity, it would be natural to dress up and feel proud of how you had pulled yourself up by your bootstraps. To earlier Americans, it was a pleasure and a sign of respect to look neat and clean when you went out or when you had company over.

I remember I was in Cardiff, Wales, a few years back, hosted by a very gracious Christian man named Vernon Higham. To give you an idea how distinguished Vernon was, he happened to be good friends with the great preacher D. Martyn Lloyd-Jones. He and all those he associated with dressed up everywhere they went, not just to church. To give one example, we all got up early one morning at 6:00 a.m. to find Vernon already sitting at the table in a three-piece suit, ready to go. And there we were in our dungarees and sneakers, looking much less professional than he did.

Of course some of this is cultural, but that's more or less my point. When we don't respect ourselves enough to put on some dress pants and a nice shirt or a suit every now and then, what are we saying to ourselves about ourselves? Certainly there is a time to "let your hair down" (for those of you who still enjoy a head of hair) and hang out and relax in your favorite blue jeans, or slip on your favorite shorts and sports jersey and watch the game, but the line between work clothes and leisure clothes has grown gray and faded.

We have all seen kids who wear their jeans around their thighs, so we all have the blessing of seeing what brand underwear they have on. (The Marks boys would not dare.) This is flat-out a display of rebellion, period. How do I know? Show me one well-mannered young man like Tim Tebow or Cam Newton who would dress in such a way. My point is this: How we dress affects how we behave, and how we behave affects the way we see ourselves. If you wore pajamas and slippers to the airport or out to Olive Garden for dinner, would you feel sharp, successful, and confident? Probably not. I'm not saying we need to dress up everywhere we go and draw attention to ourselves; we don't need to "one-up" all our friends when it comes to clothing. But we should dress well to feel well.

For men, a professional appearance is a clean shave, neatly groomed hair, and business attire. In my experience, when you see a successful woman making an address at the front of the room, she is dressed conservatively, not in a casual or provocative outfit. Guys are usually in a dark suit, white shirt, and a red, blue, or yellow tie. (Note: I don't want to debate what is fashionable; this is simply for professional relatability in business. This is what politicians wear. In spite of how they act, we still elect them. Imagine if they wore black suits with black shirts. Everyone would think they were crooks!)

With that said, let's talk about how women should dress to show self-respect. (I realize this is a very dangerous topic.) Thankfully, most women don't run around with their underwear hanging out (although some do). The issue with women is typically that of drawing attention to themselves through wearing clothes in public that really should only be worn to bed. What we see today is either the "Walmart shopper uniform," which is sweatpants and slippers, or shorts that she has had since high school even though she is now in her late thirties. I am certainly no fashion mogul, but ladies, you want men thinking about your brains, and not your body. I wouldn't recommend blouses that are cut too low or skirts that are cut too high. I realize that this can be difficult for some people to clearly define, so allow me to be clear: don't have any part of your body exposed that people shouldn't be staring at, such as your cleavage. (There. I said it. No other book has the confidence to come out and say it!) In fact, if you want to be really conservative, go with business pants or slacks. You don't need to show skin to show confidence; in fact, sometimes showing skin can demonstrate a lack of confidence. Remember, to have confidence, we want a high level of self-worth. You are a worthwhile person regardless of your body, whether you're a soccer mom or a supermodel.

Develop Some Posture

"It's not what you are in life that holds you back; it's what you think you are not."

– Denis Waitley

One of the most powerful concepts in confidence is the idea of *posture*. Physically speaking, posture is how you hold your body—whether you are slumped over or standing straight like a soldier on duty. Confident people walk with their shoulders back and head held high. This alone can boost your confidence and improve your mood. In martial arts, posture is a powerful stance that ensures no one can push you around.

> *Posture is a powerful stance that ensures no one can push you around.*

But what I am describing here is something even more powerful: the idea of *mental* posture. This is how we hold ourselves mentally and emotionally when talking with other people. Posture is the outward expression of our level of confidence. When we have posture, we don't just feel confident, we look and speak with confidence. We might secretly feel confident inside, but our "posture" is how well the other guy senses that feeling from us.

Sometimes I meet guys who think that posture means stepping on other people and pushing them down; remember, having posture isn't being a jerk or a bully. My friend Chris Brady has a great definition of the idea of posture: it lies somewhere between "wimp" and "jerk." You can hold your own against anyone without being rude or aggressive. No one can eat your lunch, and you still come across diplomatically. You stand up for yourself.

I say posture is somewhere between Rambo and George McFly. If you remember the great 1985 movie *Back to the Future*, Marty McFly came home to find his wimpy dad George being chewed out by his bullying co-worker Biff. Biff had been pushing George around since high school, and nothing had changed in adulthood. Biff was a total jerk, demanding that George work overtime to finish Biff's report to

178

make him look good. But by the end of the movie, George's confidence had grown. He stood up to Biff, and things changed forever. George was transformed from a doormat into a guy with posture; he was confident and wouldn't let Biff push him around. Their roles reversed dramatically; Biff was reduced to waxing George's BMW and tried to lie to George about finishing the second coat of wax. George called him out on it, saying, "Now, Biff, don't con me," and Biff sheepishly fessed up that he really was just *starting* the second coat. George McFly had transformed into a perfect example of a guy with *posture*.

Now, I can relate to being a little hard on people and drifting into "jerk" territory. In my first book, *Voyage of a Viking*,[126] I describe how sarcastic and hurtful I was in speaking to the guys who worked for me at the automotive manufacturing plant. I might have thought I had posture, but in reality I was just being a bully. If standing up for yourself involves being rude or hurting other people's feelings, and particularly if you enjoy being hurtful, you've drifted too far away from true posture. Confident people have no need or desire to be hurtful to others in daily life. So always remember, anytime you see a loudmouth jerk, you see a person who is hurting and has low self-worth.

Posture is born from our sense of self-worth and self-confidence, but in some situations, it can be helpful to have a few tools in the toolbox that help you stand and speak with posture while you are still doing the hard and enduring work of changing who you are as a person. Posture draws on the "Know Your Worth" concepts we already discussed at the beginning of the book regarding honestly believing that you are valuable and that what you have to offer others is valuable. If, for example, you are an amazing singer and your church needs singers, you have something of value to offer your church. Posture comes from knowing what you have to offer is of value to others.

Just as being a bully is not showing posture, neither is being a doormat. If you have a begging, pleading personality, no one will respect you. If you approach your boss asking to work on a project at the office, and your pitch to her is, "Please, boss, please let me work on the project. I really need this break. I'm feeling really down and don't know if I offer any value to the company; it'll be good for me. Honest, I promise to try hard. Just give me a chance, please!" That would turn off anyone. Most people wouldn't use those words per se, but they would communicate this kind of message with their words and poor posture.

Rather, you should approach your boss and make a solid business case why it would be to her benefit to select *you* to lead the project. People with posture wouldn't beg; they would point out how it would be to the other's advantage to take them up on their offer for support. You might say, "I've taken a look at the XYZ report, and I've got some ideas that might save the department money. If you'd like, **I'd be willing** to take some time over the weekend and put my thoughts down on paper for you to review." Doesn't that sound more confident? Don't beg; *offer.*

When you say, "I'd be willing," it means that you are being gracious to extend your expertise and assistance, that *you* are doing *them* a favor. Your whole spirit suggests that it's no skin off your back if they say no, but they'd be crazy to miss the chance to get your support. When you've got posture, others feel they'd be lucky to get to work with you, that *you* are offering to help *them*, as opposed to feeling that *they* are doing *you* a favor. Posture shows other people that you value yourself and that they would be wise to do so as well.

> When you've got posture, others feel they'd be lucky to get to work with you.

SUMMARY

You can always spot confident people when they walk into a room. They carry themselves like winners. They make eye contact, smile, and introduce themselves to the people around.

Their shoulders are back and their head is held high. They know they have something of incredible value to share with others: themselves. And their words and actions reflect this value. Whenever they strike up a conversation with a stranger, make an important phone call, or speak from a podium, self-assured people take action and carry themselves with confidence.

Key Points

1. Don't worry about failing in life; every successful person does. The opposite of success isn't failure; failure is part of the success journey. The opposite of success is quitting.

2. People who lack confidence tend to be held hostage by fear. While confident people may experience negative emotions, they certainly don't take advice from them.

3. Say yes to life more often. Most people regret what they *didn't* do more often than what they tried. The word *no* carries an awful burden. It shuts the door to opportunity. I'm not concerned you won't say no to life when you *should*; I'm concerned you won't say yes to life when you *could*.

4. Use the magic of momentum, just like Jaime Escalante did while teaching his high school math class. Get on a roll and use those results as rocket fuel. Never squander a victory; always use it to propel you to the next victory.

5. To become successful, people need an army of others who want to see them succeed behind them. Winners don't look at people as objects to manipulate or obstacles to overcome; they look at people and see an opportunity for friendship.

6. Learn to connect with strangers. Decide to like them and imagine they'll like you. Take a chance! Strike up a conversation by making a comment, offering a compliment, or asking a question.

7. If you are nervous making important phone calls, use these tips: Determine the exact time and place you will call. Have the phone numbers ready. Take a deep breath, imagine the call will go well, and get the other person talking.

8. When speaking in front of an audience, remember *you* are there to serve *them*. Take the time to meet some of the audience members before you start. Remember, the story trumps the details, and passion trumps polish. Have a friend in the audience who keeps smiling. And no matter what, be proud you had the guts to get up there and speak.

9. The way you carry yourself is a billboard declaring your confidence. Walk tall with your head held high. Look people in the eye and smile. Dress like a winner, and you'll feel like a winner.

10. Posture is a powerful stance that ensures no one can push you around. When you've got posture, others feel they'd be lucky to get to work with you. Posture comes from knowing what you have to offer is of value to others.

5

CUT YOUR ANCHORS

"Our past is a story existing only in our minds. Look, analyze, understand, and forgive. Then, as quickly as possible, chuck it."
— *Marianne Williamson*

Webster's Dictionary defines an anchor as "a device usually [made] of metal attached to a ship or boat by a cable and cast overboard to hold it in a particular place...."[127] Simply put, an anchor is something that stops you from moving forward and making progress. While that may serve us well when trying to moor our yacht at a faraway harbor, in our personal or professional life, anything that holds us back from making progress can be cause for concern.

For our purposes in building confidence, I am going to borrow the term "anchor" and use it to mean something a little different. For this book, an "anchor" is the negative thinking or hang-up that gets created when we go through an emotionally upsetting experience. After that event, the way we view ourselves, other people, the world, and even life in general, can be tainted. Our behavior changes as a result. We might grow fearful and timid the next time we encounter a situation that reminds us in some way of those past events, even if we aren't

> *An "anchor" is the negative thinking or hang-up that gets created when we go through an emotionally upsetting experience.*

consciously aware of what is causing these feelings and behaviors. Anchors affect us even if we don't know they are present.

I have worked with people who had received years of counseling and believed they were "cured," only to discover that getting rid of an anchor can be harder than it seems. Some people mistakenly believe that if they can grin and bear it, it means the anchor has lost its hold over them. Unfortunately, anchors can dig deep into the core of our souls. As I have personally watched and mentored people who haven't dealt with their past experiences, I have seen firsthand the terrible pain caused by unresolved issues. In some cases, the reason these people didn't deal with their past was because they didn't know how much their past was affecting them, rather than that they had a desire to avoid changing. I have watched people endure all sorts of difficult issues in their lives because of a failure to "cut their anchors," not the least of which was a massive lack of confidence. I've seen people struggle with building any sort of lasting relationship, fear taking action in their career or business, lose focus, lose belief in themselves, and even lose faith in God.

I cannot release a book on confidence without digging deep into the topic of anchors. In this chapter, we're going to highlight some common anchors, give you a chance to consider your own, and illustrate the process of redefining your anchors. As a big disclaimer, this is not meant to be a counseling book, and I am not a psychologist. I also don't believe that psychology, though it can help, is the only answer. But I do know, as I sit here, that failing to address the scars or "anchors" of the past is a major reason people struggle to have the success and confidence they desire. So, from one friend to another, let's have a personal and important conversation about some of the deeper stuff that might be holding you back.

Failing to address the scars or "anchors" of the past is a major reason people struggle to have the success and confidence they desire.

Even Top Leaders Have Anchors

"There is nothing you can do about your early life now, except to understand it. You can, however, do everything about the rest of your life."

— *Warren Bennis*

Anchors can be created by many different experiences, from early trauma to an upsetting event we have endured recently. Most often, however, the anchors we face are created by negative experiences in our childhood.

A very common example of an event that could create an anchor is giving a speech in school. As we discussed earlier, young children may have felt embarrassed in an early public-speaking experience. As a result, they've created a story about that experience that they've told themselves repeatedly, often amplifying their own experience of embarrassment. Thus, they created a long-lasting fear of speaking in front of an audience again.

Orrin Woodward had this very experience in speech class in college; he absolutely choked in front of an audience when giving a speech on John F. Kennedy and received a failing grade. Orrin was convinced he couldn't do public speaking, and that was a huge barrier to his belief many years later that he could build a business and speak on a stage in front of a business audience. Most of us progress through life with a similar anchor holding us back. Fast forward five, ten, even twenty years later, and you might be invited to give a presentation in front of your sales team, offer a toast at a wedding reception, or give your testimony in church. As you stand up and face the crowd, you feel a wave of panic grab you. You can feel a fire alarm going off inside, warning you of the danger. Your brain remembers how awful it felt back in school to be embarrassed in front of the kids and is trying to protect you from ever going through that again.

In my case, I had struggles with learning in school. At one time in my life, I could barely read a book, much less write one. As I mentioned in *Voyage of a Viking*, I was an undiagnosed dyslexic at the time. When I looked at the page, the numbers and letters would move around on me, and it was confusing. My mom and the teachers thought I was being lazy; if I would just apply myself, they reasoned, everything would improve. But sitting in class was like torture. I was terrified to be called to the front of the class to solve a math problem, knowing everyone would stare at me as I struggled. Reading was even worse; I would screw up a word, and the other kids would laugh at me. I could feel my face burning with embarrassment. I prayed the teacher would call on anyone else to continue.

For years, I thought I couldn't read and couldn't make it through school. Graduating high school with a 1.8 GPA is not exactly an indicator of the next great writer coming down the road! Because of my low self-image due to all of my struggles in school, I just gave up on believing in myself academically. I didn't go after a college degree until my job required it because I was too uncomfortable with learning.

Chuck Norris Finally Stood Up for Himself

Many people know Chuck Norris as a classic Hollywood hero, fighting off the bad guys and saving the day in a string of popular action movies through the '80s. His expertise in martial arts is the stuff of legend, with online communities making grand claims about the near superhero-like strength of his roundhouse kick. These wild, hilarious, and obviously fictional claims have taken on a life of their own in the form of "Chuck Norris Facts," a string of jokes that suggest Chuck Norris has superhero-level powers. As an example, one humorous "fact" suggests that when Chuck Norris does push-ups, he doesn't lift *himself up*; he pushes the *earth down*. Chuck Norris takes all these jokes in stride. As a man firmly grounded in his Christian faith and an outspoken political advocate for personal and economic freedom, Chuck is not afraid to stand up for himself and what he believes in. But that was not always the case.

In his autobiography, *The Secret of Inner Strength: My Story*, Norris tells the story of growing up with an alcoholic and emotionally abusive father. His dad, a WWII vet, was clearly affected by the war, as many men were when they returned home. He was not a friendly drunk, often exploding in a rage by the time he hit the bottom of the bottle. He would disappear for months at a time, abandoning the family and leaving Chuck, his mom, and his two brothers to fend for themselves.

Chuck was deeply embarrassed by his father's alcoholic behavior and the family's obvious poverty and avoided bringing friends over to his house as a boy. His mom took any job she could find, and the young boys went with her. By the time Chuck was ten, they had moved sixteen times, never settling long enough for Chuck to develop any relationships. Between his father's alcoholism, the family's poverty, and constant moves from house to house, Chuck grew painfully shy. His self-image suffered, and he grew afraid of saying the wrong thing in social settings. Soon, it became easier just to say nothing at all.

Without a father around to take care of the younger boys, Chuck had to grow up faster than other kids. When he was sixteen, his father punched his mom. That was the final straw. She divorced Chuck's dad, officially turning him out of the family home once and for all; then she found and married a nice man.

Later that year, Chuck's dad came by the house to confront the new husband and "take him out." At sixteen, soft-spoken Chuck Norris, who had grown up terrified of his father, finally decided to stand his ground. He told his dad he would have to go through him first before he could hurt his stepfather. He was about to be forced to square off in a fistfight against his own father outside the family home. At the last second, his dad relented and drove off. Except for a chance encounter outside a bar years later, it was the last time Chuck ever saw his father until the day of his funeral.

Chuck eventually enlisted in the Air Force. While in Korea, he was exposed to martial arts and grew fascinated. It was a discipline that could teach people, no matter their size, to defend themselves against an aggressor. Chuck threw himself into it wholeheartedly, earning his black belt in karate. That accomplishment was a major victory in his life and a huge boost to his self-esteem and self-confidence.

He began getting requests to teach classes. Standing up in front of an audience was terrifying for the boy inside who had been afraid of saying the wrong thing. He recalls shaking and pouring with sweat. Despite his fear, he forced himself through his first class and found that the more he spoke in front of audiences, the more confident he became. It served as a springboard to launch a career in movies and television that has inspired many millions of people. And Chuck and his wife went on to create a charity, the Kick Start Foundation, which teaches martial arts to disadvantaged youth and helps them build their self-confidence while learning proper values.

In the course of his life, Chuck decided to stand up for himself, and his confidence grew as a result.[128]

ORIGINS OF ANCHORS

"What you need to know about the past is that no matter what has happened, it has all worked together to bring you to this very moment. And this is the moment you can choose to make everything new. Right now."

— *Anonymous*

The events that shape our lives come from many different places, and they help to define our sense of personal identity. The positive events propel us to have confidence and believe in our strengths; they often support our choices in career and relationships. Unfortunately, our negative experiences are just as powerful, contributing to (or contaminating) our self-identity and influencing our behavior. And in those negative experiences is where an anchor is created. It is possible to be aware of the anchor and the exact experience that created it; it is also possible that the anchor is operating at a subconscious level, without our even being aware that we are being driven by forces from the past.

There is a story of a Russian worker leaving the factory each night pushing a wheelbarrow filled to the brim with sawdust. The guard at the gates, on the lookout for sticky-handed workers taking advantage of lax security, was convinced that the worker had something valuable hidden in the sawdust and was attempting to steal it. He stopped the worker and ordered the man to dump out the sawdust. The man, sighing, dumped the sawdust onto the ground. The guard was shocked to discover nothing was hidden in the sawdust! He allowed the man to scoop up the sawdust and wheel it home. The next day, the scene was repeated: The worker approached with a wheelbarrow filled to the brim with sawdust. *Aha*, the guard thought. *Now I'll catch him red-handed!* Again, the guard made the worker empty the contents of the wheelbarrow, and again it was shown to be only sawdust. This went on for days, with the guard growing more frustrated each day. Finally, the guard relented. He said to the man, "I am sure you are stealing something! I just know it! But I give up. I promise to stop asking if you'll just tell me!"

The worker smiled and replied, "I'm not hiding anything in the sawdust. Each night, I am stealing the wheelbarrow!"

The point is that the very problem we face can be right in front of us, but unless we have identified it correctly, the problem will continue. In order to make a positive change and cut our anchors, we must first identify the anchor. Despite many of the great things that we likely each experienced in our past, our view of life can be tainted easily by setbacks, hurts, and disappointments. As Warren Bennis wrote in his book *On Becoming a Leader*, "Most of us are shaped more by negative experiences than by positive ones. A thousand things happen in a week to each of us, but most of us remember the few lapses rather than our triumphs, because we don't reflect. We merely react."[129]

In no particular order, here is a laundry list of some of the events that may have created an anchor for you. You may wish to put a checkmark next to the ones you relate to.

- ❏ You struggled in school in some way, academically, socially, or athletically.
- ❏ You had trouble making friends or were shunned at school; you were the outcast.
- ❏ You were actively teased or bullied at school.
- ❏ You were treated poorly by teachers.
- ❏ You have suffered major setbacks before:
  - o You have lost a job.
  - o You have endured bankruptcy.
  - o You have lost a business.
  - o You have lost a major relationship.
  - o You have been through a divorce.
- ❏ You faced major illness or injury.
- ❏ You have made a grave mistake and hurt yourself and your loved ones because of it.
- ❏ You quit something, and now you regret it.
- ❏ You saw your parents struggle and fail.
- ❏ You lost a pet that was like a family member.
- ❏ You endured a traumatic experience, such as a fire or natural disaster or the loss of a loved one: a parent, a spouse, a child, a sibling, or a best friend.
- ❏ You were the victim of a crime.
- ❏ You were assaulted physically or sexually.
- ❏ You were treated poorly by your parents or other family members:
  - o Your parents were highly critical, saying, "You're a disappointment."
  - o Your parents were perfectionists; nothing you did was ever good enough.
  - o Your parents never paid attention to you.
  - o You were told you were bad or worthless.
  - o You were blamed for family problems.
  - o You were compared unfavorably to siblings and told, "Why can't you be more like Johnny?"

o   Your parents divorced.

o   Your parent(s) abandoned you in some way.

o   Your parent(s) suffered from an addiction.

o   You were abused mentally, emotionally, physically or sexually by a parent or family member.

o   Other: _____

While this is not an exhaustive list, I believe it covers some of the common situations that a great number of people have faced.

MY TOP 5 NEGATIVE EVENTS IN LIFE

In order to cut your anchors, you first need to identify and define them. We aren't discussing this in order to *cause* further pain but to begin the process of understanding what has happened and how it has affected you in order to seek solutions. Take a little time right now to determine what the top five most embarrassing, painful, or traumatic events that have occurred in your life are. These may include single events, such as a house fire or the loss of a family member. They could include ongoing series of events, such as bullying or abuse that lasted for weeks, months, or even years. They may include a traumatic event that happened recently, such as a divorce or a home invasion. Big or small, such experiences can have an impact on your view of yourself and the world. These moments aided in defining who you are today.

In the space provided below, write down five of the most negative experiences in your life to date.

1. _____

2. _____

3. _____

4. _____

5. _____

In a moment, we will come back to this list to look at how these events affected your thinking and discuss how to rewrite your internal dialogue. But first you need to identify not only the negative events but any other negative influence that may have affected you.

VOICES FROM THE PAST

Words can leave scars that last long after physical scars have disappeared. Words said in a moment of anger or thoughtlessness can wound so deeply that decades later, even after family members or teachers who said them may have passed away, we remember them. In taking steps to cut our anchors, it can be helpful to briefly remind ourselves of what those people said to us (while being careful not to wallow in that criticism). Then we can use the tools in this book to rewrite those statements and eventually reframe their meaning in our minds.

Consider what hurtful words may have been said to you by your parents, classmates, teachers, or anyone else. Write your thoughts in the spaces below.

My _____ said I am _____.
My _____ said I am _____.
My _____ said I am _____.
My _____ said I am _____.
My _____ said I am _____.

FAILURES, MISTAKES, AND REGRETS

Sometimes the biggest anchor isn't what someone has done to us; it's what we've done to *ourselves*. If we are saddled by guilt, sadness, fear, and regret, the emotions surrounding the actions we've taken can hamper our path to success.

If you could go back in time and rewrite something you did, what mistake would you correct? Maybe you chickened out on going after a job you wanted. Maybe you quit a sport you loved. Maybe you lied. Maybe you broke the law. Maybe you had an affair. Maybe you had an abortion. Regardless of what your mistake was, perhaps the guilt surrounding your action is seeping into everything and causing you to hold back on pursuing success.

Unearthing these fearful and emotional memories can be one of the most liberating experiences possible. In the space provided below, write down your top failures, mistakes, and regrets.

I wish I hadn't _____.

I wish I hadn't _____.

I wish I hadn't _____.

Our regrets can also be caused by the actions we *failed* to take.

I wish I had _____.

I wish I had _____.

I wish I had _____.

If you have done things you regret, and you are carrying around that baggage of guilt and hypocrisy, don't think you are alone. One example of a regretful action of mine (which may seem small to some people) occurred because of my former alcoholism. I emphasize *former* because as of March 29, 2013, it will have been thirteen years since I've had a drink. However, in my late teens and early twenties, I was a very heavy drinker. I would get drunk three and four nights a week, and this destructive behavior continued well into my twenties. I was an alcoholic, though I didn't see it at the time. I regretfully remember one time taking some change from my grandmother's bedroom to pay for my addiction. She had a wastebasket that she used only for collecting change. Periodically, she would toss her loose change in there. So, as an alcoholic looking for a few extra bucks before payday in order to purchase a forty-ouncer, I rationalized my behavior by telling myself, "It's just change, and Grandma won't care anyway."

Years later, I was standing in front of a group of people teaching them about integrity. I cited the Ten Commandments and reminded them that "thou shalt not steal." Just as I made that comment, the memory of stealing change from my grandmother popped into my head. I felt like a total hypocrite. My grandmother had since died, and I had no way of apologizing to her or atoning for my actions.

I needed to call it what it was: a sin. I could minimize it and rationalize it to myself all day long, saying, "Tim, it was only taking change out of a trashcan," but in the end, it was still stealing from my grandmother. I could fall back on the excuse, "Hey, I was an alcoholic. Alcoholism is a disease! My behavior wasn't really my fault." But I know in my core that such an excuse doesn't justify my actions.

If I was willing to steal from my grandmother's trashcan, it forced me to consider how low I could go to feed my addiction. What was next: stealing cookies from a Girl Scout? The fact was, I had sinned. And I could choose to drag that anchor around, or I could choose the only real solution: to fall to my knees, beg God for forgiveness, and lay that sin on the cross. I asked God to help me cut away that anchor. As you examine each of these ideas above to help define your anchors, you may still find you are at a loss to discern what is holding you back. If you feel stumped regarding what your specific anchors are, complete the following statement as a starting point from which to work backward:

I feel I can't succeed in life because _____

_____

What did you come up with? Was your natural reaction to reject the statement altogether, saying, "I can succeed," or did you find yourself reflecting on a painful personal "truth"? If so, where do you think that "truth" came from? Can you remember the first time you thought it about yourself? What was happening in your life at that time? Who influenced you the most? What were your hopes and fears at that time?

What was your financial, familial, and friendship situation? What was your relationship with God? Answering these questions may awaken some memories and provide some insight into what your anchors are.

What Is This Anchor Costing You?

In order to make a change, we have to reach a point where we decide the cost of carrying our anchors around is too great a price to bear. It can be helpful to ask ourselves, "What is this anchor costing me?" Dan Hawkins, one of my business partners and a great friend, offers a perfect example of the cost in his life of carrying an anchor. On the audio he produced to encourage people entitled "Keep Your Eye on Your Dream and Swing,"[130] Dan shares the story of stepping up to bat as a young boy in school.

He was good enough to play baseball, but he was terrified to take a swing at the ball. Why? Because he was scared he would strike out. He was often walked to first base, getting rewarded for not swinging, but no one realized he wasn't doing this strategically; he was scared!

With each passing year, the other baseball players got better. But when Dan did swing at the ball, he found himself striking out often. He began telling himself every reason why he would strike out, why he would fail. He kept visualizing failure and then created the failure that he had seen in his imagination. Each time the ball was thrown across the plate, he froze. *"Strike one!"* the umpire called. Dan gulped and watched the second ball fly past him. *"Strike two!"* Then he would begin panicking. He couldn't react at all when the final ball sizzled past him and the umpire declared, *"Strike three! You're out!"* Dan walked away from home plate, crying.

In those moments of failure, an anchor was formed in Dan. Over the following years, opportunities to "take a swing" at making a better life came his way, and each time he panicked and froze. He recounts how he felt timid in many situations. He was gripped with fear at the thought of attending an automotive tech-school orientation day alone and needed his mom to go with him. He couldn't make a phone call to a barber to set up his own hair appointment; his mom needed to do it for him, and later his wife Lisa took over the responsibility. Dan had wanted to become an engineer. But it meant having to move away from home to go to college, so he gave up on that dream.

His stepfather was an automotive mechanic, and because of his fear, Dan thought being a mechanic would be a relatively easy path. But he was so fearful of talking to people that he would hide in the back of the shop when new customers entered hoping someone else would serve them. He also passed up an opportunity to work at another shop because rather than "take a swing," it seemed more comfortable to stay where he was. Every time Dan acted in fear, the strength of the anchor grew.

In my case, my mom had passed away, and her passing was very painful for me. What I didn't realize at the time was that it was actually causing problems in my marriage to my wife, Amy. The problem was that Amy reminded me of my mom, plain and simple, and being reminded of my mom at that time hurt deeply. Amy and I were already struggling in our relationship, and this was just one more reason I wanted to avoid being around her. It was too painful for me to bear.

What's amazing is that I didn't consciously realize that all this was going on in my head. It all came out in therapy some time later. It took a trained counselor to be able to ask me the questions that would help me piece this puzzle together. Often, it can be difficult for us to consciously diagnose our thoughts and feelings. But when the counselor asked me, "How does being around Amy make you feel, Tim? What is it about Amy that is making you feel pain and sadness? Why do you feel that way?" it all became clear. It was like doing a verbal "5 Why," the technique we discussed in Chapter 3: "Manage Your Self-Talk."

While it can be extremely helpful to sit down with a psychologist, we can still do some of the initial work ourselves. Since it can be tough to keep all your thoughts clear, you may want to start a journal and jot your thoughts and feelings down on paper. Below, I have posed a series of questions and provided space for you to write your answers.

I recognize, in suggesting these writing exercises, that they may be met with skepticism or resistance.

You aren't likely to fix all your problems just through a few moments of journaling, though it can help greatly. In many cases, cutting your anchor isn't a one-time chop with a machete. Sometimes it can take months or even years to cut every fiber of the anchor's rope. If you have a massive anchor with a large rope, you probably won't fully cut it by reading one book or saying one prayer. Some anchors, such as the shame and loss of trust that often accompany sexual abuse, have created such deep wounds that merely journaling about the experience is often not enough of a remedy. I recognize that and have provided an Appendix with some suggested reading that may shed light on a variety of traumatic scenarios and offer wisdom, perspective, and solutions.

With that in mind, take a moment and consider what your anchor is and what it is costing you in your life. What opportunities have you missed out on because of the limits you have placed on yourself? How have your relationships suffered because of this anchor? How has your career suffered? How has your health suffered? How has your mental and emotional well-being suffered because you have been carrying around this anchor? In order to cast off an anchor, sometimes we need to "get leverage on ourselves," as Tony Robbins says, and consider how painful it is to not change. Orrin Woodward says, "When the pain of staying the same becomes greater than the pain of changing, we're going to change." When you reach the point where you no longer merely *should* cut away your anchors but *must* cut away your anchors, you will throw open the doors to becoming the greatest possible version of yourself.

> "When the pain of staying the same becomes greater than the pain of changing, we're going to change."
> – Orrin Woodward

WHAT IS THIS ANCHOR COSTING ME IN MY:

Marriage? _____

Relationship with my kids? _____

Career? _____

Emotional well-being? _____

Level of confidence? _____

Physical health? _____

Finances? _____

Faith? _____

What have you missed out on because of holding this anchor? How much have you endured? Are you *tired* of dragging the pain and anguish around through your life? Have you reached a point where you finally want to be rid of the anchor? If you don't cut away this anchor, what will the rest of your life hold? Imagine five more years of dragging this anchor around. What about ten years? What about twenty? Have you reached a point where you are done with carrying this burden?

Now, resolve to break loose from the anchor. Resolve that you *must* be free of the pain, fear, embarrassment, sadness, guilt, and any other negativity that is being dragged behind you. Resolve that your life is *worthwhile* and you *deserve* to make a change. Resolve that you will unearth the meaning you have attached to these events and, using the tools we've discussed so far, create a new and empowering meaning to attach to them.

REWRITE WHAT YOUR PAST MEANS

"There are lessons in everything, and if you are fully deployed, you will learn most of them. Experiences aren't truly yours until you think about them, analyse them, examine them, question them, reflect on them, and finally understand them. The point, once again, is to use your experiences rather than being used by them, to be the designer, not the design, so that experiences empower rather than imprison."

–Warren Bennis

Now that you've identified some of the negative events, voices, and regrets of your past that might have become anchors, it's time to rewrite the script in your mind. Take all the skills we used in chapter 3 and rewrite the words you use when communicating with yourself. What do you say to yourself about those tough experiences? You need to dig into your old hang-ups to uncover any irrational beliefs and thought patterns that resulted from those experiences.

In order to "prime the pump," I am going to offer a series of examples of negative experiences, voices, and regrets, followed by my suggestion of a new and positive script. If it serves you, you may use these examples as a model for rewriting your own scripts. Here is the basic structure to help you get started. Simply fill in the blanks according to what you've experienced, and then create a new and empowering statement of belief that focuses on the positive.

Because of (negative event), **I thought it meant that** (what you used to tell yourself about it). **But now I know** (the new script you have written to attach to the event).

Here are some examples to consider.

Negative event: I failed math class.

"Because I failed math class, I thought it meant that I might fail high school and wouldn't get accepted to college. It left me worried I wouldn't be able to get a job. But now I know that failing math isn't the end of the world; my dad failed math, and he had a

199

successful career. This one math grade doesn't dictate my future. I can work hard and make up for it!"

Negative Event: I was very shy in school.

"Because I was shy in school, I had a tough time making friends. I thought it meant I was a loser. But I know now that being shy doesn't have to be a permanent thing, and I have a lot of great qualities to share with other people. I've read some great books and listened to some self-improvement audios, and my confidence is growing every day. Every time I interact with people, I am more successful, and I am going to keep improving. I have a lot of value to offer the world, and I'm going to give it!"

Negative Event: I had a teacher who was mean to me.

"Because I had a teacher who said terrible things to me, I thought it meant that I was stupid. But I know now that teacher was wrong, and I was just as smart as anyone else. My grades in school are just a stepping-stone to success. Right now, I'm learning a lot associating with positive and successful people. I'd love to run into that teacher someday so she could see how wrong she was and how successful I have become. Rather than feel anger toward that teacher, I will pray for her because she must be hurting inside. I will choose to pity her rather than feel hostility."

Negative Event: I grew up hating my body.

"Because I felt ugly when I was growing up, I thought it meant that the whole world was staring at me and thinking what they saw was disgusting. I resorted to unhealthy actions, such as purging, to try to change my body so that I felt better about myself. But now I know several things: First, my irrational view of what a perfect body should be was inspired more by edited magazine covers than reality. Second, many people consider me very attractive. Finally, what someone looks like is only a small part of who he or she is. People should be judged more by their character, actions, and spirit than by their height, weight, or complexion. I have learned to love myself and love my body, and I know I am attractive both inside and out."

Negative Event: I lost my job.

"Because I lost my job, my family suffered a lot of financial hardship. I thought it meant I was a failure. But I know now that everyone faces setbacks, and my worth as a man and a husband isn't defined only by my employment. I am focusing on being a more loving husband and father, and my family is better because of the time I am spending at home. Besides, that job wasn't my dream. Now I am free to go after what I really want in life."

Negative Event: I got a divorce.

"Because I got a divorce, my kids' lives were turned upside down. It was crushing financially and beat the stuffing out of my self-esteem. But the biggest pain came from the thought of hurting them. I thought it meant I couldn't look anyone in the eye because I would feel like I was just pretending to be successful when I had actually faced such a big failure in my life. But I have learned that good things can come from tough experiences. I can take this to God and know there was a purpose for my divorce. If I hadn't divorced my last wife, I wouldn't have been available to fall in love with my current wife and create a life together. Having gone through divorce before, I can have a more successful marriage to my new wife since I can spot the snares that once tripped me up. In addition, I know I am a better leader and coach to the guys I know because I have gone through the fire myself. I can try to help them avoid some of the mistakes I've made."

Negative Event: I watched my parents go bankrupt.

"Because my parents went bankrupt, we lost our home and had to move in with my grandparents. The other kids made fun of my used clothing, and I felt embarrassed to be poor. I thought it meant I should be afraid of doing anything that might be financially risky. But now I know how to manage my finances well, live a debt-free lifestyle, and have savings built up for a rainy day. It wasn't fun going through it, but my parents' bankruptcy made me stronger. Looking back on it, it helped me learn that we still cared for each other through the tough times, so we were always rich in love."

Negative Event: My father always told me I was stupid.

"Because my father always put me down, I thought it meant that I was worthless and couldn't do anything right. It made me second-guess myself for years. I carried around a feeling of insecurity. But now I know my father's criticism wasn't indicative of my worth; it was just a symptom of his own low self-esteem. Today, I feel sorry for him that he is so down on himself, but his opinion of me doesn't have to be my reality. I have my own identity, free from his criticism, and I know I am a good and worthwhile person. I am also careful to be a loving and encouraging father to my own kids."

Negative Event: My mother was an alcoholic.

"Because my mom was an alcoholic, our home was chaotic. I had to grow up fast and learn to take care of myself. I couldn't count on her to take care of me the way other moms took care of their kids. I tucked her into bed instead of the other way around. Therefore, I thought it meant that I couldn't count on anyone. Now I know that although my mom let me down, that doesn't mean other people will. Many people are responsible, caring, and reliable. Many people keep their word. I have learned to slowly let my guard down and trust other people again."

Negative Event: My father beat me up.

"Because my father was abusive, I grew up feeling terrified. I thought it meant I deserved being treated that way because I was worthless or had done something bad. I now see my father's behavior had nothing to do with me. He was a hurting, hate-filled, and sorry man who was beaten by his own father. He deserves my pity. Every child deserves to grow up feeling safe, secure, and loved, and my father failed in his duty to me. I know I am a good, worthwhile person who is entitled to receive love and should be treated with respect. I am able to stand up for myself today and am stronger because of the terrible experience of my childhood. And as a result, I love on my kids and have broken the cycle of abuse."

Now that you've read some examples, take a moment and consider three anchors you've been dragging around. What did you say to yourself about these events, and how could you rewrite the meaning you attach to the events to create a new and empowering thought?

Because _____, I thought it meant that _____
_____.
But now I know _____
_____.

Because _____, I thought it meant that _____
_____.
But now I know _____
_____.

Because _____, I thought it meant that _____
_____.

But now I know _____

_____.

I am proud of you for taking the time to identify your limiting thoughts and starting to put them in proper perspective. I hope that doing this has challenged you to look at the meaning you attach to the events of your past and take control of any limiting beliefs that have been an unfair burden to you.

CUTTING ANCHOR AND SETTING SAIL

"No one can go back and make a brand-new start. Anyone can start from now and make a brand-new ending."

– Anonymous

There are a multitude of potential anchors. There are literally thousands of books covering every possible situation, but it's obviously not possible to dig into that vast level of detail here. What I hope to do is expand on *some* of the common experiences you may have faced. Many of these examples are focused on your childhood and your relationship with your parents." n this next section, we are going to focus on a select list of anchors to provide some strategies to managing your current behavior. The anchors we will focus on are:

** As we dive into some common anchors typically established during childhood, I want to add one important disclaimer: While we do discuss your parents' behavior, this next section is not a discussion on how you should parent. That isn't the focus of this book. Though I am going to be talking about parenting, in no way is this meant to be a sermon about where you might be slipping up.

- My parents never praised me.
- I received too much praise.
- My parents expected perfection.
- My parents often criticized me.
- I was pushed around.
- My parents were unkind toward me.
- My parent/relative abused me.

My Parents Never Praised Me

Praise is a powerful motivator to take action. It also helps affirm our worth. For many of us, the first and most critical people to whom we look for encouragement are our parents. As kids, we run to catch the football and hope that our dad saw us do it. We study hard for the math quiz and hope that Mom mentions how proud she is of our grade.

It is only natural that we hope to hear our parents speak well of us. Sadly, some parents do this poorly, if at all. Parents burdened with failure in their own life can be slow to praise and quick to criticize, and their children may bear the brunt of their unforgiving viewpoint. Research backs this up. Betty Hart and Todd R. Risley, authors of *Meaningful Differences in the Everyday Experience of Young American Children*, wrote "Research highlights a striking link between encouraging child-raising and class. Half of working-class parents' interactions with their 12-18 month-olds were affirming, versus 80% among the affluent and 20% among those in poverty."[131]

> *Parents burdened with failure in their own life can be slow to praise and quick to criticize.*

I've always found that successful people are quicker to point out what you've done right than other people are. They can often point to an encouraging mentor or parent who nurtured them along the way. When we hope to get that praise from our parents but don't, it can wound deeply.

If a child deserves praise and *doesn't* get it, obviously that can hurt the child's feelings. For example, if a sixth-grade boy who typically gets Cs and Ds decides to study really hard for a math test and instead earns a B+, it is natural that he will come home feeling excited about his accomplishment. The boy is seeking praise from his parent(s). Any normal parent can and should praise such efforts and results. However, if a parent doesn't respond with praise, it shouldn't be surprising that the boy is no longer motivated to go through the same effort again. Failure to praise someone when it is deserved can sting and be remembered for years. How do I know that? Because I am describing the exact situation that happened to me. That isn't to say it shaped my whole view of myself, but here I am, writing this book thirty-eight years later, and I still remember it.

The self-image of a child is developed very early in his or her life. Consider children playing a game with blocks. When they figure out how to put the round wooden peg in the circular hole, they are pleased with themselves, and they look around to any family member who might have seen them in action. They want someone to notice their accomplishment and praise them for it. I have literally witnessed children, including my own, come and look for praise when they accomplish something small. If, for whatever reason, I hadn't noticed what they had done, my kids actually sought out praise. If that need for validation and approval isn't met properly when we are children, we may grow into "approval junkies" when we get older.

Many people in this world are "approval junkies" who can't seem to accomplish even the smallest task without requiring some sort of approval and recognition. They might explain away their craving by saying, "That's just the way I'm wired; I like to receive praise." Now certainly every human being likes to receive praise; please don't misunderstand what I am saying. But some people cannot take action in business, in a marriage, at church, at work, or in their neighborhood until they receive praise for whatever they have done. It's really a tough way to live because no matter how much praise someone receives, it is just never enough.

Mark Goulston and Philip Goldberg, authors of *Get Out of Your Own Way*, write:

> Men long to hear their [fathers] say, "I'm proud of you, son." Men who, as kids, did not have the admiration of their dads feel a gaping deprivation; those who did have it long for sweet boyhood moments they can never recapture. That is why, if you want to see a grown man cry, get him to talk about his father."[132]

It isn't uncommon that grown men will still be working long hours at the office, hoping to hear the words, "I'm proud of you, son," from parents who are out of touch or who might have even passed away.

The antidote for an addiction to praise is to recognize that you don't need someone else to validate your worth. You can validate your own worth. How? By noticing all the things that are good, strong, intelligent, creative, and uplifting about yourself. You may choose to print out a copy of your "Top Five Victories" and "Top Five Talents" that we discussed in Chapter 1: "Know Your Worth" and hang it up on the wall of your office for you to see throughout the day. Or you may choose to paste it to your steering wheel. You may share your list with a friend. You could read it out loud to yourself as an affirmation statement, and you could even make an audio recording of yourself reading the list so you can listen to your personal affirmation statement while commuting.

> *The antidote for an addiction to praise is to recognize that you don't need someone else to validate your worth.*

There are many great ways to keep your mind focused on what is *right* about you instead of what is *wrong* with you. Listen to yourself and ignore the criticism of others. Why would someone else's opinion about you matter as much as, if not more than, your own opinion about yourself? For me personally, I know my worth comes from realizing that I am doing the best I can, according to what God has called me to do. If I have His approval, it's enough.

I Received Too Much Praise

"Our dependency makes slaves out of us, especially if this dependency is a dependency of our self-esteem. If you need encouragement, praise, pats on the back from everybody, then you make everybody your judge." – Fritz Perls

Contrary to what many people believe, praising too broadly or generally can actually cause low self-esteem in children. Some parents give their children a golden star for eating their cereal in the morning or for picking up their socks in their room, and they might even give them a new bicycle if they do their homework on time. The ridiculous list goes on and on.

In extreme cases, the parents don't believe in correcting anything their child does, and they don't believe in spanking. (By the way, I do believe in spanking when it is done in love, to teach the child. I do not condone it if it is done in anger.) If a child is brought up in a home where every action is treated as cause for celebration, the child loses perspective on what praiseworthy behavior actually is. As Tom Ascol says, our kids already think they are the center of the universe. They don't need further help from us to keep them there.

If children grow up in this artificial atmosphere, when they actually get out into the real world and get their first job, they are in for a rude awakening. They will quickly discover they are *not* as good as they've always been told they are and they do *not* get a gold star for every single thing they do. The "house of cards" they've built their self-esteem upon (Mom and Dad's ceaseless and inflated praise) is revealed for its flimsy foundation. Their proverbial self-esteem bubble is burst. As Norman Vincent Peale said, "The trouble with most of us is that we'd rather be ruined by praise than saved by criticism."[133]

From my experience, having mentored many hundreds of people, those individuals who were told through their childhood that they "walked on water" actually do have confidence—for a while. They'll have some initial success, buoyed by the "hot air" that's been pumped into their psyche; perhaps they are good at football or tennis or some other sport. But after a time, they'll notice in other areas of life that reality has set in.

Most importantly, they are not able to cope with setbacks, failure, or criticism. Kids who receive ceaseless praise have no mental callus later to protect themselves against minor criticism; their emotional skin is paper-thin. The first setback or disapproval crushes their false self-image. Because they can't accept criticism, they can't learn and grow as fast as they ought. False self-image is as bad as low self-image because it comes crumbling down so easily.

> *Kids who receive ceaseless praise have no mental callus later to protect themselves against minor criticism; their emotional skin is paper-thin.*

This is not to say that you *shouldn't* praise your kids. By all means, if they do something praiseworthy, let them know! While this isn't a book on parenting, please allow me to offer some friendly suggestions or guidelines on the topic of praise. If your son does a great job mowing the lawn, perhaps you might say, "Jimmy, I noticed how well you cut the grass this time. Last time, you missed a bunch of spots, and we had to talk about it. And this time, it's nearly perfect! What an improvement; I am so proud of you!" That praise is specific and realistic; offering praise in that way is exactly the right thing to do.

Inevitably, each of us will endure a situation that fails to earn praise. That doesn't mean we need to feel discouraged; it's a normal part of everyone's life. Failure to earn praise shouldn't be a soul-crushing experience. We can choose to calmly assess our true strengths and weaknesses and resolve to improve those areas in which we are weak.

For example, if our checkbook is filled with errors and we struggle with handling our finances, we can get help. We can reach out to a friend or colleague who is skilled in the area in which we are not.

We are not a "loser" or a "failure" because we discover we aren't automatically the best at everything we do, for no one ever is. It just means we have a problem in a specific area in our life, a problem which is solvable with proper guidance.

My Parents Often Criticized Me

"The final proof of greatness lies in being able to endure criticism without resentment."

– Elbert Hubbard

Our parents may have not only failed to say many positive things; they may have actively pointed out everything we did wrong. They may have said, "You're such a disappointment. You'll never amount to anything. You're no good. You're a loser." These words are hurtful, and anyone who speaks that way to their children is wrong to do so.

It's always sad to me when I hear of this, let alone see this bad behavior. For example, our sons play football, and at their games and practices, we get to associate with all different kinds of people: some fun, some nice, and some who are, well, *interesting*. This next story is not to criticize a mother but rather to illustrate how damaging a parent can be without even knowing it.

At the football games and practices, we have seen a mother by herself with two boys, one about eight years old and the other only three years old. This mother routinely lets the three-year-old run amuck at practices and games, many times allowing him to go places where he risks getting hurt (and sometimes does get hurt). On top of her poor supervision of him, she sadly appears to have a very short fuse with this three-year-old boy. She frequently yells at him, insulting him in a worse way than two drunken football fans watching a game in a bar. On one occasion, my wife Amy and I actually heard her say to her friend about her younger son, "You want to see the dumbest kid in the world? Here he is; look at this little douche bag." Her friend seemed shocked, but didn't appear to know what to say. This little boy is only three! If this is how she speaks about her boy to her friends in public, can you imagine how she speaks to her children alone in private? Can you imagine how this will shape his view of himself as he grows older, listening to the person who is supposed to be the most nurturing person in his life? (The mother I've described is most likely a massively stressed-out mom who loves her kids but just doesn't have a clue.)

I am embarrassed to even write those words but felt it necessary to illustrate how negative influences can affect our lives, and often we don't even know it. I hope your parents didn't treat you this way, but I know that many people reading this book might have been on the receiving end of such treatment. While no one has perfect parents, it is wrong for people to speak that way of their children. If your parents did so, I empathize. However, you do not need to be limited by their beliefs about you.

This sort of unrelenting criticism is going to have an effect on anyone, particularly a child. If you've had to go through this, there is a chance that you feel more sensitive than others to the criticism you face as you get older. Injuries someone faces in childhood can stain their self-esteem for years. As Sally Field said, "It took me a long time not to judge myself through someone else's eyes."[134]

Criticism you faced as a child can leave you even more sensitive to criticism in adulthood. Without thick skin to handle critics, you might feel that you can't embark on a bold new adventure in relationships, in your career, or in business. If you are going to be successful, you are going to have your share of critics throwing tomatoes at you. Knowing that this is inevitable and arming yourself with defense measures are the best ways to prepare for what's to come. As LeBron James says, "I like criticism. It makes you strong."[135]

> *If you are going to be successful, you are going to have your share of critics throwing tomatoes at you.*

In his book *Healing the Shame That Binds You*, author John Bradshaw shares four strategies for dealing with critics. He refers to these techniques as *clarifying, confessing, confirming,* and *confusing.*[136] The next time you face a critic, you might choose to pull one of these responses out of the toolbox and use it.

- **Clarifying**. Whenever a critic starts to cut into you, simply reply with clarifying questions. For example, if someone says, "I don't like the brown pants you are wearing," you could ask, "What is it about my brown pants you don't like?" This will probably surprise them. Usually people respond defensively to critics, but you aren't going to be suckered into doing so.

  Returning to our example, the critic might reply, "Well, I think they look cheap."

  So then you could ask, "What is it about cheap pants you don't like?" By asking these kinds of questions, you force the critic to think logically. This is exhausting for many people and especially critics, and they are going to run out of steam long before you do.

- **Confessing**. When you actually do something wrong, own up to it. If you forgot to refill the coffee pot, own it. Simply say, "You're right. I forgot to refill the coffee pot. I apologize." And leave it at that. Every human being makes mistakes, and this shouldn't come as a surprise to your critics. They have made many mistakes as well. Once you've apologized, that's the end of it. If they bring it up again, you can let them know you've already apologized for it once, and it's time to move on.

- **Confirming**. This technique involves confirming your worth to yourself and to your critic during the height of their verbal attack on you. Remember you are a worthwhile person, regardless of what a critic says. We can't be hurt unless we believe some of the criticism is true. When it comes to hearing criticism and being hurt by it, as Ram Dass said, "Your problem is you're too busy holding onto your unworthiness."[137] We have discussed how to recognize our worth in chapter 1. Remember those ideas and what you've learned. When someone is being unfairly harsh in their criticism, even attacking your character, it's time to confirm your worth. You can say, "No matter what you say or do to me, I am still a worthy person. I know what I'm doing is right in God's eyes, and you aren't God."

- **Confusing**. The final strategy should only be used in specific situations when the relationship is not very important to you (i.e., you don't care about finding resolution or having a long-term relationship with this person). When the other person says something critical, say something confusing. If they point out you did a poor job on your report in front of your boss, say something out of left-field, such as "Wow, this office is replete with vacuous sycophants!" (That translates to "Wow, there sure are a lot of empty-headed boot-lickers working here!") As your head-scratching critic stands there looking totally confused at the meaning of the big words you've used, just stroll away with a happy smile on your face.

By applying some of these techniques, you can deflect the sting of criticism. Just remember, critics are fallible too. They aren't all-knowing and all-powerful; they're just the guy in the cubicle beside you, or the jock from high school, or your dad. Learn to ignore what they say because they are managing their own self-esteem issues. Remember always the words of Robert Brault: "We all have our limitations, but when we listen to our critics, we also have theirs."[138]

My Parents Expected Perfection

The mother of a friend of mine recalls a time she brought home her report card from high school. Beaming with pride, she showed her dad, a military veteran from World War II, that she had received a 98 percent. Her gruff father simply snorted and said, "What happened to the other 2 percent?" She was crushed. It was just one example of the critical environment that set up a pattern in her life. No matter how hard she tried, she couldn't be perfect and never measured up in her father's eyes. His love for her, among other things, was conditional on her perfect performance. This was obviously an impossible task, as absolutely no one is going to get it right all the time.

Authors Susan Forward and Craig Buck say in *Toxic Parents*, "Perfectionistic parents seem to operate under the illusion that if they can just get their children to be perfect, they will be a perfect family."[139] This is obviously not correct and is a damaging belief to hold. Once the seed of perfectionism is planted, it opens up Pandora's Box to a host of psychological anchors. Because perfectionists fear making mistakes, they are less likely to take risks. When the inevitable mistake does occur, they treat it as a strike against their personal worth rather than a normal incident that befalls everyone.

> *Because perfectionists have a fear of making mistakes, they are less likely to take risks.*

Consider this excerpt from an article from *Psychology Today* entitled "Pitfalls of Perfectionism": "Concern with mistakes and doubts about actions are absolute prerequisites for perfectionism. Perfectionists fear that a mistake will lead others to think badly of them; the performance aspect is intrinsic to their view of themselves."[140] Fear of making mistakes also paralyzes someone's ability to learn and grow. You can't master anything, including hitting a baseball or playing piano, if you can't be at peace with striking out or hitting a bad note. It's a great quality to aim high, but know that everyone stumbles at some point. As actor Michael J. Fox says, "I am careful not to confuse excellence with perfection. Excellence, I can reach for; perfection is God's business."[141] Finally,

> *When the inevitable mistake does occur, perfectionists treat it as a strike against their personal worth rather than a normal incident that occurs to everyone.*

214

perfectionists may quit something too quickly because they won't allow themselves to be bad at something long enough to learn how to be good at it.

If you have lived your life with a perfectionism anchor and are fearful of making mistakes, here are some strategies to help you reclaim your confidence and ward off excessive perfectionism. These strategies are:

1. Understand the Law of Diminishing Returns.
2. Weigh the Actual Consequences of Imperfection.
3. Survey Other People.
4. Indulge in Imperfection.

1. Understand the Law of Diminishing Returns.

To combat perfectionism, consider the idea of the Law of Diminishing Returns. The basic idea of this principle is that the closer you get to perfection, massive increases in your effort produce smaller and smaller improvements in the quality of your work. For example, let's suppose a college student needs to expend a certain amount of effort on writing a paper to get a grade of 80 percent. To get a 90 percent doesn't require a 10 percent increase in effort but more like a 50 percent increase in effort. To get from 90 percent to 95 percent on the paper requires another massive increase in effort, and getting from 95 percent to 98 percent requires a crushing amount of extra effort. At a certain point, you may want to ask yourself, "Is the increase in quality worth it for the effort I am about to expend?"

One way to manage this is to assign yourself a deadline. You can say, "By 5 p.m. today, I will submit this report, whether it is perfect or not." That way you won't get trapped into perfectionism paralysis. Another technique is to resolve to be satisfied with 90 percent. An employee who is satisfied with 90 percent perfection is likely to deliver much more output than someone who is obsessed with getting 100 percent and gets bogged down in the details on one single project.

John Lasseter, head of famed movie studio Pixar, famously said, "Our films don't get finished; they just get released."[142] If a movie studio like Pixar that produces some of the most amazing movies in Hollywood can be satisfied with releasing an unfinished product, surely we can too!

2. **Weigh the Actual Consequences of Imperfection.**

If you are paralyzed with worry about not being perfect, ask yourself what the consequences will be if you do something that isn't perfect. One challenge for perfectionists is they imagine a worst-case scenario and exaggerate the consequences of an error in their mind.

One challenge for perfectionists is they imagine a worst-case scenario and exaggerate the consequences of an error in their mind.

Imagine the worst possible scenario. Consider handing in a report that you have done a good job on, but you worry it isn't yet perfect. If you are thinking, "If this report isn't perfect, I will be fired," you may want to test your theory. The chance that you will be fired for a report that is only 99 percent perfect might be exaggerated. Check your report for errors *once*, double-check it, and then hand it in. You might be relieved to discover the world continues turning even though you used a semicolon where a period would have been a better choice.

3. **Survey Other People.**

How imperfect are other people? It may surprise you to discover that fully functioning adult human beings actually walk around making mistakes all day long without spontaneously combusting. Your co-worker only spends four minutes doing her hair, and several hairs are now out of place. Surprise! She is still enjoyed and respected at work and able to do her job with absolute professionalism and effectiveness. You visit your sister's home and notice the laundry piling up in her children's closet. Surprise! They are well-adjusted and delightful kids who are healthy and happy and doing well in school.

Think about the job that you believe *must* be perfect, and ask the people around you what amount of time or effort they put into doing it. Maybe you spend twelve hours every Saturday cleaning your home top to bottom, in crevices other people could never even find. Maybe you actually clean *under* the stove and fridge. Maybe you clean your house before the maid service arrives to clean it for you! (I had to work through that one today with my wife, Amy.) Take a survey at work and ask people, "How long do you spend cleaning your home each weekend?" You might be shocked to discover that, compared to others, you are overdoing it. And the shocking truth is that most people are surviving just fine with a "pretty good" effort in many areas.

> *The shocking truth is that most people are surviving just fine with a "pretty good" effort in many areas.*

4. Indulge in Imperfection.

Notice the areas of your life where you indulge in perfectionism, and resolve to push your limits. Deliberately do something that isn't perfect, and monitor your thinking and your emotions. Do this as a way of weaning yourself off your psychological habit. With practice, you can gently teach yourself to lighten up, let your hair down, and not feel a need for everything to always be right. Here are some examples of things that may cause you anxiety and of actions you can take to shake off perfectionism.

Perfectionistic Anxiety	Imperfect Action
"Before ever trying to do a business presentation, I must first be able to do it perfectly."	Learn by doing. Every time you do a business presentation, you get better. Consider how you can improve each time.
"My kitchen must be picture-perfect."	Deliberately leave a dish in the sink.
"I must match all my socks before putting them away."	Stuff all your socks in the dresser drawer without matching them.
"When someone makes a mistake at work, I must correct them."	When someone makes a mistake, let someone else correct them.
"My child's clothing is not color-coordinated."	Let them dress themselves.
"I don't want my spouse to do a certain chore because he or she won't do it as perfectly as I do."	Let her or him handle it, and no matter what the outcome, just smile and say nothing!

I Was Pushed Around

Whether the schoolyard bully, a rough older brother, or really unpleasant parents are responsible, it can be very damaging to our psyche to be pushed around. We might believe that this treatment is universal and ceaseless and that we will never escape it. Obviously that's not correct because over time, our life situation changes. But while the bullying is happening, it can be crushing to our spirit.

We may start to believe it's easiest to just accept it, to swallow our wounded pride, and to say nothing that will rock the boat. We may even believe we have, in some way, caused such treatment. However, accepting unfair and abusive treatment can cause lasting damage to our confidence.

You may have developed the habit of letting other people push you around. Now it's time to stand up for yourself. Earlier we discussed the concept of posture. It lies somewhere between being a bully and being a doormat. The underlying principle of posture is *respect*. You have respect for yourself, which a doormat lacks, and you have respect for others, which a bully lacks. If you have posture, you stand up for yourself when someone else is being rude, unfair, overly aggressive, or even abusive. You take accountability for any mistake you have made, but you don't accept any extra guilt the other person may wish to burden you with. You expect and demand, diplomatically, to be treated fairly and politely.

> *The underlying principle of posture is respect. You have respect for yourself, which a doormat lacks, and you have respect for others, which a bully lacks.*

Let's imagine an unfair situation where someone has crossed the boundaries and is taking advantage of you. How about intrusive family members who constantly stop by without notice and invite themselves into your home?

Doormat response:

"Hey guys, what a surprise. Please come in. We are just in the middle of dinner. It was very thoughtless of us not to have planned enough extra food in case of surprise guests; here, you can have ours. We should be cutting back on our meals anyway to keep up with our diets."

Response with *posture*:

> "Hi, guys; nice to see you. Man, I wish you had called in advance because we are just finishing dinner. We are always happy to see you. But in the future, please give us a quick call if you are planning on stopping by. That way, we can make sure to have enough food to invite you to join us for dinner."

You aren't getting angry, but you are clearly requesting a change in behavior and setting some boundaries.

Keep in mind that doormats have a bad habit of making up a false reason why they can't honor a request. This might create a new problem because they risk having the aggressor offer a solution to their false objection. For instance, they might say, "I'd like to stay late and do your report, but I can't because my laptop is broken. Otherwise, I'd work all weekend on it!"

The aggressor might say, "Hey, no problem. You can borrow *my* laptop!" Now the doormat is stuck because the false objection has been handled. The next stammered false response might be handled just as well.

If you don't want to do something, simply say no and leave it at that. You don't need to explain or defend your position. In fact, you can tell the other person exactly that. When relatives ask you why you can't work all through the weekend baking cookies for their fund-raiser, you

> *If you don't want to do something, simply say no and leave it at that.*

might simply say, "I can appreciate your curiosity. The reason is personal; what I am telling you is I am unavailable to work overtime this weekend but would be happy to help you with your project on Monday." That's not to say you shouldn't serve others and sacrifice to move ahead, but please draw the line at being a doormat. Stand up for yourself!

In their book *Impossible to Please*, authors Neil Lavender and Alan A. Cavaiola offer some rapid-fire phrases for communicating with posture with controlling co-workers, bosses, and family members:

➤ "I know how busy you are. I have a lot of work to do as well, which I know is important to you. Which task would you rather I do?"

➤ "I was thinking about our plans for the holidays. I know how committed you are to going to your mother's. I was thinking about us going to my mother's instead."

➤ "I see the predicament you are in with getting the Jones report done tonight. Unfortunately I have a prior commitment this evening that I cannot reschedule. Perhaps I can come in early tomorrow, and we can work on the Jones report then?"

➤ "I know your mind is made up about what you concluded is the right thing to do, but I'd like to ask you to consider my point of view as well."

➤ "I know you've been dead-set against my proposal. The one thing I ask is you keep an open mind and give some consideration to my ideas."

By standing up for yourself and exhibiting mutual respect, you stop the intrusive or disrespectful behaviors of others.

If you've been pushed around your whole life, it's time to cut that anchor. Recognize that you deserve to be treated with respect, and, in coming to that realization, you know that others deserve the same. You aren't just going to feel empowered and start to act like a bully. Your newfound confidence will allow you to carry yourself with grace and diplomacy. Resolve to stand up for yourself!

My Parents Were Unkind toward Me

"When you hold resentment toward another, you are bound to that person or condition by an emotional link that is stronger than steel. Forgiveness is the only way to dissolve that link and get free."

– Catherine Ponder

Some parents are flat-out unqualified for the job. They might be prone to angry outbursts, struggle with addictions, or level unfair criticism. Some irritating parents might have simply nit-picked your wardrobe choices, and some horrific parents we will talk about in the next section might have been brutally violent criminals. Whatever your experience, how they treated you can create massive anchors.

Dan Neuharth, author of *If You Had Controlling Parents*,[143] has this to say about accepting responsibility for the treatment we endured at the hands of our parents:

> ➢ You aren't responsible for what your parents did to you; *they* are.

However, once you've recognized that truth, here is Neuharth's follow-up thought:

> ➢ Your parents aren't responsible for what you do with your life now; *you* are.

We own our current reality. We own our current decisions. We own the results of our behavior. Just as our parents were responsible for how they treated us in the past, we are responsible for how we treat ourselves today. We can finger point and cast blame until we reach our deathbed, and it won't change one moment of our childhood experience. However, we can look back on that experience and learn, grow, and become stronger because of it.

It's possible your parents were self-absorbed, focused on popularity or on keeping up appearances. They may have had low self-esteem themselves or wished to live vicariously through you. Some parents want to see you score the game-winning touchdown to relive their high school glory on the gridiron, while other parents may sabotage your goals out of their own jealousy. There is an insidious saying: "Don't rise above your raisin's." Translated without the Southern drawl, that phrase means, "Don't outshine your parents." In other words, if they didn't go to college, start a business, have a happy marriage, or whatever else, neither should you. To do so, some parents wrongly conclude, would be disrespectful to them.

It's possible that your parents were or are controlling. Parents who are controlling often feel that they are right to be so. In her book *Controlling People: How to Recognize, Understand and Deal with People Who Try to Control You*, author Patricia Evans says, "Perpetrators usually believe that their oppressive actions are necessary, even right. Their behavior is actually the opposite: unnecessary and wrong."[144]

Controlling parents can define themselves and their worth through their child's behavior. If the child makes a mistake, controlling parents think, it must mean *they* (the parents) are bad. If the child succeeds, the parents reason, it means their controlling behavior is validated. This unhealthy connection can lead the parent to meddling in the child's affairs, second-guessing the child's decisions, and standing in as the Monday-morning quarterback after the game: "If you'd only listened to me, this wouldn't have happened. I'm your mother, and Mother knows best." In their book *Toxic Parents,* authors Susan Forward and Craig Buck describe the problem of controlling parents:

> *Controlling parents can define themselves and their worth through their child's behavior.*

Children who are not encouraged to do, to try, to explore, to master, and to risk failure, often feel helpless and inadequate. Over-controlled by fearful, anxious parents, these children often become fearful and anxious themselves. This makes it difficult for them to mature. When they develop through adolescence and adulthood, many of them never outgrow the need for ongoing parental guidance and control. As a result, their parents continue to invade, manipulate, and frequently dominate their lives.

The fear of not being needed motivates many controlling parents to perpetuate this sense of powerlessness in their children. These parents have an unhealthy fear of the "empty nest syndrome," the inevitable sense of loss that all parents experience when their children finally leave home. So much of a controlling parent's identity is tied up in the parental role that he or she feels betrayed and abandoned when the child becomes independent.

What makes a controlling parent so insidious is that the domination usually comes in the guise of concern. Phrases such as, "this is for your own good," "I'm only doing this for you," and, "only because I love you so much," all mean the same thing: "I'm doing this because I'm so afraid of losing you that I'm willing to make you miserable."[14]

There are so many things our parents may have done wrong. They may have been alcoholics, they may have walked out on us, they may have exposed us to crime, or they may have cheated on each other. The list of potential failings is long and heartbreaking. Whatever our parents' behavior, it is likely caused by the script they adopted due to the garbage they themselves faced as children.

Trying to manage your parents' behavior is like the hurting child in *you* trying to deal with the hurting child in *them*. We can't cut away our own anchors while we are more worried about Mom and Dad's emotional well-being than our own. That means that while it may risk upsetting them, standing up for yourself, setting boundaries, saying no, refusing to accept guilt, or having a difficult conversation should be the higher priority.

> *Trying to manage your parents' behavior is like the hurting child in you trying to deal with the hurting child in them.*

In order to reach a place of healing and cut your anchors loose, it can be helpful to examine the source of your parents' behavior. For example, if your parents never said, "I love you," it may be that their parents never said it to them. If your parents were cold or overly critical, it may not come as a surprise that their parents were probably critical of them. Mark Goulston and Philip Goldberg have this to say on how such a lack of affection can be perpetuated:

> In many cases, what you do not get from your parents is precisely what your parents never received from their own. Because it is hard for them to give what they haven't received they end up mimicking their own upbringing or perpetuating the deprivation in other ways. The key to breaking the family cycle is: ...give to your parents what they never got. By tapping into their hidden yearning, you might just free them to give you what you need.[146]

Each generation has a choice to pass down bad behavior, and unfortunately, some parents may never learn how to be better. You have a choice to stop any bad behavior in its tracks. Maybe it's something as small as your parent never saying, "I love you" or "I'm proud of you." Perhaps they were also starved of love as children. If that is the case, one thing you may choose to do is say to them what they yearned for from their parents. Greet them at the door and surprise them with a warm hug, saying, "I love you." You may be surprised to find this is sometimes a highly emotional and cathartic experience.

Another key principle in managing the damaged relationship with a parent is to simply give up hope that they will change. This comes from Dr. Laura Schlessinger's excellent book *Bad Childhood, Good Life*. In it she writes, "If I have a Chihuahua and want him to be a Doberman, he will not turn into a Doberman no matter how nicely I treat him, or how much I hope it were true."[147] She goes on to mention that some parents just don't have the intelligence, insight, integrity, or desire to change their behavior or beliefs. If your dad no-shows every family outing, there is a good chance he will no-show the next one, no matter how much you wish he would change. If your mom criticizes the way you dress your kids, fold your laundry, or manage your checkbook, she isn't likely to change, no matter how badly you wish her to. Choose instead to give up hope of your parents ever changing, make peace with that fact, and move on.

Finally, we can also choose to forgive. This is particularly appropriate if the person's behavior toward you has been frustrating, irritating, or even hurtful. However, if someone's behavior was violent or evil, such as physical or sexual abuse, you shouldn't feel forced by anyone to forgive your abuser if you don't wish to do so. Forgiving someone is not an *obligation*; it is a personal decision to help with *your* healing. However, I *encourage* you to forgive.

Please understand: there's a big difference between forgiveness and reconciliation. The person you forgive may never desire to reconcile with you, and that's okay. But if you don't forgive, you're the one left carrying the emotional baggage around. Unfortunately, it's likely that the person who sinned against you *doesn't care* whether you ever forgive him or her; that's just further evidence that *you're* the one carrying the baggage. As I wrote in *Voyage of the Viking*, forgiveness has less to do with whether the person should be let off the hook for his or her bad behavior than with letting *yourself* off the hook.[148]

Ann Landers says, "Hanging onto resentment is letting someone you despise live rent-free in your head."[149] We might be angry with our parents. We might want them to apologize for something they did. We might even want to be rid of them and the negative memories they've created. But the truth of the matter is that hanging on to anger just means hanging on to the hurt. Laurel Lee said, "A personal offense is like a scratch on a phonograph record. I couldn't move my thoughts beyond my pain. It kept repeating, as if I were stuck within its grooves. There was only one way to play beyond it. I had to forgive them, so my heart could take its form again."[150]

It takes a tremendous amount of energy to be angry. It is exhausting. It consumes your focus, when your focus could be directed to priorities like loving your family and doing a great job. Being angry changes the way you treat the people around you. Eventually, you need to decide that focusing on how you've been wronged isn't the best way to live an exceptional life. Forgiving your parents for their bad behavior frees you to direct your mental focus, energy, and love elsewhere.

Remaining angry with someone is like locking yourself in a prison of resentment and hatred and throwing away the key. You are simply punishing yourself. You need to give yourself permission to move past the hurt, resentment, and anger and move on. As Henry Ward Beecher said, "'I can forgive, but I cannot forget,' is only another way of saying,

> *Remaining angry with someone is like locking yourself in a prison of resentment and hatred and throwing away the key.*

I will not forgive. Forgiveness ought to be like a cancelled note—torn in two, and burned up, so that it never can be shown against one."[151]

My Parent/Relative Abused Me

"Although the world is full of suffering, it is also full of overcoming it." – *Helen Keller*

Parents have a very important and specific job: to love us, nurture us, protect us, help instill into us proper morals and values, and prepare us to face the world as adults. Children have a right to receive love, shelter, and safety. Sadly, some parents are woefully unprepared for the rigors of caring for and guiding a human life. Because of this, many children grow up in tough situations, and the treatment they receive at the hands of their parents may leave scars that last forever.

If you have suffered abuse of any kind, whether verbal, emotional, physical, or sexual, it is important to understand that you aren't to blame. You were the child, and your parents were grown adults with the responsibility to love and protect you. If they failed to do so, it isn't because you are not worthy of love; *you are*. It isn't that you don't

227

have value; *you do*. It isn't that you did something bad to deserve it; you *did not*. If you suffered any form of abuse, *it was not your fault*.

In some ways, we must learn to remember, and in other ways, we must learn to forget. We need to remember all the good things we have ever done and manage our thinking around those bad things that may have been done to us that we think somehow devalue us. Obviously, any form of abuse severely affects people. If someone reading this book has endured any abuse, I am truly sorry that has happened. Those events do affect someone's confidence and self-image, but they shouldn't.

Your worth as a person is not determined by what other people do

> *Your worth as a person is not determined by what other people do to you.*

to you. We certainly don't want to make light of it, and this book is obviously not a place to "fix" those issues, but no matter what you've gone through, it wasn't your fault. I am reminded of what Robin Williams's character in the movie *Good Will Hunting* says to Matt Damon's character Will, a troubled but brilliant young man who was severely beaten by his father. Robin Williams's character keeps repeating, "Will, it's not your fault," until Matt Damon's character breaks down sobbing in release.[152] In their book *The Courage to Heal: A Guide for Women Survivors of Child Sexual Abuse*, authors Ellen Bass and Laura Davis have this to say about accepting blame:

> Children often believe that they are to blame for being sexually abused. Many adult survivors continue to hold this belief. Although large numbers of children and adolescents are abused, it is never the fault of any of them. Yet there are many reasons why survivors assume that blame.

The authors go on to share some common reasons for accepting blame:

- Survivors were told explicitly by their abuser that it was their fault, either for being a "bad" girl, for dressing provocatively, for not doing enough to stop the abuser, or for secretly wanting the abuse.

- Survivors might have been punished when someone did find out.
- The religion of the survivor might have actually blamed the survivor. As the authors put it:

Your religion might have told you that you were a sinner, unclean, damned to hell. You might have become convinced you were unlovable, even to God. One woman said: "That little incested girl inside of me is still waiting for the lightning to strike because I told people what happened to me. If I say, 'I think it was my dad,' I'll burn up in hellfire."

The authors conclude by saying:

There are less obvious reasons why survivors blame themselves. It is a stark and terrifying realization for a child to see how vulnerable and powerless she actually is. Thinking that you were bad, that you had some influence in how you were treated, gave a sense of control, though illusory. And perceiving yourself as bad allowed for the future possibility that you could become good and thus, things could improve.

In truth, nothing you did caused the abuse; nothing within your power could have stopped it. Your world was an unsafe place where the adults who abused you were untrustworthy and out of control, where your well-being, and sometimes your very life, was in danger. This perspective, though more realistic, is more distressing for many children than thinking that they were bad and somehow responsible for the abuse.[153]

In the words of Dr. Patti Feuereisen, author of *Invisible Girls: The Truth about Sexual Abuse*, there are three things to remember for a survivor of sexual abuse:

1. The abuse was not your fault.
2. You have nothing to be ashamed of.
3. You deserve great love and happiness in your life.

One of the most insidious aspects of any kind of abuse is how it diminishes your self-worth long after the abuse has ended. You may feel at some level you were bad and deserved it. You may even feel that you are worthless because of the horrific treatment you endured. Hear me loud and clear: Every child deserves to be treated with love, respect, and dignity. Every child deserves to feel safe, secure, and protected from harm.

> *Every child deserves to be treated with love, respect and dignity. Every child deserves to feel safe, secure and protected from harm.*

If you question your worth, the best antidote is to read your Bible and get closer to God. He is the one who made you, and we can all draw our worth through the finished work of His Son, Jesus Christ. Review the content we've discussed in Chapter 1: "Know Your Worth." Please also review the Appendix, where I include a list of recommended reading on this and other topics.

Remember, you have tremendous gifts, talents, and intrinsic value. Remember that a crumpled dollar bill still retains its full value, no matter how it is treated. You can stomp a diamond into the mud, and it's still worth a great deal. You are irreplaceable.

FORGIVE YOURSELF FOR PAST MISTAKES

"You can't undo anything you've already done, but you can face up to it. You can tell the truth. You can seek forgiveness. And let God do the rest."

– Author unknown

Some of the greatest tragedies are not what other people have done to us but rather what we have done to ourselves. We all make mistakes, but some errors seem so great that the effects are tough to shake off. Situations such as adultery, addictions, crime, divorce, bankruptcy, or even failed relationships with friends and family can leave the weight of regret sitting heavily on our shoulders.

We can't go back and make yesterday any better, but we can make amends today. We have control over today and what we do now. We can turn over a new leaf. We can apologize to anyone we've hurt and learn from our mistakes to become a better person.

Whatever you feel you have done wrong, real or imagined, ask yourself this: *"When will I have punished myself enough?"* If you feel you must continue to bear the burden of your error, consider what Joshua Loth Liebman said: "We achieve inner health only through forgiveness—the forgiveness not only of others but also of ourselves."[154] In order to help others, to be a blessing in the lives of people around us and make the world a better place, we must start by forgiving ourselves.

When we have made a grave error, especially a moral error, the anchor that drags us down is guilt.

If you are carrying guilt, please consider whether any of it was bestowed upon you by other people. If so, drop it. Nathaniel Branden, author of How to Raise Your Self-Esteem, asks, "By whose standards am I judging [myself]?" Consider the example of a family that has a strict doctrine that dictates the parents induce an arranged marriage for their daughter. The daughter stands up for herself and chooses a mat whom she loves dearly. The parents, based on their value system, feel a profound sense of shame and embarrassment in their community and cast a pall of guilt over their daughter. Should she feel guilt? According to her parents, *yes*. And if she chooses to accept that guilt, she will diminish her sense of self-esteem. By accepting the guilt

> *If you are carrying guilt, please consider whether any guilt you carry was bestowed upon you by other people. If so, drop it.*

231

placed upon her by other people, she cripples her self-esteem, and in turn, her self-confidence suffers.

Are you feeling guilty because you haven't lived up to someone else's expectations? Maybe your father expected you to take over the family farm, and you wanted to go to college and become a doctor. Your parents bemoan your choice at every family gathering and are quick to point out the hardships your "selfish" decision has caused. Should you accept their guilt?

Branden goes on to ask a follow-up question: *"What do I really think about this issue?"* Maybe if you dig down deep enough, you aren't really feeling guilt; perhaps you are feeling resentment or frustration at being forced to make a decision against your wishes or anger at the unfairness of the treatment you are enduring. Maybe you are feeling fear. Perhaps you are scared of someone exploding in anger at your actions, and you fear the inevitable conflict.

However, let's consider when you have failed your own standards and made a genuine mistake, big or small. What is the value in vilifying yourself and beating up on yourself? Certainly you want to make sure you don't repeat your mistake. But is punishing yourself the key to ensuring you don't relapse in your regrettable behavior? You might feel you deserve punishment, but feeling bad doesn't really arm you with the tools to be strong the next time you face temptation.

> *What is the value in vilifying yourself and beating up on yourself?*

Consider the example of people dealing with a drug addiction. Imagine they have managed to go a couple of months in a row staying clean, but then they relapse. It would be normal for them to beat themselves up. And they certainly should face the consequences of their actions.

But imagine what happens to their ability to stay strong in the face of temptation if they habitually punish themselves with a verbal beating: "I'm such a loser. I can't believe I did drugs again. I have totally failed. I am a screwup. No wonder I can't get my life on track."

Would it be any surprise if their very next thought was: "I may as well do drugs again. Who cares if I wreck myself even more? I am a screwup anyway."

This negative thinking can be applied to almost any mistake or failed goal. Whether you fall off the wagon with addiction, cheat on your diet, fight with your spouse, or fail to call a client when you said you would, the greatest predictor of whether this will be a momentary and isolated slipup or a new pattern of repeated behavior is the story you tell yourself about it. Is it a defining moment to chart a new and positive course toward your goals, or is it a mistake that dooms you to a life of misery and failure? *You get to choose!*

If you decide to indulge in beating up on yourself, your self-criticism can further weaken your self-esteem to the point that you relapse and repeat the original bad behavior. There is a point where punishing yourself actually makes the problem worse. Consider that you are more likely to follow through on correct values and principles when you hold yourself in high esteem. That does *not* mean you condone your bad behavior. It means you *affirm* your inherent worth and resolve to improve.

Here is the internal thinking when you are feeling strong and confident and assured in your self-worth: "Hey, I've screwed up before, but I deserve to treat myself with more respect. I am capable of better behavior than this. Inside I am a good person. I've licked this before, and I am going to stay strong."

Kick the monkey off your back, no matter what the problem is. Maybe it's gambling. Maybe it's being a compulsive liar. Maybe it's not spending enough time with your kids. Maybe it's drug addiction. I believe the ultimate and final fix is to surrender to God. Here is an example prayer to help overcome your sin:

"Father in Heaven, I have sinned again. I am not able to beat this addiction alone. I want to turn from these drugs and put my faith in Jesus. I know He has paid the price for me. I surrender to Him now. I ask for the power to resist these drugs. I fill my heart with Your Spirit. I give my life to You now."

Forgive yourself, stay strong, and commit to living by the standards you know you are capable of reaching.

SUMMARY

We've dealt with some very deep and even uncomfortable topics in this chapter. I truly believe that, for you to have the confidence you desire, at some point it is necessary to confront the demons of the past and take back any control you may have lost. Everyone has anchors that are holding them back. By recognizing what your anchors are and where they came from, you can change the script running in your mind and move forward with your life. No matter what has happened to you in the past, it is not the complete definition of who you are, and you can create a brighter future because of your awareness and courage.

Key Points:

1. An "anchor" is the negative thinking or hang-up that gets created when we go through an emotionally upsetting or even scarring experience.
2. Even top leaders can have anchors and probably do.
3. Anchors can be caused by a current event or experience, but often they are caused by upsetting childhood experiences, negative voices from the past, and guilt or regret we have over mistakes we've made.

4. To cut an anchor loose, we must first know the meaning we've attached to the event. Use the following statement template to help you discover your anchors and rewrite their meaning: "Because [this happened], I thought it meant [something bad]. But now I know [it can mean something more positive]."

5. If you crave praise from others, realize you don't need others to validate your worth.

6. If you struggle with perfectionism:
   a. Understand the law of diminishing returns,
   b. Weigh the actual consequence of imperfection,
   c. Take a poll, and
   d. Indulge in imperfection.

7. If you struggle with criticism, remember four options in your toolbox to handle a critic: clarifying, confessing, confirming, and confusing.

8. If you have been pushed around, remember that people with posture have self-respect as well as respect for others. Stand up for yourself!

9. If a parent hurt you either emotionally, verbally, physically, or sexually, remember that you aren't responsible for that behavior, past or present; *the perpetrator* is responsible. Survivors are not at fault and should not blame themselves. However, your parents aren't responsible for your current behavior either; *you* are.

10. Forgive yourself for past mistakes, and hold yourself to a higher standard of excellence.

6

FIGHT FEAR WITH FAITH

We have nearly come to the end of our time together. Throughout this book, I have shared principles of examining our true worth, principles of success thinking, methods of communicating with others, ways of changing how we walk and dress, and even some of the tough events of our past that hold us back. We have analyzed how our own thinking and behavior may be a barrier to achieving massive success. We have done all these things with the specific goal of developing more confidence in our lives.

Despite all the well-researched and time-tested methods we have covered so far, we need to conclude this book by circling back to the critical point I first made in the introduction. While I would never shy away from sharing the truth that I have learned, I am sensitive that you may think and feel very differently than I do. I pray that I do not offend you by sharing my beliefs. I realize that many of you reading this book may not be Christian. You may be Jewish, Muslin, Hindu, atheist, agnostic, or of another faith entirely. However, if I didn't share these points from my heart, please understand I would be a hypocrite. So, taking a deep breath, I repeat what I said at the beginning of the book: my ultimate confidence comes not from belief in myself, but from belief that I am doing what God has called me to do and living, to the best of my ability, for His honor and glory.

> *Ultimate confidence comes not from belief in oneself, but from belief in God.*

I may choose to fight off my fears only by using people skills, positive attitude statements, better posture, or saying no to my overbearing relatives. These are still excellent strategies which will *aid* me in my confidence. But I must keep them in proper context: those strategies are still only "behavior modification" of a sort. Not one of those behavior strategies comes close in comparison to my confidence in God.

Since I have found Christ, I am way more confident than I was before. I am confident because I know I am called to serve Him—as a Christian, as a husband, as a father, as a leader in God's world, in church, in my community, and in business. Now, let me be abundantly clear: *faith in God is* not *a means to an end,* if my goal

> *Once I knew my eternal salvation was assured, the day-to-day stuff no longer rattled me.*

is only to build confidence. Having faith in God alone does not mean I am guaranteed to close the real estate deal, make the game-winning touchdown, or be brave in combat. The Bible doesn't even suggest these things. Rather, faith in Jesus Christ is ultimately a means to *eternal salvation.* Why then would my confidence be affected in a positive way because of my faith in Christ? Simple. Once I knew my eternal salvation was assured, the day-to-day stuff no longer rattled me. I know I am just passing through this world. By accepting this, I can now keep the setbacks and hardships I face in proper perspective.

There really isn't a way I can accurately explain how my faith in Christ has changed the way I view things, but here is a silly example that may help for comparison: Imagine I had won a lottery prize of $50 million and while driving to collect the money, I spilled my coffee on my lap. How much would I really care? My daily struggles are so ridiculously tiny in comparison to the ultimate goal of eternal salvation that they are hardly worth noticing. That's why my confidence in God is the *ultimate* confidence; my faith in Him brings the *ultimate* reward: eternal life.

Confidence in God Never Comes Up Lacking

To achieve the greatest confidence, I need to deal with the core of who I *am*, not just what I *do*. Throughout history, from biblical accounts to current events, many millions of people have faced the worst of circumstances in their lives and found that their faith in God gave them the confidence to make it through.

Why does Jesus Christ give me ultimate confidence, whereas *confidence in myself* can be fleeting? Because I am flawed, and God is flawless. I am only human, and I can't compare myself to His perfection. I am a fallen man filled with contradictions, weakness, and sin. In comparison, God is perfect, all-knowing, and all-powerful. There is no weakness to be found in God, no contradiction, no fear, no flaw whatsoever, because He is perfect.

I can visualize any situation that may have shaken my confidence. Maybe it was standing up in front of an audience and speaking. Maybe as I began to speak, I recalled the snickers of the kids back in grade school. Now I compare the miniscule power of those childhood snickers against the fact that I believe what I am doing is what the Creator of the universe has called me to do. It seems ridiculous to compare, doesn't it? I might describe it as "spitballs against a battleship," but it's more like "spitballs against all of creation."

I can imagine a family member chuckling at my exploits in business or in life. Again, I compare his ignorant chuckles against the certainty of my calling from God. Imagine if I had a low estimation of my worth. Now I view my worth through the eyes of God, my Creator, who fashioned me in His image. It would be like a twelve-year-old boy sneering at the beauty of the Sistine Chapel. It would be ludicrous to place more weight on a child's negative critique than the work of the recognized master. My confidence in God never comes up lacking.

HAVE CONFIDENCE IN YOUR CALLING

For me, what I have found is that lasting confidence is faith that my *calling* is worthy. Following that initial thought is the belief that I am worthy of my calling. If I still struggled with confidence in my own worthiness, I could fall back on the worthiness of my ultimate purpose. If I doubted my plan-developing ability, I could fall back on the certainty of God's plan for my life. Once I knew that God's plan for me is perfect, the burden of worry was lifted from my shoulders.

The obstacles put before me aren't always *my* obstacles to remove;

> *The obstacles put before me aren't always my obstacles to remove; sometimes I have to be patient and wait for God to remove them.*

sometimes I have to be patient and wait for *God* to remove them. If He doesn't, He is refraining for a reason. As my own children grew from diapers to running shoes, it could have been easy to do everything for them. For example, many times they struggled with putting on their shoes. They might have grown frustrated with the "obstacle" I placed in front of them. They might have moaned, "Daddy, please help me with my shoes!" They might have felt that because I forced them to put on their shoes, I was being unkind or unfair toward them.

In fact, it was just the opposite. I knew that I needed to let them struggle in order for them to grow. I was showing my confidence in my children by *not* always helping them. I often believed more in them than they believed in themselves. By forcing my children to stand on their own feet, I helped them have a personal victory, and their confidence blossomed as a result. When God forced me to stand on my own two feet, I began to feel my confidence growing.

I'd like to share the stories of two men, one from ancient times and one from today, who showed confidence in their calling by following God's plan for them. The second man we will discuss is Tim Tebow;

first we will consider Joshua. Both showed great faith and obedience to God and experienced confidence because of it.

God Showed Confidence in Joshua

When Moses died, God chose Joshua to succeed Moses. He was the man God selected to lead the people of Israel into the Promised Land. If you aren't familiar with the story, I'd like to share the highlights with you because I believe it really illustrates how a person who has been rather ordinary his entire life can be used by God to do amazing things.

Joshua struggled with having confidence in himself and his own ability. It is said that everyone believed in Joshua except Joshua. Joshua gained confidence through his faith in God and his conviction to follow his calling. Because of that, he had the confidence to do what was asked of him.

The Israelites had wandered, aimlessly it seemed, through the wilderness with no idea how long their journey would last. (This is probably when the children of history started to ask their parents, "Are we there yet?") God had promised them a vast plot of land, from the desert in the south to the Lebanon Mountains in the north. The Euphrates River would form their eastern border, and their land would stretch west until they reached the Mediterranean Sea. Unfortunately, there were two immediate barriers to reaching their ultimate destination: the swollen waters of the River Jordan and the city of Jericho, which blocked their passage through the mountains. If they didn't go through the city of Jericho, they would be forced to attempt to bring their tribes over the surrounding mountains, a seemingly impossible task for their weakened flock. Few among them could accomplish this. The Lord had said to Joshua:

No man shall be able to stand before you all the days of your life. Just as I was with Moses, so I will be with you. I will not leave you or forsake you. Be strong and courageous, for you shall cause this people to inherit the land that I swore to their fathers to give them. Only be strong and very courageous, being careful to do according to all the law that Moses my servant commanded you. Do not turn from it to the right hand or to the left, that you may have good success wherever you go. This Book of the Law shall not depart from your mouth, but you shall meditate on it day and night, so that you may be careful to do according to all that is written in it. For then you will make your way prosperous, and then you will have good success. Have I not commanded you? Be strong and courageous. Do not be frightened, and do not be dismayed, for the Lord your God is with you wherever you go. (Joshua 1:5–9)

Joshua ordered two spies to go into the enemy lands of Canaan and bring back information on the enemy, specifically focusing on the city of Jericho. When they reached the city of Jericho, what they saw was an impregnable fortress with massive walls that couldn't be scaled by hand. The spies also knew that their own army didn't have any ladders to scale the walls or battering rams to break down the main gate.

They sneaked into the city and saw how the people of the city worshipped a pagan god named Baal. The city was a cesspool of debauchery and sin. During their mission, they were discovered by a prostitute named Rahab, whose dwelling had a window on the outer wall of the city. She was sympathetic to their plight.

She, along with the people of Jericho, had heard the report of God parting the waters of the Red Sea to allow the Israelites to escape the soldiers of Egypt and then of God's wrath brought down upon the Egyptian army by crushing them with those very waters. Such a terrible display of power had the people of Jericho whispering in fear about God.

Rahab hid the two Israelite spies in her home as the soldiers of Jericho searched every dwelling. She lied to the soldiers, admitting that the spies had visited her, but saying that they had escaped into the mountains. She hid the spies on her rooftop under stalks of flax until nightfall and then helped the men escape. In return, the spies told her that because she had helped them, she and any of her family who stayed in her home during the upcoming battle would be spared. The spies instructed her to tie a red sash to the window to let the army of Israel know to spare the lives inside.

Once the spies returned to the Israelite camp and briefed Joshua, he prayed to the Lord for guidance. The Lord said to him:

And as for you, command the priests who bear the ark of the covenant, "When you come to the brink of the waters of the Jordan, you shall stand still in the Jordan." (Joshua 3:8)

Joshua then took those orders back down to his people. He readied them to cross the River Jordan.

Again, for anyone without faith in God, what Joshua was suggesting must have looked like suicide. The river waters were swollen and rushing with the harvest flood. Any nonbeliever trying to cross them would surely be swept away and drowned. Crossing the river must have seemed like certain death. But Joshua and the people of Israel were not counting on *their* ability to cross the rushing waters. Their confidence came from their faith in the Lord. The Lord had parted the waters of the Red Sea and spared their lives once before; the Lord again would show His power and halt the waters of the River Jordan.

Joshua directed the priests to carry the Ark of the Covenant into the river and wait in the middle of the riverbed while everyone else crossed. Joshua told his people:

And when the soles of the feet of the priests bearing the ark of the Lord, the Lord of all the earth, shall rest in the waters of the Jordan, the waters of the Jordan shall be cut off from flowing, and the waters coming down from above shall stand in one heap. (Joshua 3:13)

When the priests stepped into the water, a miracle occurred. The raging river calmed, and just as the Lord had promised Joshua, the water receded. The people of Israel successfully crossed the River Jordan into the land of Canaan. The priests carrying the Ark of the Covenant remained standing in the middle of the riverbed, their faith in the Lord being the toll required to allow their people to cross the riverbed unharmed. Once everyone else had finished crossing the river, the priests lifted the Ark of the Covenant and also crossed. They made sure to bring twelve stones from the riverbed, as commanded by God, which would serve to remind the people of Israel of God's power and mercy.

Soon, the people of Israel marched and came upon the city of Jericho. It was just as the spies had described it: seemingly impenetrable. Again, to any nonbeliever, it would have been. But Joshua and the people of Israel had faith in the Lord to stand by them. As commanded by the Lord, for the next seven days, they circled the walls of the city, sounding their trumpets. On the seventh day, they circled the city seven times, sounding their trumpets and praying for the Lord to stand by them.

The people of Jericho must have watched this procession in amusement. *Surely,* they must have thought of the Israelites, *you guys are kidding yourselves. Sounding horns and saying prayers? No one,* they thought, *can knock down towering walls of impenetrable rock with a few prayers to God.*

At that moment the Lord crashed down upon the walls of Jericho, knocking them flat. I would imagine the citizens of Jericho were starting to doubt themselves and their pagan god Baal at that moment. But Baal wasn't anywhere to be found that day. The army of Israel poured across the shattered defenses of Jericho and put the city to the sword, sparing no one except Rahab and her family, the prostitute who had earlier protected the Israelite spies.

How did Joshua have the confidence to cross the raging waters of the River Jordan and attack the towering walls of Jericho? He didn't have the confidence that he could do it; he had confidence in the Lord.

His confidence in the Lord gave him the strength to overcome his obstacles.

Obedience to God's Calling Brings Confidence

Many of the great stories in the Old Testament are about obedience to God's calling. Many of us have attempted things that don't feel like a "fit" and decided to drop them. However, there is a world of difference between my declining an invitation to sing karaoke because it doesn't feel like a fit versus declining an invitation by God to use my life for part of His greater plan.

Recently, I was talking with a business leader I work with who is a Christian. He was struggling to go out and do the work he needed to do for his business, which included making phone calls and scheduling business meetings. Anyone who sells insurance or promotes timeshares, etc., knows what I mean. It's not unusual for people to feel some fear of rejection through these activities. However, when someone like him is hesitant to pick up the phone, clearly there are two disconnects: one obvious and surface-level, the other subtle but much more meaningful.

First, and most obvious to bystanders, this business leader is someone who has enough results and experience that making a phone call shouldn't faze him in the slightest. He should pick up the phone and laugh out loud at the thought of rejection. That's the first and more obvious disconnect. The second and deeper issue at stake? He professes that working on his business is what he feels *God has called him to do*. And if this person is truly a Christian and is avoiding what God has called him to do, he's moved past merely avoiding discomfort into something more menacing.

I recall several years ago I was looking at a snapshot of my own life and my own financial situation. I had achieved a certain degree of financial success, and I could literally sit back and do nothing for the rest of my life if I lived wisely. It would have been easy to justify my inactivity and not do what God had called me to do because in the world's eyes, I had already done it. I could have filled my time with things that would seem, to outsiders, to be highly commendable: I could go on mission trips; I could spend more time at church, etc. I could have easily done all these good things.

But I have long believed in the saying, "Everything good in life is the mortal enemy of everything great in life." I have not been called by God to be a full-time missionary. Though I have been on missionary trips in the traditional sense, my "mission field" is right here where I live. I have been called by God to lead men, build a business community, and serve Him by serving His people to the best of my ability. To shirk that duty, to casually shrug off the responsibility God has placed on me, would be nothing less than disobedience to God.

Without mincing words, the Bible gives us a great example that disobedience is a sin. In Joshua 5:6 we read, "For the people of Israel walked forty years in the wilderness, until all the nation, the men of war who came out of Egypt, perished, because they did not obey the voice of the LORD...." Disobedience doesn't simply mean you failed to do what God called you to do. There is a vast difference between *failing* to follow God's calling and *choosing* not to follow God's calling.

Consider the difference between struggling to bench-press two hundred pounds and failing versus not even going to the gym to try. The physical result is the same (you didn't end up bench-pressing two hundred pounds), but the moral implications are vastly different. If you try to press two hundred pounds and fail, you can be forgiven for trying and failing. If someone struggles desperately to follow the will of God and fails, that's one thing. Disobedience, however, carries with it the added concern of *willfully* going against God's wishes.

As 1 Corinthians 10:31 reads, "So, whether you eat or drink, or whatever you do, do all to the glory of God." If God called me to be a hockey player, and I was *not* a hockey player, I would be showing obvious disobedience to God. (It's a good thing He didn't because I can't skate very well.) On another level, if I was called to be a hockey player, and I showed up on the ice and gave a half-hearted effort, knowing that I held back and was *not* playing the very best I could, then I would still be disobedient to God. I would not glorify God with a half-hearted effort.

Additionally, those around me might not realize that I was only giving a half-hearted effort; they would only see that I was skating on the ice. In fact, they might applaud my effort at even lacing up my skates. "Wow," they might say, "you are really doing what God called you to do. Look at you skate!" By allowing them to think that, my heart would ache with the burden of lying by omission. I would know I wasn't truly the champion they thought I was. I would not be honorable in my actions. That further sin of dishonesty would be another strike against me in my mind. My confidence and self-esteem would be weakened even more. I see this in my own life and in many others' lives. Unfortunately, most people don't even know it's happening.

If I am called to be a pastor, can I really just do it halfway? Can I be a business leader in my community and do it halfway—not full-throttle, but only fifty percent? If I am professing to be one of Christ's children, I need to give it 100 percent and do it for His glory. I feel I am in my strongest and most confident state of mind when I am obedient to God, when I am following that calling to the best of my ability. I am not talking about getting my priorities out of whack, but I am saying I need to be into what I am into. This is not to say that my vocation or career goes above God or my family; I am called to serve them first. A half-hearted effort on my part is, I would argue, a sin against God and will erode my confidence. My attempted obedience to God and His plan has built my confidence.

The Faith of Tim Tebow

"PHIL 4:13," as written on Tim Tebow's game-day eye black[155]: "I can do all things through him who strengthens me." *Philippians 4:13*

Tim Tebow is one of the most famous and, because of his very public devotion to God, one of the most controversial NFL players today. From winning the Heisman Trophy in 2007 to being unceremoniously dumped from the New York Jets in 2013, Tebow has always managed the ups and downs of his life with his faith in the Lord to see him through. This last year has proven one of the most challenging for Tebow. In 2011, he led the Denver Broncos to the semifinals; they were two wins from reaching the Super Bowl. By 2012, he had strangely been traded to the New York Jets, often left on the bench, passed over for time in the game, and eventually dropped by the Jets. Through this period of time, arguably his greatest career challenge yet, Tebow has maintained grace and a spirit of wanting to follow God's plan in his life.

The attacks on Tim began even before his birth, in his mother's womb. When his parents were in the Philippines doing missionary work, his mother, Pamela, became pregnant. It quickly became obvious this would not be a normal pregnancy; she experienced constant pain and bleeding. Soon they would learn that the placenta had almost completely separated from the wall of the uterus. This is called a placental abruption and is one of the leading causes of maternal mortality worldwide, particularly in developing countries where the medical care is less advanced.[156] In other words, there was a very good chance the baby would die in the womb, his food supply from his mother cut off, and Tim's mom might also die. The doctor, viewing the unborn Tim only as fetal matter, grimly recommended an abortion to ensure the survival of his mother. Tim's parents, both devout Christians, wouldn't consider it. They walked out of the doctor's office and decided to place their faith in the Lord to see them and Tim safely through this.

A few months later, Tim Tebow was born. Tim showed a natural athleticism at an early age, fostered by the competitive spirit of his siblings. Whether it was playing T-ball as a five-year-old that morphed into Little League baseball or throwing the football in the backyard with his Uncle Dick, Tim had an early appetite to win at whatever he chose to do. He eventually settled on football and discovered an innate genius at handling the pigskin.

In time, Tim became a high school football superstar, easily the most committed on his team. He out-trained anyone and everyone in his off hours and gave 110 percent in practice. In one famous example, Tim sustained an injury to his leg during a game that left him in agonizing pain. Yet he continued to play, and made a 25 yard run for a touchdown. Afterward, he discovered he had played the game with a broken leg! This heart and determination did not go unnoticed, and he was heavily courted by several colleges to join their football programs. In the end, it came down to a choice between Alabama and Florida.

Making the decision between which of the two colleges to attend and play for initially showed none of the characteristic Tebow confidence. In the end, he had to trust that the Lord would guide him. Of his nail-biting last-minute decision to go with the Florida Gators, Tebow had this to say:

> People often seem to think that when you're following the Lord and trying to do His Will, your path will always be clear, the decisions smooth and easy, and life will be lived happily ever after and all that. Sometimes that may be true, but I've found that more often, it's not. The muddled decisions still seem muddled, bad things still happen to believers, and great things can happen to nonbelievers. When it comes to making our decisions, the key that God is concerned with is that we are trusting and seeking Him. God's desire is for us to align our lives with His Word and His Will.[157]

In his tenure as a Gator, Tebow rose to national prominence at the college level. He went on to become the first sophomore in college football history to win the coveted Heisman Trophy. He was soon courted by NFL teams to join their franchises.

In 2010, against all the predictions offered by the experts, Tebow defied expectations and was drafted in the first round by the Denver Broncos. What followed over the next two years was a fantastic spectacle of prowess on the field and record-shattering results for an NFL rookie, culminating in Tebow helping bring the Broncos to the doorstep of the playoffs. He began 2011 as the backup quarterback, but finally, five weeks into the season, got his chance to lead the team. Along the way, he drew a massive fan base, his number-15 jersey outselling every other NFL jersey in 2011. He popularized "Tebowing," praying on one knee on the sidelines of his games (something he had started doing in high school). He drew even more viewers during his after-game remarks than during the games themselves. He appeared on magazine covers, and he launched a bestselling memoir titled *Through My Eyes*.

Through this media whirlwind, he spoke of his devotion to God at every opportunity, drawing both praise and disdain, but always drawing attention. Tebow has said, "I have so many things to work on, and so many ways that I fail. But that's what grace is all about. And I constantly wake up every morning trying to get better, trying to improve, trying to walk closer to God."[158] Detractors thought Tebow, always polite both on and off camera and demonstrating a squeaky-clean lifestyle, was too good to be true. Opinionated ESPN commentator Merril Hoge called Tebow "phony as a three-dollar bill."[159] Sports radio host Morris O'Kelly said of Tebow in an interview, "There's a lot of Tebow resentment, part of which is [due to the fact that] he is very upfront about his Christianity, he was homeschooled as a child, [and] he has been very separated in many ways from regular folks. How many people actually get to tour the world or do missionary work before they're twenty-two? How many people win national championships also before they're twenty-two?

Or get drafted in the first round in the NFL? Each step he has been successful."

To describe Tebow as a football phenomenon would be a mild understatement. Wikipedia.com shares some of the many highlights of what Tebow accomplished with the Broncos. Here are just a few:

- Tebow and the Broncos struggled in the first three and a half quarters of a game against the Dolphins, but rallied from a 15–0 deficit in the last three minutes to win the game, 18–15, in overtime. Denver became the first team in NFL history to win a game after being down by at least 15 points with three minutes to play in a game.

- In the 10th start of his NFL career, Tebow led the Broncos to their third consecutive come-from-behind win of the season after trailing going into the fourth quarter, as Denver beat the Minnesota Vikings on the road, 35–32. The following Sunday, Tebow once again guided a comeback victory, this time at home over the Chicago Bears. Denver won 13–10 in overtime after facing a 10–0 deficit with just over two minutes to play in regulation. Tebow's sixth come-from-behind fourth-quarter or overtime victory in his 11 career starts was the most in NFL history for any quarterback in that time span.

- On January 8, Denver hosted the Pittsburgh Steelers during the first round of the NFL playoffs. Tebow threw for a career high 316 yards and two touchdowns, including an 80-yard TD to Demaryius Thomas on the first play of overtime, as the Broncos won 29–23. Tebow completed 10 of 21 passes in the contest, setting the franchise record for quarterback rating in a playoff game (125.6) and an NFL record for yards per completion (31.6) in a playoff game. Media sources noted Tebow's passing yards (316) and yards per completion (31.6) evoked the Bible's John 3:16. The Nielsen ratings for the game also peaked at 31.6. *John 3:16* was the top search item on Google the next morning, followed by *Tebow* and *Tim Tebow*.[160]

With such a stunning display of talent and results on the gridiron, and having brought the team so close to the Super Bowl, Tebow might have been thought to have found a home in the Denver Broncos for the foreseeable future. But it seemed that a different ending to the story would unfold. In a dramatic move, Denver decided to sign Peyton Manning to their roster. With a salary cap in effect upon every team, someone had to be trimmed in order to make up for Manning's paycheck. Tebow got the call that every player dreads: he was being cut, traded to the New York Jets to make room for Manning.

Tebow handled the news with the same grace and deference to the Lord's plan with which he handled everything. The Jets promised they had something special in mind for Tebow, something that would draw on his unique talents as an aspiring quarterback who had an unusual penchant for taking the ball and running with it. But the Jets never seemed to be able to decide what to do with Tebow on the field. Game after fruitless game saw Tebow's abilities wasted, either on the sidelines or in situations that didn't utilize his strengths. Critics were left scratching their heads, and fans howled to have him put in the game. Through it all, Tebow focused on his faith in the Lord. An article in the *Washington Times* stated:

> But maybe this is the moment to point out just how deep Tebow's faith seems to run. If it's easy to be a Christian in the sunlight—to turn the other cheek, to speak the mild word, to convert every loaded question shouted out by a reporter into an occasion to name the name of Jesus—it's harder when life isn't going well. But still Tebow speaks as he always has, saying things like "the team comes first," "the Jets' players are giving their best," and "the Lord has a plan." Tebow told us last year about the reality of his faith. He's proving it this year.[16]

Tebow, to his credit, remained steadfast in his public commitment to serving the Jets as they thought best. Tebow was forced to run a wildcat play (direct snap to a runner) that hammered him repeatedly, leaving him with cracked ribs and injuries to prove his commitment to the team. And yet he would not be handed his coveted chance to play as the team's quarterback. When quarterback Greg McElroy was sidelined in December 2012 due to a concussion, it seemed Tebow finally would have his chance to step up into the quarterback position. But at the time of this writing, the Jets coach has passed Tebow over, giving the coveted position back to Mark Sanchez. Tebow is facing the grim truth: he may not have a future with the Jets.

Through all Tim's struggles and heartaches, he has looked to God to give him the confidence to push on. Tim's poor treatment in his time with the Jets has come to the great dismay of the many fans who cheer for him. Personally, I believe the NFL doesn't want Tebow because he attracts much more attention than other players, he leads a moral lifestyle, and he doesn't hold back in sharing his love for the Lord. Critics would point out that the mechanics of Tebow's left-hand throw are unusual, and he takes the ball and runs more than pretty much any other quarterback in the game. But I believe petty politics are having their way with him. On handling adversity, Tim wrote in his memoir:

Sometimes, people are able to see more of your witness when you're facing adversity than when everything is going your way. People expect you to be a good winner, but they know how agonizing it is to lose. When you are able to reflect God's light during those times of great disappointment, it can have quite an impact. I try to keep that in mind.[162]

> "I don't know what my future holds, but I know who holds my future."
> – Tim Tebow

Although this is not an easy time for him, it is certainly not the end of the story for Tim Tebow. No matter what the future holds for him, he has proven to everyone who knows him where his strength comes from: his faith in the Lord. The *Washington Times* quoted Tebow as saying, "I don't know what my future holds, but I know who holds my future. And, in that," he added, "there is a lot of peace and a lot of comfort."[163]

MY FAITH IS MY PROTECTION

"My faith and my protection are in Jesus Christ." – *Tim Marks*

During the American Civil War, the lines of battle would lurch back and forth as Union and Confederate troops traded victories, losing land only to reclaim it later. Entire towns would often be caught in the middle of those exchanges. The town of Moorefield, West Virginia, was one such example of a town that saw its leadership change hands throughout the years-long contest.

At an old home that still stands to this very day, enemy troops came calling one morning on the old woman who lived there. She had refused to be uprooted by the battle that swirled around her. The stomping of Yankee boots on her porch alerted the old woman that she had guests. Although the troops had her at their mercy, there was no sign of fear on her face as she politely welcomed them into her modest home. They seated themselves at her dining table, demanding to be fed. As she graciously set breakfast before them, she announced that it was her custom to always say grace before a meal. She picked up her Bible, selected a passage at *random*, and began to read out loud:

> The LORD is my light and my salvation;
> > whom shall I fear?
> The LORD is the stronghold of my life;
> > of whom shall I be afraid?

When evildoers assail me
  to eat up my flesh,
my adversaries and foes,
  it is they who stumble and fall.
Though an army encamp against me,
  my heart shall not fear;
though war arise against me,
  yet I will be confident. (Psalm 27:1–3)

When she finished reading the passage from the Bible, she said softly, "Let us pray." The soldiers, armed to the teeth and outnumbering the frail old woman, were struck by the power of the Lord's written Word and the woman's faith. They glanced at each other uneasily, having lost their bravado and their appetite. As the old woman prayed quietly to herself, eyes closed, she could hear the soldiers slowly getting up from the table and walking quietly out of her home. She concluded her prayer to God, said, "Amen," and opened her eyes to discover the soldiers had slinked away. Her confidence in the Lord to protect her had proven to be a greater power than their muskets and bayonets.[164]

I would never want to compare my hardships with that story, but if you asked both that old Civil War lady and me, we would both say that our faith pulled us through difficult circumstances. Having faith in God doesn't remove the circumstances. It helps me manage my spirit within them. Because of my faith in Jesus Christ, if one of my kids were to get a life-threatening illness, I would still know that God had a plan. It doesn't make the pain go away, and it doesn't always "make sense," But it makes difficulty a lot more palatable. That is the protection my faith offers me.

My Testimony and Why I Am Confident

In my line of work, it's a big deal to all of us involved to leave a legacy—to make our lives count for something great. I am sure it is for you as well. While I certainly want to leave a legacy here on earth, my greatest goal doesn't concern things of this world. I'm going to be dead a lot longer than I'm going to be alive, so I'd better get this part right. Some may ask, "What does this have to do with confidence?" The answer is: everything! Please allow me to explain.

As I first shared in my book *Voyage of a Viking*, I used to believe that I was a Christian because I lived in the United States, said I was a Christian, and went to church. That thinking is as off-track as believing that standing in a garage will automatically make me a car. I grew up going to a parochial school and was taught by nuns. A teacher at my school, Sister Judy, first opened my eyes and my heart to God's love for me. As a youngster in her class, I was a troublemaking, vandalizing rascal, and still she showed me grace and forgiveness. She told me that God had a plan for me and that she wouldn't give up on me. The grace she showed opened the door many years later to accepting the Lord into my life, and I am forever grateful to Sister Judy for all she did in my life.

I finally realized one day that in order to get into heaven, I have to be *perfect*. Unfortunately, *no one is*; like everyone else, I am a sinner. I used to think that I could get to heaven through all my good deeds on earth. I sometimes went to church seven times in one week and incorrectly thought, *Surely that will get me into heaven!* I just somehow believed that. But God revealed to me from the Scriptures that I cannot get to heaven on my own. It doesn't matter if I have been baptized, if I go to church every week, if I carry a Bible everywhere I go, if I can quote scripture, if I tithe 50 percent of my income, if I build schools in third-world countries, if I donate all my money to women's shelters, or if I serve as a deacon at my church. While all those are great deeds to do, doing all of them, and a million times more, will *still* not buy me passage into heaven. The only way into heaven is by accepting Jesus

Christ as my personal Lord and Savior. God sent His only son, Jesus Christ, to live a perfect, sinless life on earth and die on the cross for my sins. Because He did that and rose from the grave three days later, it is only through placing my faith in Jesus Christ that I will find my eternal salvation.

As I grew older and wiser, I became more discerning and discovered that different churches preach different messages. The church I attended in my younger years was more focused on good works than on God's grace. Because I didn't understand the gospel in my younger years, in my teens I actually fell away from the church. I thought I knew "how things were"; I actually got to a point where I was basically agnostic. I needed to "see it" in order to believe it. I felt that if someone could have shown me proof of God's existence, then I would believe in Him again.

The irony of my argumentative thought is that everything, everywhere, through all eternity, is the proof of God. God reveals Himself through His Scriptures, through changed lives, through the miracle of all creation. The book you are holding is proof of God. The molecules that bind together to form the paper, ink, and glue that make up the book are proof of God. The computer used to type these words is proof of God.

God created the heavens and the earth, and like it or not, He created you. God created the human mind that has the ability to form thoughts, the vocal cords that allow us to express ideas in the form of spoken words, and the printed word. When a nonbeliever says, "There is no such thing as God," the irony is that that person's brain and vocal cords and the very words used to express disbelief in God were all created by God in the first place!

When I was going through management training for work years ago, I came across a tape set by the world-renowned motivational speaker Zig Ziglar. He has since gone to be with the Lord, but during his time here, he touched many thousands of lives, including my own. In fact, Zig was instrumental in leading me to Christ. I was listening to his tapes and loving them when I noticed a flyer promoting one of his other products entitled *Christian Motivation for Daily Living*. I had recently started going back to church at the time, and I felt I related to the tape.

Zig started talking about a plan for salvation and being "born again," an idea which was totally foreign to me when I first heard it. Then he quoted a verse from the Bible that literally saved me. It was Ephesians 2:8–9, and it reads, "For by grace you have been saved through faith. And this is not your own doing; it is the gift of God, not a result of works, so that no one may boast." When I heard that, it was like a ton of bricks hitting me. I realized going to church and praying to God were not enough to save me. I realized I was a sinner, like all people, and that I wasn't going to heaven until I had a Savior who I would put faith in and give my life to. There was no earthly limit to how many good deeds I would have to do to *earn* my way into heaven; doing so was an impossibility. The one and only way to eternal salvation was by accepting Jesus Christ as my Lord and Savior.

I became more aware of God's presence in my life during some of my darkest hours. In an effort to create financial freedom for my family, I had purchased thirty-three rental homes in a period of nine months. It seemed we would find success through real estate investment.

And then disaster struck: Some of the people I trusted to help me with my properties were not honest in their dealings with me, and all of a sudden I found myself $1.3 million in debt, including my primary residence. It was a crushing experience. We didn't have money to cover our bills. We couldn't make our mortgage payment. I was sending away for every credit card I could get just to get some cash in our hands and survive another day. I remember being cooped up in my basement for hours, making phone calls, weeping at my desk, as I desperately tried to borrow from Peter to pay Paul and cover the notes on my properties.

One time, my lovely bride Amy was standing in line at the grocery store and didn't have any money in any account or on any credit card that would work to even buy food. A year and a half before I launched my current business, I remember coming home late one night to find my little boy Cameron curled up asleep on the couch. He had tried to wait up for me. I was overcome with emotion. I sat down beside him and whispered to him, "I'm so sorry, little buddy. Daddy messed up. We are out of money, and I don't know what to do."

While all this had been going on, two of my co-workers had been pestering me to check out another business venture. I finally relented, saying to Bill, "If I agree to this deal, will you stop bugging me?"

He said, "Yes," so I paid the money and joined the "weight-loss program": getting Bill off my back. However, every Tuesday night, these guys would meet for their business association get-together and invite me to come. And every Tuesday, I would turn them down. This went on for weeks. I share this because at the height of my real estate business falling to pieces around me, I found myself one night in a church praying to God. I prayed for hours. I prayed for wisdom, for a way out of the mess I had created. I prayed for any possible way to earn the money to save my family's bacon. As the hours wore on, I realized that it was Tuesday and grumbled to myself, "Darn it, those guys are going to bug me again about going to their stupid Tuesday night meeting to learn how to make money."

Suddenly, it hit me. It was like the heavens parted and the angels started singing (well, not *really*). I had been at church praying for hours for the Lord to show me a way, and all of a sudden, He did! I raced home and told Amy to get dressed, and we rushed off to that business meeting. It opened the door to building a business that has created incredible financial blessing for my family and many others.

I can honestly say that I grew closer to Christ during a time of massive financial struggle and personal debt than during any other time in my life. When I was broken, when I had nothing, I turned to my faith in Jesus Christ. When I was born again, and I understood who Jesus

> *When I was broken, when I had nothing, I turned to my faith in Jesus Christ.*

Christ was, I had my eternity secured. During my struggles, when He brought me to my knees, when I was truly humbled, God made it blatantly clear through the events of my life both *who* I was and *whose* I was. I realized God had called me in a new direction, and I followed that calling. By acting in His will, I found a sense of strength and confidence I had never experienced before.

Some of you who are reading this are Christians, and you already know what I am saying is true. I would wager to say that you have had an experience similar to mine: you were once broken, and in professing your faith in Christ, you were saved and life became more clear. Some of you are nonbelievers, either atheists or agnostics. I would challenge you to really think through how you have arrived at your conclusions. Know why you believe what you believe. Ask a trusted friend, your local pastor, or a Christian you know for information to help you as you begin to seek answers. If you are atheist or agnostic, and particularly if you have a logical or scientific mind, I would encourage you to investigate a discussion on the idea of irreducible complexity, the flagellum motor,[††] and the concept of intelligent design as a starting point to asking bigger questions.

The reason I share my testimony isn't to show you that I faced terrible struggles in real estate and went *broke*; it's rather to show you that I was *broken*. There is a massive difference between being broke and being broken. My whole life, I lived for myself—my goals, my dreams—and I operated solely on my abilities and talents and the things I could do. A couple of years before the second time I went broke in real estate, I found Jesus Christ. And only because of Him did I have confidence to continue on. I went through my second set of real estate struggles, and I have faced major struggles since then. But when I was in my darkest hour, when I had nowhere to turn, I couldn't even buy groceries. I felt like a horrible husband, father, leader, businessman, and employee; I was just at the end of myself. And honestly, although I never contemplated suicide, emotionally I probably wasn't far from it. I felt that hopeless. I just felt totally

---

†† The flagellum is a tail-like propulsion structure, similar to the tail of sperm, found on certain bacteria. Under an electron microscope, we can see its motor has over forty parts and has been clocked moving at speeds of over 20,000 rpm. For comparison, consider that the average man-made engine in a car would likely explode at only 10,000 rpm. The idea of irreducible complexity is straightforward: The motor wouldn't function with any fewer parts than it has now. It only functions when all of the parts are present. Therefore, it couldn't have evolved from a smaller motor with fewer parts. Another example would be a mousetrap. It has a base, a holding bar, a hammer, a spring, and a catch. Remove any of these pieces, and the mousetrap won't function.

worthless—worthless in myself. And it was at that moment that I put my faith in Christ.

That doesn't mean that everything was peaches and cream the rest of my life. It means that I finally understood that I am just a pilgrim in this world. I am a sojourner. I am only here for about a hundred years (hopefully a few more than that). But I will be in eternity forever. So once I put my faith in Christ and knew I was inside His will (to the best of my discernment and ability), then I had confidence in myself because I wasn't worried about all the mamsy-pamsy things that happened to me on this earth. I was focused on eternal things.

Now that's not to say there aren't going to be some major situations that knock you on your heels or flatten you on your bottom. You may have a cherished loved one who faces a major illness or even dies unexpectedly. I have had those things happen, and I can tell you they make more sense because I have put my faith in Christ.

As we close our time here together, let me say: When you know your eternity is secure, I believe you'll have confidence to handle the things of this world. God bless you.

SUMMARY

"Even though I walk through the valley of the shadow of death, I will fear no evil, for you are with me; your rod and your staff, they comfort me." – *Psalm 23:4*

My ultimate source of confidence is my faith in God. When I have God on my side, no earthly obstacle can shake me, no matter what it is. As long as I am obedient to God and do everything for His glory, I will be filled with the confidence to face any challenge before me.

Key Points:

1. My ultimate confidence comes not from belief in myself but from my belief that I am living according to God's will.

2. I can have confidence in God because He is all-knowing, all-powerful, and flawless.

3. I have faith that my *calling* is worthy. I believe that *I* am worthy of my calling. If I ever struggle with confidence in my own worthiness, I can fall back on the worthiness of my ultimate purpose.

4. Because Joshua had faith in God, he had the confidence to do what was asked of him.

5. My obedience to God and His plan builds my confidence. Disobedience is a sin, and giving a half-hearted effort is just another form of disobedience to God.

6. My faith in Christ to protect me gives me greater strength when the adversaries of life appear.

CONCLUSION

"Believe in yourself and there will come a day when others will have no choice but to believe with you."

– Cynthia Kersey

Congratulations! By reaching the end of this, or any, book, you've done something critical to one's sense of self-esteem and self-worth: You have followed through on what you decided to do. Any goal attained is a step toward success. As my friend and business partner Wayne MacNamara says, "Nothing breeds confidence like results."

In closing, allow me to share one final story of choosing confidence in all our actions:

When Henry Ward Beecher was a young boy in school, he learned a lesson in self-confidence which he never forgot. He was called upon to recite in front of the class. He had hardly begun when the teacher interrupted with an emphatic, "No!" He started over and again the teacher thundered, "No!" Humiliated, Henry sat down. The next boy rose to recite and had just begun when the teacher shouted, "No!" This student, however, kept on with the recitation until he completed it. As he sat down, the teacher replied, "Very good!" Henry was irritated. "I recited just as he did," he complained to the teacher.

But the instructor replied, "It is not enough to know your lesson; you must be sure. When you allowed me to stop you, it meant that you were uncertain. If the world says, 'No!' it is your business to say, 'Yes!' and prove it."[165]

You have now been armed with the tools to say "Yes!" to the world. You will find that some of the ideas we've discussed will come back to you quickly and easily. Pick out your top nuggets and apply them as you meet with people today, tomorrow, and throughout this week. Make it a point to use this information *now*. Don't just read this book for entertainment or to get a "gold star" for having read a book this month. Apply the lessons you have learned.

I have shared with you the **six principles for building self-confidence** *and how to implement them* in business and in life. To review, they are:

Principle #1: Know Your Worth.
Principle #2: Stop Comparing.
Principle #3: Manage Your Self-Talk.
Principle #4: Take Action.
Principle #5: Cut Your Anchors.
Principle #6: Fight Fear with Faith.

The ball is in your court. You *can* become a person of great confidence. Remember to see your inherent worth, know that you measure up, speak well of yourself, get off the couch, make peace with your past, and fearlessly pursue your calling for the glory of God.

ADDITIONAL READING

This book has hopefully challenged you to look at or think about yourself in ways that you may have struggled with or even avoided in the past. In particular, Chapter 5: "Cut Your Anchors" will, for many people, begin a conversation about their past that could be quite challenging. With so many different life experiences, the scope of this book won't allow us to go into the level of detail desired by some people. In response to this, I have provided a list below of some additional books to review that have helped many people I know and have worked with. I hope these books can offer insight and relief to you as well.

CHILDHOOD SEXUAL ABUSE

Rid of My Disgrace: Hope and Healing for Victims of Sexual Assault. Justin S. Holcolm, Lindsey A. Holcomb, and Marc Driscoll.

The Wounded Heart: Hope for Adult Survivors of Childhood Sexual Abuse. Dr. Dan B. Allender.

SPIRITUAL QUESTIONS / ISSUES

Ashamed of the Gospel. John MacArthur.

Be Sure What You Believe. Joe Nesom.

Brokenness. Nancy Leigh Demoss.

Faith Tried and Triumphant. D. Martyn Lloyd-Jones.

Holiness. Nancy Leigh Demoss.

Reason to Believe. R. C. Sproul.

Surrender. Nancy Leigh Demoss.

EATING DISORDERS

Love to Eat, Hate to Eat: Breaking the Bondage of Destructive Eating Habits. Elyse Fitzpatrick.

Made to Crave: Satisfying Your Deepest Desire With God Not Food. Lysa Terkeurst.

ROUGH CHILDHOOD GENERAL / ALCOHOLIC FAMILY / DIVORCED

Bad Childhood, Good Life: How to Blossom and Thrive in Spite of an Unhappy Childhood. Dr. Laura Schlessinger.

When Bad Things Happen. Kay Arthur.

Trusting God - Even When Life Hurts. Jerry Bridges.

ENDNOTES

1   Zig Ziglar, "The Zig Ziglar Weekly Newsletter," January 24, 2012, Edition 4, accessed May 31, 2013, http://www.ziglar.com/newsletter/january-24-2012-edition-4.

2   Norman Vincent Peale, "BrainyQuote," BookRags Media Network/tend Glam Media, copyright 2001-2012, accessed December 23, 2012, http://www.brainyquote.com/quotes/quotes/n/normanvinc132560.html.

3   Norman Vincent Peale, *How to Handle Tough Times* (Peale Center for Christian Living, 1990).

4   Helen Keller, "BrainyQuote," BookRags Media Network/tend Glam Media, copyright 2001-2012, accessed December 23, 2012, http://www.brainyquote.com/quotes/quotes/h/helenkelle164579.html.

5   Sydney Smith, The Quote Garden, last modified September 3, 2012, accessed December 23, 2012, http://www.quotegarden.com/confidence.html.

6   Anna Freud, The Foundation for a Better Life, copyright 2000-2012, accessed December 17, 2012, http://www.values.com/inspirational-quotes/value/81-Confidence.

7   Glenn R. Schiraldi, *10 Simple Solutions for Building Self-Esteem* (Oakland, CA: New Harbinger Publications, 2007), 3.

8   Nathaniel Branden, *Honor the Self* (New York: Bantam Books, 1985), 4.

9   Brian Tracy, "BrainyQuote," BookRagsMediaNetwork/tendGlam Media, copyright 2001-2012, accessed December 30, 2012, http://www.brainyquote.com/quotes/quotes/b/briantracy386522.html.

10   Maxwell Maltz, MD, FICS, *Psycho-Cybernetics* (New York: Pocket Books, 1960), ix.

11   Author Unknown, The Quote Garden, last modified September 3, 2012, accessed December 23, 2012, http://www.quotegarden.com/confidence.html.

12   Orrin Woodward, *RESOLVED: 13 Resolutions for LIFE* (Flint, MI: Obstaclés Press, 2012).

13   Damon Throop, Goodreads Inc., copyright 2013, accessed May 30, 2013, http://www.goodreads.com/author/quotes/5862566.Damon_Throop.

14   Meryle Gellman and Diane Gage, *The Confidence Quotient: 10 Steps to Conquer Self-Doubt* (New York: St. Martins Press, 1986).

15   Wikimedia Foundation Inc., last modified March 28, 2013, accessed May 30, 2013, http://en.wikipedia.org/wiki/John_D._Rockefeller.

16   Charity Vogel, "The Angola Train Wreck," originally published by American History magazine, published online November 30, 2007, accessed December 23, 2012, http://www.historynet.com/the-angola-train-wreck.htm.

17   Ida M. Tarbell, "John D. Rockefeller: A Character Study," accessed December 23, 2012, http://www.reformation.org/john-d-rockefeller.html.

18   T.J. Stiles, *The First Tycoon: The Epic Life of Cornelius Vanderbilt* (New York: Vintage Books, 2010), 475.

Chapter 1

19   Joni Eareckson Tada, *A Place of Healing:Wrestling with the Mysteries of Suffering, Pain and God's Sovereignty* (Colorado Springs: David C. Cook, 2010).

20   Larry Crabb and Dan B. Allender, *Encouragement: The Key to Caring* (Grand Rapids, MI: Zondervan Publishing House, 1990).

21   Denis Waitley, Nightingale-Conant Inc., copyright 2011, "Nightingale-Conant presents Denis Waitley," accessed May 30, 2013, www.nightingale.com/Auth_Bio~author~Denis_Waitley. aspx.

22   *The Guardian*, "Paralysed Claire Lomas finishes London Marathon 16 days after it began," Guardian News and Media Limited, copyright 2012, accessed July 22, 2012, http://www. guardian.co.uk/sport/2012/may/08/paralysed-claire-lomas-london-marathon.

23   Nick Collins, The Telegraph, "Eye implant restores vision to blind patients," Telegraph Media Group Limited, copyright 2012, accessed July 22, 2012, http://www.telegraph.co.uk/ science/science-news/9243223/Eye-implant-restores-vision-to-blind-patients.html.

24   Alan Henry, "New Japanese supercomputer is the world's most powerful," Ziff Davis Inc., copyright 1996-2012, published June 20, 2011, accessed July 22, 2012, http://www.geek.com/ articles/chips/new-japanese-supercomputer-is-the-worlds-most-powerful-20110620/.

25   Myra Brooks Welch, "The Touch of the Master's Hand," All Poetry, copyright 2012, accessed May 30, 2013, allpoetry.com/ poem/8601687-The_Touch_of_the_Masters_Hand-by-Myra_ Brooks_Welch.

26   Og Mandino, *The Greatest Miracle in the World* (New York: Bantam Books, 1977).

27   Robert Johnson, Class Act Media, LLC, "Inspirational Encouraging Quotes," accessed May 30, 2013, www. inspirationalspark.com/inspirational-encouraging-quotes.html.

28   John Templeton, "Inspirational Quote of the Day Archives," copyright Jim and Audri Lanford, accessed May 30, 2013, www. famous-quotes-and-quotations.com/john_templeton.html.

29   Maxwell Maltz, MD, FICS, *Psycho-Cybernetics* (New York: Pocket Books, 1960).

30   Margherita Stancati, *The Wall Street Journal*, "Would a Major Quake Wipe Out Delhi?," published online September 28, 2011, accessed May 30, 2013, http://blogs.wsj.com/indiarealtime/2011/09/28/would-a-major-quake-wipe-out-delhi/.

31   Joe Batten, iWise Wisdom On-Demand, accessed May 30, 2013, www.iwise.com/uS5fS.

32   Wikimedia Foundation Inc., last modified http://en.wikipedia.org/wiki/Dendrology; accessed July 23, 2012.

33   Zig Ziglar, Goodreads Inc., accessed May 30, 2013, www.goodreads.com/author/quotes/50316.Zig_Ziglar.

34   Wikimedia Foundation Inc., last modified February 21, 2013, accessed May 30, 2013, http://en.wikipedia.org/wiki/Nelson_Mandela.

35   Orrin Woodward and Chris Brady, *Launching a Leadership Revolution* (New York: Business Plus, 2007), 177.

36   Wikimedia Foundation Inc., last modified May 30, 2013, accessed May 30, 2013, http://en.wikipedia.org/wiki/Schindler's_List.

37   Stephen R. Covey, *7 Habits of Highly Effective People*, (New York: Fireside, 2004), 35.

38   Search Quotes, copyright 2012, accessed July 23, 2012, www.searchquotes.com/quotation/The_depth_of_your_belief_and_the_strength_of_your_conviction_determines_the_power_of_your_personality/266982.

39   Quotegreetings, copyright 2011-2012, accessed August 7, 2012, http://quotegreetings.com/2012/abraham-hicks-quotes/.

40   Henri J.M. Nouwen, Goodreads, Inc., "Quotes about Feelings," copyright 2012, accessed November 1, 2012, http://www.goodreads.com/quotes/tag/feelings.

41   David A. Seamands, *Healing for Damaged Emotions* (Colorado Springs, CO: David C. Cook, 1981).

Chapter 2

42 Jill Coody Smits, "Field Guide to the Overachiever," *Psychology Today*, November/December 2011, 33–34.

43 Jim Courier, "BrainyQuote," BookRags Media Network/tend Glam Media, copyright 2001-2013, accessed May 30, 2013, http://www.brainyquote.com/quotes/quotes/j/jimcourier182782.html.

44 Blaise Pascal, *Pensees*, Goodreads Inc., accessed June 3, 2013, http://www.goodreads.com/quotes/10567.

45 Les Giblin, *How to Have Confidence and Power in Dealing with People*, (New York: Reward Books, 1956), 13.

46 Ralph Waldo Emerson, *Self-Reliance*, Goodreads Inc., accessed June 3, 2013, http://www.goodreads.com/quotes/259136.

47 Tim Layden, SI.com, published November 2, 2012, copyright 2013 by Time Inc., a Time Warner Company, accessed November 30, 2012, http://sportsillustrated.cnn.com/2012/magazine/sportsman/11/26/usain-bolt-tim-layden/index.html.

48 Wikimedia Foundation, Inc., last modified May 28, 2013, accessed June 3, 2013, http://en.wikipedia.org/wiki/Jon_Huntsman,_Sr.

49 Martin Luther, "BrainyQuote," BookRags Media Network/tend Glam Media, copyright 2001-2012, accessed December 20, 2012, http://www.brainyquote.com/quotes/quotes/m/martinluth403720.html; accessed.

50 Orrin Woodward and Oliver DeMille, *LeaderShift* (New York: Business Plus, 2013), 88.

51 Stephen Richards, Goodreads Inc., accessed November 20, 2012, http://www.goodreads.com/quotes/tag/overcoming-fear.

52 Contactmusic.com Ltd., accessed November 20, 2012, http://www.contactmusic.com/news/streisands-stagefright-prompted-by-forgotten-lyrics_1117130.

53 Joyce J. Chansingh, Microsoft & MediaCorp, Pte. Ltd. , accessed November 2, 2012, http://entertainment.xin.msn.com/en/celebrity/buzz/asia/article.aspx?cp-documentid=5484262.

54 Howie Mandel, *Here's the Deal: Don't Touch Me* (New York: Bantam Books, 2010).

55 Editors at Netscape, Compuserve Interactive Services Inc., accessed November 20, 2012, http://webcenters. netscape.compuserve.com/celebrity/package.jsp?name=fte/celebrityfears/celebrityfears.

56 Dyslexia Help: Success Starts Here, The Regents of the University of Michigan, copyright 2012, accessed December 13, 2012, http://dyslexiahelp.umich.edu/success-stories/tom-cruise.

57 Wikipedia, Wikimedia Foundation Inc., accessed November 30, 2012, http://en.wikipedia.org/wiki/Sylvester_Stallone#Personal_life.

58 Live Science, TechMediaNetwork.com, accessed November 22, 2012, http://www.myhealthnewsdaily.com/2446-celebrity-health-illness-diseases.html.

59 QuinnStreet Inc., copyright 2005-2013, accessed June 3, 2013, http://www.citytowninfo.com/career-and-education-news/articles/study-shows-baldness-can-be-beneficial-in-the-workplace-12100801.

60 Ibid.

61 Glenn R. Schiraldi, *10 Simple Solutions for Building Self-Esteem* (Oakland: New Harbinger Publications, 2007).

62 Aline Brosh McKenna (writer), *The Devil Wears Prada*, Directed by David Frankel (Twentieth Century Fox, released June 30, 2006).

63 Edward T. Welch, *When People Are Big and God Is Small*, Phillipsburg, NJ: P&R Publishing Company, 1997).

64 Manesh Shrestha, "73-year-old becomes oldest woman to climb Mount Everest," May 19, 2012, CNN Cable News Network, Turner Broadcasting System Inc., accessed June 3, 2013, http://www.cnn.com/2012/05/19/world/asia/nepal-everest-cimb.

65 Wikipedia, Wikimedia Foundation Inc., last modified May 10, 2013, accessed June 3, 2013, http://en.wikipedia.org/wiki/James_Earl_Jones.

66 Wikipedia, Wikimedia Foundation Inc., last modified June 3, 2013, accessed June 3, 2013, http://en.wikipedia.org/wiki/Andrew_Johnson.

67   Wikipedia, Wikimedia Foundation Inc., last modified June 3, 2013, accessed June 3, 2013, http://en.wikipedia.org/wiki/Michael_J._Fox.

68   Wikipedia, Wikimedia Foundation Inc., last modified April 30, 2013, accessed June 3, 2013, http://en.wikipedia.org/wiki/Rick_Hansen.

69   Olivia Fleming, "I was conceived in jail: Hope Solo on how her mother became pregnant after conjugal visit to her father," Associated Newspapers Ltd., accessed December 15, 2012, http://www.dailymail.co.uk/femail/article-2178817/I-conceived-jail-Hope-Solo-mother-pregnant-conjugal-visit-father.html.

70   Wikipedia, Wikimedia Foundation Inc., last modified June 2, 2013, accessed June 3, 2013, http://en.wikipedia.org/wiki/Frank_Abagnale.

71   Les Giblin, *How to Have Confidence and Power in Dealing with People*, (New York: Reward Books, 1956), 14.

72   Les Giblin, *How to Have Confidence and Power in Dealing with People*, (New York: Reward Books, 1956), 143-144.

73   Naren, Spiritualpub.com, December 5, 2008, copyright 2011, accessed November 18, 2012, http://www.spiritualpub.com/5-ways-to-stop-complaining-and-criticizing-unnecessarily.php.

74   Dale Carnegie, *How to Win Friends and Influence People* (New York: Pocket Books, 1981), 128.

75   Woodrow Wilson, Quotations Book, copyright 2007, accessed December 15, 2012, http://quotationsbook.com/quote/35560/.

Chapter 3

76   Alan Chapman, Businessballs.com, "Stories and Analogies," copyright 2012, accessed June 3, 2013, http://www.businessballs.com/stories.htm#the-man-boy-hotel-story.

77   Orrin Woodward, "12 Laws of Success (Team 612)," (Flint, MI: Team, 2012).

78   Quotewise.com, accessed June 4, 2013, www.quotewise.com/zip-ziglar-quotes-9.html.

79   Charles Swindoll, Goodreads.com, Goodreads Inc., copyright 2013, accessed June 4, 2013, www.goodreads.com/quotes/1169.

80   John C. Maxwell, *The Difference Maker* (Nashville, TN: Thomas Nelson Inc., 2006), 114.

81   Robert K. Cooper, *Get Out of Your Own Way* (New York: Crown Business, 2006), 88.

82   Vince Poscente, *The Ant and the Elephant: Leadership for the Self* (Dallas: Be Invincible Group, 2004).

83   Jim Rohn, Goodreads.com, Goodreads Inc., accessed December 17, 2012, http://www.goodreads.com/quotes/tag/self-improvement.

84   Josiah Hotchkiss Gilbert, *Dictionary of Burning Words of Brilliant Writers*, Harvard College Library (New York: Wilbur B. Ketcham, 1895), 255.

85   Will Rogers, Goodreads.com, Goodreads Inc., accessed June 4, 2013, www.goodreads.com/quotes/20896.

86   Socrates, "Inspirational Quotes," Infinity Web Development, LLC, copyright 2002-2012, accessed December 17, 2012, http://www.inspirational-quotes.info/self-improvement.html.

87   Sir J. Stephen, "Inspirational Quotes," Infinity Web Development, LLC, copyright 2002-2012, accessed December 17, 2012, http://www.inspirational-quotes.info/self-improvement.html.

88   Stephen R. Covey, "Time Quotes: 66 Best Time Management Quotes," Life Optimizer, copyright 2012, accessed December 17, 2012, http://www.lifeoptimizer.org/2007/03/08/66-best-quotes-on-time-management/.

89   Muhammad Ali, "BrainyQuote," BookRags Media Network/tend Glam Media, copyright 2001-2012, accessed December 16, 2012, http://www.brainyquote.com/quotes/authors/m/muhammad_ali.html.

90 Ludwig Wittgenstein, "The Quotations Page," QuotationsPage. com and Michael Moncur, copyright 1994-2013, accessed May 30, 2013, http://www.quotationspage.com/quote/30291.html.

91 Christopher Bergland, "Choosing Positive Words Improves Mindset and Performance: Cognitive scientists confirm the power of affirmative language," *The Athlete's Way: Sweat and the biology of bliss, Psychology Today,* Published December 7, 2012, copyright 2002-2012 Sussex Directories Inc., accessed December 16, 2012, http://www.psychologytoday.com/blog/the-athletes-way /201212/choosing-positive-words-improves-mindset-and-performance.

92 Philip K. Dick, "Quotes about Power of Words," Goodreads.com, copyright 2012 Goodreads Inc., accessed December 16, 2012, http://www.goodreads.com/quotes/tag/power-of-words.

93 Melinda Beck, "Silencing the Voice That Says You're a Fraud," *The Wall Street Journal,* June 16, 2009, copyright 2012 Dow Jones & Company Inc., accessed December 16, 2012, http://online. wsj.com/article/SB124511712673817527.html.

94 David D. Burns, MD, *Feeling Good: The New Mood Therapy* (New York: Avon Books, 1999) 71–75.

95 "5 Whys" is a root-cause analysis methodology originally developed by Toyota. Wikipedia.com, Wikimedia Foundation Inc., last modified May 25, 2013, accessed June 4, 2013, http:// en.wikipedia.org/wiki/5_Whys.

96 Wikipedia, Wikimedia Foundation Inc., last modified June 3, 2013, accessed June 4, 2013, http://en.wikipedia.org/wiki/ Mental_toughness.

97 Tim Marks, *Voyage of a Viking* (Flint, MI: Obstaclés Press, 2011).

98 James E. Loehr and Peter MacLaughlin, *Mentally Tough: The Principles of Winning at Sports Applied to Winning in Business* (Manhattan: M. Evans & Company, 1988).

99 Honoré de Balzac, FinestQuotes, accessed December 17, 2012, http://www.finestquotes.com/author_quotes-author-Honore%20de%20Balzac-page-0.htm.

Chapter 4

100 Henry C. Link, Goodreads.com, Goodreads Inc., accessed June 4, 2013, www.goodreads.com/quotes/59975.

101 Eric Zorn, "Without Failure, Jordan Would Be False Idol," May 19, 1997, *Chicago Tribune*, accessed December 30, 2012, http://articles.chicagotribune.com/1997-05-19/news/9705190096_1_nike-mere-rumor-driver-s-license.

102 Pearl S. Buck, Goodreads.com, Goodreads Inc., accessed June 4, 2013, www.goodreads.com/quotes/122511.

103 Susie Steiner, "Top Five Regrets of the Dying," February 1, 2012, copyright 2013 Guardian News and Media Limited, accessed June 4, 2013, http://www.guardian.co.uk/lifeandstyle/2012/feb/01/top-five-regrets-of-the-dying.

104 Wikipedia.com, Wikimedia Foundation Inc., accessed July 18, 2012, http://en.wikipedia.org/wiki/Jaime_Escalante.

105 Ibid.

106 Ibid.

107 Ibid.

108 Ibid.

109 Ibid

110 Lowell Thomas, Quotationsbook.com, copyright 2007 Quotations Book, accessed June 4, 2013, quotationsbook.com/quote/13118.

111 Wikipedia.com, Wikimedia Foundation Inc., accessed July 18, 2012, http://en.wikipedia.org/wiki/Jaime_Escalante.

112 Leo Buscaglia, Goodreads.com, copyright 2013 Goodreads Inc., accessed June 4, 2013, www.goodreads.com/quotes/49785.

113 Les Giblin, *How to Have Power and Confidence in Dealing with People* (New York: Rewards Books, 1956), 73.

114 Dale Carnegie, *How to Win Friends and Influence People* (New York: Pocket Books, 1981), 84.

115 Chip and Dan Heath, *Switch: How to Change Anything when Change Is Hard* (Toronto: Random House Canada, 2010), 209.

116 Orrin Woodward, *RESOLVED: 13 Resolutions for LIFE* (Flint, MI: Obstaclés Press, 2012).

117 Daniel Goleman, *Social Intelligence: The New Science of Human Relationships* (New York: Bantam Books, 2006), 54.

118 Will Rogers, accessed June 4, 2013, QuotationsBook.com, copyright 2007 Quotations Book, quotationsbook.com/quote/16267.

119 Wired Science, "Top Scientific Discoveries of 2012," December 29, 2012, copyright 2013 Condé Nast, accessed June 4, 2013, http://www.wired.com/wiredscience/2012/12/top-discoveries-2012/.

120 Wikipedia.com, Wikimedia Foundation Inc., last modified June 3, 2014, accessed June 4, 2013, http://en.wikipedia.org/wiki/US_Airways_Flight_1549.

121 John Ford, "QuotationsBook," copyright 2007, accessed December 29, 2012, http://quotationsbook.com/quote/37032/.

122 Dale Carnegie, *Public Speaking for Success* (New York: Penguin Group USA, 2005), 113.

123 Richard Kline, 'Quotations about Confidence," last modified September 3, 2012, accessed December 30, 2012, http://www.quotegarden.com/confidence.html.

124 Zig Ziglar, *Ziglar*, March 10, 2009, Edition 10, accessed June 15, 2013, http://www.ziglar.com/newsletter/march-10-2009-edition-10.

125 Nicholas Boothman, *How to Connect in Business in 90 Seconds or Less* (New York: Workman Publishing Company Inc., 2002), 17–18.

126 Tim Marks, *Voyage of a Viking* (Flint, MI: Obstaclés Press, 2012), 45–67.

Chapter 5

127 Merriam-Webster Online Dictionary, copyright 2013 Merriam-Webster Incorporated, accessed January 21, 2013, http://www.merriam-webster.com/dictionary/anchor.

128 Chuck Norris, *The Secret of Inner Strength: My Story* (Diamond Books, 1989).

129 Warren Bennis, *On Becoming a Leader* (New York: Basic Books, 2003), 228.

130 Dan Hawkins, "Keep Your Eye on Your Dream and Swing," copyright Team (Deluth, GA: PSI Discs Inc., 2012).

131 Betty Hart and Todd R. Risley, *Meaningful Differences in the Everyday Experience of Young American Children* (Baltimore, MD: Paul H. Brooks Publishing Co Inc., 1995).

132 Mark Goulston and Philip Goldberg, *Get Out of Your Own Way* (New York: The Berkley Publishing Group, 1996), 23–45.

133 Norman Vincent Peale, Goodreads.com, copyright 2013 Goodreads Inc., accessed February 14, 2013, http://www. goodreads.com/quotes/tag/criticism?page=2.

134 Sally Field, "BrainyQuote," BookRags Media Network/tend Glam Media, copyright 2001-2013, accessed June 4, 2013, brainyquote.com/quotes/quotes/s/sallyfield104637.html.

135 James LeBron, "BrainyQuote," BookRags Media Network/tend Glam Media, copyright 2001-2013, accessed February 6, 2013, http://www.brainyquote.com/quotes/keywords/criticism. html.

136 John Bradshaw, *Healing the Shame That Binds You* (Deerfield Beach, FL: Health Communications Inc., 2005), 243–246.

137 Ram Dass, "The Quote Garden: A Harvest of Quotations for Word Lovers," copyright 1998-2013, last modified September 3, 2012, accessed June 4, 2013, http://www.quotegarden.com/ confidence.html.

138 Robert Brault, "A Robert Brault Reader," (blog) accessed January 17, 2013, www.robertbrault.com.

139 Susan Forward and Craig Buck, *Toxic Parents: Overcoming Their Hurtful Legacy and Reclaiming Your Life* (New York: Bantam Books, 1989), 104.

140 Hara Estroff Marano, "Pitfalls of Perfectionism," *Psychology Today*, published March 1, 2008, last reviewed May 17, 2013, copyright 1991-2013 Sussex Publishers, LLC, accessed June 4, 2013, http://www.psychologytoday.com/articles/200802/ pitfalls-perfectionism.

141 Michael J. Fox, Goodreads.com, copyright 2013 Goodreads Inc., accessed February 6, 2013, http://www.goodreads.com/quotes/tag/perfection.

142 John Lasseter, copyright 2005 – 2012 toplingo development, accessed February 12, 2013, http://collider.com/pete-docter-note-up-monsters-inc-pixar-john-lasseter/.

143 Dan Neuharth, *If You Had Controlling Parents* (New York: Harper Collins, 1998), xxii.

144 Patricia Evans, *Controlling People: How to Recognize, Understand and Deal with People Who Try to Control You* (Avon, MA: Adams Media Corporation, 2002), 17.

145 Forward and Buck, *Toxic Parents,* [pg.#].

146 Mark Goulston and Philip Goldberg, *Get Out of Your Own Way* (New York: The Berkley Publishing Group, 1996.), 2.

147 Dr. Laura Schlessinger, *Bad Childhood, Good Life* (New York: Harper Collins Publishers, 2006), 95.

148 Tim Marks, *Voyage of a Viking* (Flint, MI: Obstaclés Press, 2012), 178.

149 Ann Landers, Goodreads.com, copyright 2013 Goodreads Inc., accessed June 4, 2013, http://www.goodreads.com/quotes/273322.

150 Laurel Lee, "BrainyQuote," BookRags Media Network/tend Glam Media, copyright 2001-2013, accessed January 20, 2013, http://www.brainyquote.com/quotes/authors/l/laurel_lee.html.

151 Henry Ward Beecher, "BrainyQuote," BookRags Media Network/tend Glam Media, copyright 2001-2013, accessed January 20, 2013, http://www.brainyquote.com/quotes/authors/h/henry_ward_beecher.html.

152 Matt Damon and Ben Affleck (writers), Good Will Hunting, directed by Gus Van Sant, Miramax Films, released December 5, 1997.

153 Ellen Bass and Laura Davis, *The Courage to Heal: A Guide for Women Survivors of Child Sexual Abuse* (New York: Harper Collins, 1988), 121-122.

154 Joshua Loth Liebman, "Joshua Loth Liebman Quotes," copyright 2013 SearchQuotes.com, accessed June 4, 2013, http://www.searchquotes.com/quotation/We_achieve_inner_health_only_through_forgiveness_-_the_forgiveness_not_only_of_others_but_also_of_ou/225354/.

Chapter 6

155 Tim Tebow, *Through My Eyes* (New York: Harper Collins Publishers, 2011), 178.

156 Wikipedia, Wikimedia Foundation Inc,, last modified February 26, 2013, accessed June 4, 2013, http://en.wikipedia.org/wiki/Placental_abruption.

157 Tim Tebow, *Through My Eyes* (New York: Harper Collins Publishers, 2011), 85-86.

158 Ibid., 238.

159 "Merril Hoge: Tebow as Phony as a Three Dollar Bill," 2013 *USA Today*, a division of Gannett Satellite Information Network Inc., copyright 2013 Gannett, accessed February 20, 2013, http://www.usatoday.com/story/gameon/2012/12/24/nfl-tebow-merrill-hoge/1789529/.

160 Wikipedia, Wikimedia Foundation Inc., last modified June 4, 2013, accessed June 4, 2013, http://en.wikipedia.org/wiki/Tim_Tebow.

161 Joseph Bottum, "Tebow's Faith Helps Him Adjust to Tough Season: Christian Quarterback Has Patience of Job While on Bench with N.Y. Jets," December 19, 2012, *The Washington Times*, copyright 2013 The Washington Times, LLC, accessed February 18, 2013, http://www.washingtontimes.com/news/2012/dec/19/tebows-faith-helps-him-adjust-to-tough-season/?page=all.

162 Tim Tebow, *Through My Eyes*, (New York: Harper Collins Publishers, 2011), 299.

163   Dennis Waszak Jr., "Tim Tebow, Suddenly Unwanted, Awaits Next Career Move," January 15, 2013, *The Washington Times*, copyright 2013 The Washington Times, LLC, accessed February 20, 2013, http://www.washingtontimes.com/news/2013/jan/15/tim-tebow-suddenly-unwanted-awaits-next-career-mov/.

164 J. Hampton Keathley III, "Crossing the Jordan (Joshua 3:1 – 4:24)," *Studies in the Life of Joshua*, copyright 2013 bible.org, accessed February 17, 2013, http://bible.org/seriespage/crossing-jordan-joshua-31-424.

Conclusion

165 Stephen, "Improving Self-Confidence," *Moral Stories*, copyright 1999-2013 AcademicTips.org, accessed March 4, 2013, http://academictips.org/blogs/improving-self-confidence/.

VOYAGE OF A
VIKING

HOW A MAN OF ACTION
CAN BECOME A MAN OF GRACE

Are the struggles of life causing you to feel like you are in bondage to fear, stress, sorrow, and doubt? It doesn't have to be that way. ***You can live the life you have always wanted!***

Let bestselling author Tim Marks help you start the journey to a place of joy, hope, and success with his book ***Voyage of a Viking***, which details his dramatic personal achievement in the face of adversity—with a little dose of humor.

Tim Marks is a nationally acclaimed speaker, activist, mentor, co-founder of LIFE, happily married man of faith, and a dedicated father of four with a highly successful leadership business that has helped thousands of families rekindle the dreams, hope, and joy in their lives.

In *Voyage of a Viking*, Marks candidly shares his personal tragedies and triumphs in the hope that others can gain wisdom from the mistakes he has made and the lessons he has learned as he has worked to sand off the rough edges of his Viking personality in order to become a man of grace. Laugh with him, cry with him, and get inspired by his personal success to **reach for and attain your own dreams and goals**.

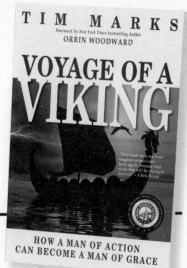